An Introduction to the Australian Novel 1830–1930

An Introduction to the Australian Novel 1830–1930

BARRY ARGYLE

OXFORD
AT THE CLARENDON PRESS
1972

Oxford University Press, Ely House, London W. 1

GLASGOW NEW YORK TORONTO MELBOURNE WELLINGTON
CAPE TOWN IBADAN NAIROBI DAR ES SALAAM LUSAKA ADDIS ABABA
DELHI BOMBAY CALCUTTA MADRAS KARACHI LAHORE DACCA
KUALA LUMPUR SINGAPORE HONG KONG TOKYO

PRINTED IN GREAT BRITAIN
AT THE UNIVERSITY PRESS, OXFORD
BY VIVIAN RIDLER
PRINTER TO THE UNIVERSITY

THIS BOOK IS DEDICATED
TO MY PARENTS

Our present age is essentially one of understanding and reflection, without passion, momentarily bursting into enthusiasm, and shrewdly relapsing into repose. . . A revolutionary age is an age of action; ours is the age of advertisement and publicity. . . No one is satisfied with doing something definite, every one wants to feel flattered by reflection with the illusion of having discovered at the very least a new continent.

SØREN KIERKEGAARD: *The Present Age*

Lord Byron and Sir Walter Scott are among writers now living the two, who would carry away a majority of suffrages as the greatest geniuses of the age.

WILLIAM HAZLITT: *The Spirit of the Age*

Acknowledgements

I SHOULD need another book to acknowledge fully my debt to friends and colleagues, especially those with whom I disagree. Here, I should like simply to record my gratitude to Brian Elliott, Bryn Davies, E. J. Vickery, and the late Gustav Cross, who first introduced me to Australian literature when I was a student in South Australia; to G. Wilson Knight, Arnold Kettle, Douglas Jefferson, Randolph Stow, and the late Douglas Grant, who, at Leeds University, provided me with many a lastingly useful insight into literature; to my former colleagues, Hans Häusermann of Geneva University, and William Empson, William Mainland, Roma Gill, and Christopher Heywood of Sheffield University, whose friendship and conversation helped stimulate and sustain my interest in this work; to Edmund Blunden, for his criticism of it; and to A. Norman Jeffares, to whose friendly encouragement it, like so many other things I have undertaken, owes its genesis.

I am also grateful for the patience and advice of my publishers, my students, and especially my wife.

York University
Toronto, Ontario

Contents

Introduction

SCOTT and Byron still dominated English literature in 1832, when the first novel published in Australia appeared; and Australian literature grew out of English literature. Scott provided the pattern for adventure—the result of two societies in conflict—and the scenery. Byron provided the typical heroes, who admitted no social allegiance. Expressed thus bleakly, the situation offers one clear explanation why the influence of Scott and Byron was to last longer in Australian fiction than in English. Colonization is the process by which a stronger society overcomes a weaker. In Australia, the process caused the virtual disappearance of the aborigines and the establishment of a white settlement.

Early Australian settlement, unlike that of America, was not an expression of liberty, but of captivity. The settlers brought their conflicts with them. The convicts were on one side, their military gaolers on the other; and between were the bars of a prison. The cruelty that increasingly shocked the various House of Commons Select Committees in the first half of the nineteenth century has a very modern quality, derived from the care with which the System was administered, and memories and observations of it documented. This element of bureaucracy, which stemmed from the fact that the whole enterprise was official—inspired by Government and therefore enforced out of a sense of duty and loyalty—is an aspect of the present century's history. Obviously, in the past men have been equally cruel to each other, but to record that cruelty in detail, in order to approve or condemn it, is a characteristic of a society both literate and cohesive. H. P. Heseltine can thus rightly refer to the 'peculiarly modern element which . . . Australian literature so early laid hold on,' as 'the rationalization of cruelty', borrowing the phrase from Lionel Trilling.[1] Few countries in recent times have had origins so charged with drama.

[1] 'The Australian Image: The Literary Heritage', *Twentieth Century Australian Literary Criticism*, ed. Clement Semmler, Melbourne 1967, p. 90.

Such origins produced a history of culture in Australia which the increasing immigration of free men affected but could not change. As Scott again and again implied, the past conditions the present. Being brutal, Australia's early past produced a society and a fiction which deployed a cruelty to match a climate and terrain often cruel. In the search for respectability, Australia, in its fiction and its history, has often endorsed that cruelty. No death is too bad for a bad man, no life too good for a good one. This is what I have chosen to call the conflict between the Byronic hero and the gentleman.

It may be said that Australia's convict origins in 1788 can have had little effect on Australian fiction of 1888, and even less on that of 1968. It is worth recalling, then, that transportation to this 'young country' did not end till 1868; that, in 1828, convicts and freed convicts, or emancipists, formed sixty-three per cent of the population of New South Wales, the most populous of the states and the earliest settled; in 1841, thirty-nine per cent; and in 1851, the last year of transportation to New South Wales, they were still fifteen and a half per cent of the population.[1] Secondly, history, while not repeating itself, sometimes records an experience so powerful that it assimilates earlier and weaker experiences which, in retrospect, take on an importance they did not have at the time. Thus Hiroshima, from poisonous rubble, has become a symbol.

In the 1967 postscript to his novel, *In Praise of Older Women*,[2] Stephen Vizinczey writes—with profound sense, it seems to me—that 'the man who is not bound to anyone has no one bound to him; as he renounces his obligations to others, so he forfeits his claims upon them; his relationships being transitory, his alienation becomes permanent'. He is writing of the philanderer, the Don Juan, what Mario Praz calls the Byronic hero. Thus Vizinczey can continue: 'The libertine has become (from an extraneous "odd" character on the fringes of society) the representative hero of our time.' He becomes so because of his alienation. In other words, the Byronic hero becomes the Outsider, not because he is a libertine—that was Byron's own fate

[1] These figures are quoted by Russel Ward in *The Australian Legend*, Melbourne 1958, p. 14, from *General Report on the English Census of N.S.W.*, Sydney 1894, and *Votes and Proceedings of the N.S.W. Legislative Council*, 1841 and 1851.

[2] London 1967, p. 184.

—but because in the libertine's life there can be seen most clearly the question with which Vizinczey concludes: 'Can our haste to succumb to joy, regardless of all other longings, reveal anything beyond the measure of our forlornness and despair?'[1] Joy comes to denote not simply sexual pleasure, but any attempt to 'make a break' out of our confinement.

Observing this, we can see why the Byronic hero in Australian fiction should be more than a literary convention. Australia began with every outsider 'inside'. Freedom, of the most elementary physical kind, became his aim; in claiming it, he established his heroism. And, in achieving it, he confirmed his 'forlornness and despair'. A gentleman would always try to shoot him down, even though that gentleman, as Richard Mahony was, should be his own *Doppelgänger*. I have said elsewhere that 'in English literature, the image of the prison is specifically of the last century, ranging from Scott's *Heart of Midlothian* through *Little Dorrit* and *Barnaby Rudge* to Wilde's *Reading Gaol*, as prevalent as Kafka's courtroom has been in this'.[2] When we recognize how literally a prison was the heart of Australia, we can see why the image should last longer in Australian fiction. Even the feel of the country often sustains it: 'In Australia . . . one can be lonely, and . . . the land almost calls one to be lonely —and then drives one back again on one's fellow-men in a kind of frenzy.'[3] D. H. Lawrence has here defined, more clearly than most whose overt theme it was, the struggle between the old convict urge to 'make a break for it' and the realization that to abandon the bitter conformity of prison will end in despair, madness, or death. Voss may despise the 'huddlers', those who cling to Australia's coasts, but his end is 'Death by torture', and not only 'in the country of the mind',[4] but physically. The climate and the land torture him. This fact is often overlooked even by those such as Judith Wright who have written most intelligently of Voss's condition, pursuing its implications for Australia's spiritual condition. The implication which is overlooked is that a similarly tortured death can even today overtake

[1] Ibid., p. 851.

[2] 'Problems in Studying Nineteenth Century Australian Fiction', *Commonwealth Literature: Unity and Diversity in a Common Culture*, ed. John Press, London 1965, p. 58.

[3] *Kangaroo*, Harmondsworth 1950, p. 76.

[4] Patrick White, *Voss*, Harmondsworth 1960, p. 446.

those who refuse to huddle in Australia. This is the reason the country's population is so small and must remain small in comparison with its extent. Land and climate may be inspiring, exciting, beautiful, or simply accepted; but often they are harsh. Thus Judith Wright's condescension seems misplaced when she says: 'So Marcus Clarke wrote in all seriousness: "What is the dominant note of Australian scenery? That which is the dominant note of Poe's poetry—Weird Melancholy".'[1] But this *is* the scenery's 'dominant' note: weird, or unearthly; and that is why so many thousands drive from the coasts today to have a look at it, camp in it, and pretend. They pretend they could settle there, but, because they recognize its melancholy, its threats of tragedy which are even today sometimes fulfilled, they return to the habitable coasts. Australia may be almost as large as the United States of America, but forty-three per cent of its area is classed as arid, another twenty per cent as semi-arid. Which means you can die in it, of thirst, heat, and cold. This is one reason why the country was for so long used as a prison. Today, its continuing aridity and therefore sparse population make its interior an ideal testing ground for long-range rockets.

Cruelty and isolation: these are the two interconnected themes this study attempts to trace, their existence in early Australian fiction justifying our attention. The preoccupation that binds them, the image that reflects their tangledness, is woman, as much by her absence as her presence.

One of the cruelties most easily inflicted on a man is to isolate him from women; it is a cruelty still practised in the prisons of nearly all the most advanced countries of the world. In all colonization, it is often self-inflicted. One of its results, as most colonial literatures, including the American, show, is that the few women who go, or are taken, exercise an influence on social *mores* out of proportion to their numbers. For to those free to seek them, women acquire a rarity value. When this is allied to a democratic code, as in America, which admits them as men's equals, they acquire a power that not even de Tocqueville recognized. To avoid its effects men may, as Leslie Fiedler suggests,[2] prefer a homosexual love. Instead of a wife, a mistress, or a

[1] *Preoccupations in Australian Poetry,* Melbourne 1965, pp. xii–xiii.
[2] *Love and Death in the American Novel,* New York 1966.

friend, a man may take a mate. Russel Ward seems to miss the point when he distinguishes this word from the American 'partner', a word, he says, 'connoting, basically, a business relationship'.[1] In using the word 'mate', one is using a word connoting, basically, a sexual relationship.

There were both men and women among Australia's founders. Apart from soldiers' wives, there were convicted women, housed separately from the men, and fewer. 138 were among the 736 convicts who arrived with the First Fleet in 1788. Although Australia did not begin as a democracy, women nevertheless acquired an influence far beyond their numbers and social position. They were given it by the Government. They became their masters' keepers, as both Tucker and Marcus Clarke assure us. They became the most credible of fatal women.

To escape them, or simply as substitutes, men took mates. Naturally, imprisonment encouraged this, as it inevitably encouraged *le vice anglais*. Australian history and fiction contribute to the well-documented belief that algolagnia and necrophilia have been more attractive to the English-speaking peoples than to others, despite the cases of de Sade and Masoch. Such pursuit of joy through pain goes some way to explaining de Tocqueville's civilized shock that in 1840 'the English seem disposed carefully to retain the bloody traces of the dark ages in their penal legislation'.[2] At a time more or less contemporary with de Tocqueville, English literature and art of the more advanced sort was similarly disposed. As Mario Praz remarks: 'In Rossetti there is to be found a conspicuous preference for the sad and the cruel; the Middle Ages, to him, are a legend of blood.'[3] Rossetti drew on the Middle Ages for such spiritual pabulum, but Henry Savery and James Tucker referred to those 'bloody traces of the dark ages' which they had experienced at first hand; and for Marcus Clarke and 'Price Warung' such experiences were still very recent history. What thus appears in English literature and art of 1850 as a fashionable convention, which Australian fiction used, is in reality the concomitant of Australian settlement. Without such an English predilection for lawful savagery, Australians would today be different from what they are. There is a similar connection between Lawson's and

[1] *The Australian Legend*, Melbourne 1958, p. 109.
[2] *Democracy in America* (abridged), London 1961, p. 434.
[3] *The Romantic Agony*, London 1960, p. 244.

Furphy's approval of 'mateship' and Oscar Wilde's imprisonment and vilification by 'the British public in one of its periodical fits of morality'.

Yet, in Australia today, there are few visible traces of such history. Its disappearance would seem complete to the casual observer, especially if he is an Australian. As Russel Ward so gently says: 'We Australians often display a certain queasiness in recalling our founding fathers.'[1] But if one reads the work of Patrick White, Brian Penton, Xavier Herbert, or Randolph Stow—who provide the other powerful reason for a study of this earlier fiction—one is aware that this disappearance is illusory. The cruelty has been rationalized. It comes dressed up as patriotism in the Returned Servicemen's League, as the White Australia Policy, as a nationalism that somehow justifies itself in South Vietnam, as a contempt for Australia's few remaining aborigines, as a paranoiac fear of 'Communists', and of those who used to be called 'Balts' because they too are different and thus propose an alternative and perhaps a criticism. As convicts and their gaolers knew, freedom is double-edged: one is free to accept or reject, to escape or remain, to live or die. The final paradox is that acceptance, escape, and life may still be a kind of death. The iron law of freedom is that freedom needs constant definition. Patrick White, Brian Penton, Xavier Herbert, and Randolph Stow involve themselves in this constant process of definition; and for that reason are more worth reading than almost anybody else writing in English today. Unlike so many of Australia's poets, their work is free of 'puritanism, mental colonialism, and nature worship', qualities that William Toye considers enervate much Canadian literature.[2] Writers like White have been freed by assimilating all the implications of their history. They are free enough to analyse their freedom. Such a condition is an aspect of modernity, of what Vizinczey calls 'the desolating sense of abruptness of modern life and the individual's emotional adaptation to the age of discontinuity, a way of feeling and perceiving that feeds on multiplying rather than deepening experience, and which I would call *episodic sensibility*'.[3] Which is to say, we are now all 'on the run', snatching what we can to sustain us. It is the con-

[1] Op. cit., p. 14.
[2] *A Book of Canada*, London 1962, p. 19.
[3] Op. cit., p. 185.

dition in which Australia was founded, which its earliest fiction records. Such fiction is one 'measure of our forlornness and despair'.

The phrase depends for its sense on an acceptance of the Existentialist position, one commonly held in the western world to which Australia belongs. Marxists may deny that it is thus commonly held; but few of us are Marxists, and fewer still Marxists of a kind that would deny this prevalence. It thus seems that not Marx but his contemporary Kierkegaard is the philosophical source to which we should go for an interpretation of this condition of the spirit, which Australian fiction so early defines.

There is a danger in summoning the ghost of a great man. He may not appear. And, if he does, his presence may be thought to cast magic upon the situation, whereas the magic is in him, in his coming, not in the summons. Which is to say that, to invoke Kierkegaard by name is not to attempt to invest these early Australian novels with greatness. Only one novel considered here is great, *The Fortunes of Richard Mahony*; and its quality is the more apparent from the company this book thrusts upon it. But it could not have been so great had these other novels never been written. A knowledge of Kierkegaard helps us to see how this novel is great, whereas a reading of these others substantiates Kierkegaard's greatness; and so they enlighten our present condition.

I do not consider Australian fiction as being divided into what E. Morris Miller and others call the Colonial Period and the Twentieth Century, for I question the assumption that either political status or chronology can now tell us anything new about Australian fiction. Such a division, moreover, rests on the assumption that Colonial fiction is different from English fiction, of that time or any other; or, to put it another way, that there is such a thing as Australian fiction, which is in some way distinguishable from the fiction of other societies. My purpose is to probe such assumptions.

Judith Wright has most recently summarized them in the Introduction to her *Preoccupations in Australian Poetry*, where she defines what she calls the 'Australian dream', which 'emphasizes man's duty to his brother, and man's basic equality'.[1]

[1] Op. cit., p. xxi.

I wish to know in what way this 'dream' helps define Australian fiction, when William Toye describes Canada as a 'tasteless, efficient, equalitarian society'.[1] He suggests these attributes of Canadian society have helped form Canadian literature in a dull mould; and E. H. McCormick has said much the same about New Zealand literature.[2] And how distinctive is 'the drive towards egalitarian democracy in Australian writing . . . the suspicion of heroes', as H. P. Heseltine says, if one bears in mind Toye's remark that Canada too is 'a country without heroes'? Are these perhaps only negative definitions, aspects of the same denial, 'We're buggered if we're British, and damned if we're Yanks'? The question gains point when one recalls Michael Howe, Ben Hall, Ned Kelly, and the rest of that happy band of roadside heroes celebrated in songs that begin:

> Come all Australia's sons to me—
>   A hero has been slain
> And cowardly butchered in his sleep
>   Upon the Lachlan Plain.

In the main I have directed my attention towards those novels that are considered either to mark the beginnings of Australian fiction, like Henry Savery's *Quintus Servinton*, or to be its most distinctive manifestation, like Joseph Furphy's *Such is Life*. Much has had to be ignored or touched on only lightly. I have thought it better to concentrate on those novels most widely known, or at least most generally referred to by critics, from earliest times to beyond 1900. Thus I include *The Escape of the Notorious Sir William Heans* and *The Fortunes of Richard Mahony*.

The pattern of consideration which emerged as a result of reading these novels breaks into roughly eight divisions: the attitude of an author towards England and Australia, towards women and his hero; and, in the earlier novels, the use made of aborigines, convicts, soldiers, and bushrangers.

In so far as the assumptions mentioned earlier are general, little help has been received from criticism of this subject. None of it is sufficiently objective. It appears, physically as well as metaphorically, too closely bound in the national colours of green and gold, more suited to cricket than criticism. This is not entirely the fault of Australian critics. Such an unfruitfully

[1] Op. cit., p. 18. [2] *New Zealand Literature, A Survey*, London 1959.

nationalistic approach is in part the result of the ignorance or contemptuous dismissal of these novels by English critics. Many of the novels are dull, but they possess a historical importance for both Australians and Englishmen. This has sometimes been recognized by English reviewers, but hardly at all by English critics.

The spirit now necessary for the study of fiction by or about Australians is exemplified in two short books by historians, *Australia: The Quiet Continent* by Douglas Pike,[1] and *A Short History of Australia* by Manning Clark;[2] and in Russel Ward's provocative and longer work, *The Australian Legend*.[3]

[1] Cambridge 1962. [2] New York 1963.
[3] Melbourne 1958; paperback edn. 1966.

1 Henry Savery, *Quintus Servinton*

By common critical assent, Henry Savery's *Quintus Servinton* is the first Australian novel. Written by a convict, it was published in Hobart in 1830–1 and deals with what is said to be autobiographical experience.[1] Cecil Hadgraft says of it, in the Introduction to his edition: '*Quintus Servinton* holds its position by setting, date of publication, and residence of author.'[2] Date, setting, and residence of author are the criteria by which Australian fiction is defined. It is the purpose of the first section of this chapter to draw attention to the weaknesses of such criteria and to suggest that *Quintus Servinton* can be considered an extension of English literature, a 'regional novel' comparable with Scott's work, written by a man who spent most of his life in England and acquired many of his attitudes there. It should also become apparent later that in extending the genre, Savery, the convict, offers other more dependable criteria by which his novel distinguishes itself from its origins. These criteria assume fuller expression in the work of Charles Rowcroft and Thomas McCombie, the subject of Chapters 2 and 3.

Quintus Servinton is the fifth son of a large well-to-do family. He is educated at a public school, Savery's affectionate description of it anticipating Thomas Hughes's *Tom Brown's Schooldays* by some twenty-five years. He becomes a merchant, and following a prophecy given his father by a gipsy, is successful and marries well. The prophecy also foretold that between his thirtieth and fortieth year, his private world would collapse before re-establishing itself in later years. Quintus forges a bill, is discovered, and attempts to flee to America. He is caught, and on the mistaken advice of friends pleads guilty to avoid execution for forgery. He is however condemned to death, the punishment only at the last moment being commuted to transportation to Australia.

Once there, his good behaviour allows the authorities to use his business acumen, which encourages him to send for his wife

[1] Cf. E. Morris Miller, *Pressmen and Governors*, Sydney 1952.

[2] Henry Savery, *Quintus Servinton*, ed. C. Hadgraft, Brisbane, Melbourne 1962 (hereafter referred to as *Q.S.*), p. xxx.

and son. By the time they arrive, however, he is in trouble again, this time with those who dislike him and his usefulness to others, and the fact that he is a convict in government and private employment. They successfully misrepresent his behaviour, and persuade his wife to leave him. He attempts suicide and is reunited with his wife. She leaves Australia to plead for him with the Secretary of State in England, and is successful in alleviating much of his suffering. After a number of years, his imprisonment over, he returns to England with his family, there to end his days grateful to his wife and to his God. Savery concludes the novel by repeating what he says at the beginning, namely that he defies 'the hand that might be lifted against the moral tendency of my tale'.[1] The defiance is justified.

Although many of its events are autobiographical, *Quintus Servinton* is not an autobiography. It is a novel, or a 'Tale founded upon incidents of Real Occurrence', as Savery sub-titles it. As Savery early makes clear, his purpose is to instruct and delight, but he takes good care that the delight should in no way obscure the instruction. The purpose radically affects the form, especially in the early sections. In these, Quintus Servinton meets many characters who, as Cecil Hadgraft suggests, 'are often "humours" of the line from Ben Jonson to Sheridan, with names like Crabtree, Briefless and Plausible'.[2] They contribute nothing to the progress of the narrative, and often impede it; but all serve to underline the novel's moral—what Savery calls 'the truly Christian principle, that "*Whatever is, is right*"'.[3] Although succeeding generations have had doubts about Pope's line, Savery does not share them; and because there is so much certainty that Providence, though inscrutable, is also transparently wise, the novel is without the tensions that finally dragged Savery's own life apart. Whereas Quintus is saved by his wife's appeal to the highest authority, Savery's wife returned to England and left him to attempt a suicide that may have been fatal.[4] When the facts of Savery's life are known and its obscure but certainly pathetic end compared with that of his novel, the novel becomes a moving testimony to the power of a lonely convict's hopeful dreams.

[1] *Q.S.*, p. 390.

[2] *Australian Literature*, London 1962, p. 12.

[3] *Q.S.*, p. 210.

[4] For a discussion of the uncertainty surrounding Savery's death, see Hadgraft's Introduction.

It is easy to account for so much moralizing, for so much unlikely goodness existing in those whom Savery calls the 'Local Authorities', whose concern was only with what each regarded as justice. Savery was a convict who had to take care he did not offend those Authorities as he had once already done when, as acting editor of *The Tasmanian*, he accepted articles which became the subject of a libel action. His circumstances, or rather those of Australia's foundation as a prison, account for the complete absence in the novel of a critical faculty. Thus, at the very beginning of Australian fiction, we find a constraint put upon literary expression that is not without its parallels today. There is no suggestion that the banning in Australia of *Ulysses* and *Lady Chatterley's Lover* owes anything to the cautious mood of *Quintus Servinton*, for they have been banned in places that have never heard of *Quintus Servinton*. What can be suggested, however, is that the acceptance of constraint today, as for instance the nine months' 'constraint' imposed on Frank Hardy and his novel *Power without Glory*,[1] has its origins in the unique foundation of Australia. Australian authors, in what they have said and the way they have said it, have played safe to a larger extent than might be expected of new writers in a new land. There remains a tendency to equate new civilizations with freedom, possibly because of the example of America, despite Hawthorne's work. As Quintus Servinton's experiences show, America was the land of escape, but Australia was the land of imprisonment. Australia began with 'a government designed to ensure law and order and subordination by terror, a government designed for men living in servitude rather than for free men'.[2] America was the land you went to, Australia was the land you were sent to.

In playing safe, Australian authors have tended to follow last year's fashion. To dismiss this habit as an aspect of provincialism is to ignore the literary freedom provincials like Sterne, Edgeworth, Scott, and Melville explored. Admittedly, there

[1] Realist Printing and Publishing Co., Melbourne 1950, Panther Books, Paul List Verlag, Leipzig 1956, 2 vols. 'The book was the subject of an action for criminal libel in the course of which the author, who was acquitted, was alleged to have portrayed actual persons, including some prominent in Australian public life.' *Australian Literature from its Beginnings: A Bibliography*, E. Morris Miller and Frederick T. Macartney, Sydney 1956. Macartney omits to mention that Hardy was imprisoned for nine months for contempt of court, his contempt being that he persisted in trying to sell his book in the months before the trial for libel.

[2] Manning Clark, op. cit., p. 22.

was no one else even in nineteenth-century America quite as exciting as Melville; and he paid a price in reduced sales. But the economic constraint was the only constraint imposed on his work, and he was free to ignore it.

Savery was more closely hedged about; and what he had to say defined the form of his novel. It has a narrative thread, namely how Quintus Servinton achieved ultimate peace of mind; but Savery considered the narrative as merely illustrative of his moral, which is not without its element of self-justification. The narrative is often lost in what seem to be the exigencies of the picaresque; but the hero's movements around England and the presence of various people like Crabtree, Briefless, and Plausible are not intended to delight, but to instruct. As a result of educating his hero, Savery hopes to instruct his reader, or at least confirm him in his judgements. Fielding does the same, but Savery is not thinking of Fielding.

In his preface, Savery admits 'he is aware how much further occasion he has to solicit indulgence for his temerity in entering an arena, where a mighty genius has latterly presided, chasing from the very precincts all, whose pretensions do not exceed mediocrity'.[1] The Preface is dated 1830. One mighty genius, Scott, whose example might be encouraging to a tyro, did not die, however, until 1832, his last novel, *Count Robert of Paris*, appearing in 1831. Either Savery is anticipating Scott's death, which is unlikely—though serious illness in Scotland may in Australia, under the influence of distance, have been rumoured as death—or he is referring to Byron, the only other 'mighty genius' who had at all recently retired from the arena of literature, or 'literary composition' as Savery calls it. Which of the two he had in mind it is now impossible to say; but the difficulty brings together the two influences that dominate Australian nineteenth-century fiction. When they work against each other, they are recognizable; but working together, they compound the difficulty.

Savery's Preface does make clear, however, that there is no need to be timid about ascribing influences. In the fiction of the time, unlike the poetry, there remains the classical habit of acknowledging an indebtedness to previous writers. At its lowest level, such a habit leads to the 'combination' novel:

[1] *Q.S.*, Preface, p. xxxiv.

'The combination novel enables a young author to present his public with all the brightest flowers of fiction neatly arranged into every variety of garland. I'm doing a combination novel now—the "Heart of Midlothian" and the "Wandering Jew". . . . I think you'd admit that I've very much improved on Sir Walter Scott—a delightful writer, I allow, but decidedly a failure in penny numbers. . . . Of course I don't make Aureola,—I call my Jeanie 'Aureola;' rather a fine name, isn't it? and entirely my own invention,—of course I don't make Aureola walk from Edinburgh to London. What would be the good of that? why anybody *could* walk it if they only took long enough about it. I make her walk from London to ROME, to get a Papal Bull for the release of her sister from the Tower of London. That's something like a walk, I flatter myself; over the Alps—which admits of Aureola's getting buried in the snow, and dug out again by a Mount St. Bernard's dog; and then walled up alive by the monks because they suspect her of being friendly to the Lollards; and dug out again by Caesar Borgia, who happens to be travelling that way, and asks a night's lodging, and heard Aureola's tambourine behind the stone wall in his bedroom, and digs her out and falls in love with her; and she escapes from his persecution out of a window, and lets herself down the side of the mountain by means of her gauze scarf, and dances her way to Rome, and obtains an audience of the Pope, and gets mixed up with the Jesuits:—and that's where I work into the "Wandering Jew",' concluded Mr. Smith.[1]

Mr. Smith's recipe is often followed in early Australian fiction. The need for such a 'continuous flow of incident', some of it borrowed, affects the way authors see Australia and the people, both white and black, who inhabit it.

Nor was the practice confined to the second-rate, who in the main constitute the subject of this study. It may be no more than a polite gesture born of modesty and an acceptance that, as writers of prose, their place in the pantheon was rather lower than that of poets. On the other hand, it can form an awareness of a tradition unbroken by any fictional equivalent of the Preface to the *Lyrical Ballads*. When Wordsworth said: 'The Child is father of the Man', he was stating his belief in the views Rousseau put forward in *Émile*: people, said Rousseau, 'are always looking for the man in the child, without considering what he is before he becomes a man'.[2] The earliest complaint in fiction

[1] Miss Braddon, *The Doctor's Wife*, London (no date), p. 41. I am grateful to Mr. Christopher Heywood for bringing this extract to my notice.

[2] *Émile, or Education* [1762], London 1966, Author's Preface, p. 1.

against such a view is in Scott's *Waverley*, where the young hero is described as being 'warm in his feelings, wild and romantic in his ideas and in his taste of reading, with a strong disposition towards poetry'.[1] Experience educates him into recognizing the joys of *Dulce Domum*, which also serves as the title to the last chapter.

Scott's interest in education was perhaps aroused by his reading of Maria Edgeworth, particularly works like *The Parent's Assistant* (1796–1801), *Early Lessons* (1801), and *Moral Tales* (1801), which deal directly with the kind of education she had herself experienced at the hands of her father, a keen disciple and an acquaintance of Rousseau. It was education of the kind that Rousseau summarized when he said in *Émile*: 'Experience precedes instruction.'[2]

Quintus Servinton was one for whom instruction had preceded experience; life therefore had to educate him: 'With all the excellent qualities of head and heart possessed by his parents, there were many points connected with the management of their children, wherein they differed from certain maxims that have lately obtained, sanctioned by such authorities as Miss Edgeworth, Madame de Genlis, and others.'[3] Unlike Waverley, he does not have a private tutor, but is sent to school, where he cons his books—or at least some of them. For there are books and books, as is suggested in Bishop's verse which heads the novel's Introductory Chapter:

> Books, my dear girl, when well design'd,
> Are moral maps of human kind—
> Where, stretched before judicious eyes,
> The road to worth and wisdom lies.[4]

But like Waverley, Quintus Servinton early evinces a taste for that literature which Bishop suggested was not well designed: 'As Quintus advanced towards his fourth or fifth year . . . little books, containing tales and stories, were his chief delight.'[5] His imagination, like Waverley's, further disrupts the instructive process when later, at school,

> Quintus applied himself to his studies, with diligence and attention; and in a very short time, it was manifest that a desire to emulate and

[1] Ch. xiii. [2] Op. cit., p. 29. [3] *Q.S.*, p. 14.
[4] Ibid., p. xxxv. [5] Ibid., p. 15.

surpass others was a ruling principle of his nature, and that it was leading him at a rapid rate, through the different steps or gradations of the school boy's course; but it was also remarked of him, that his spirit extended only, to objects or pursuits in which his taste or fancy were enlisted; for he regarded all others, with much indifference.[1]

Savery goes on to warn that,

With a character of this sort, it behoves those who have the care of its education, to exercise sound judgement, in adapting it to such objects, as are fit to be regarded with emulation; otherwise, a feature of the mind, capable of becoming invaluable to its owner, may oft prove a means of urging him to destruction.[1]

Scott had already delineated such a nature in the character of Wilfred in *Rokeby*:

his dream
Soar'd on some wild fantastic theme,
Of faithful love, or ceaseless spring,
Till Contemplation's wearied wing
The enthusiast could no more sustain,
And sad he sunk to earth again.
(Canto First, xxv)

He returns to it in *Waverley*:

To our young hero, who was permitted to seek his instruction only according to the bent of his own mind, and who, of consequence, only sought it so long as it afforded him amusement, the indulgence of his tutors was attended with evil consequences, which long continued to influence his character, happiness, and utility.[2]

It is Waverley's 'power of imagination and love of literature'[2] which provide him with 'the splendid yet useless imagery and emblems' later associated with the Stuart cause. Scott laments his hero's lack of 'habits of firm and assiduous application'[2] in an age when educational methods reduce 'the history of England . . . to a game of cards, the problems of mathematics to puzzles and riddles'.[2] Such education, which stems from Rousseau's proud and disconcerting cry: 'I say just what I think'[3], can only be corrected by experience. Literature, particularly poetry, is not suitable reading for an imaginative child. His imagination is the very thing that must be curbed in order that the 'whole

[1] *Q.S.*, p. 33. [2] Ch. iii.
[3] Op. cit., Author's Preface, p. 3.

man' should develop. It is a classical view, a distrust of excess; a distrust of Romanticism.

A recognition of this goes far to explain what many have noted as Scott's modest tone when discussing his own work. Fiction, we are to understand, is a relaxation from life, though equally beset with danger. He is aware that he has achieved both fame and fortune by pandering to that imagination which, at least in his first fictional hero, he is at pains to condemn quite as rigorously as did his father's 'Calvinism of the strictest kind'.[1] It causes him to tread lightly where the ground is soft, to tip like a gentleman while receiving Ireland's homage as a poet; or to support all his anecdotes with a reference to actual events and people.

A similar recognition also accounts for Savery's dull moralizing as well as his sub-title, 'A Tale founded upon Incidents of Real Occurrence'. Unlike Scott, he stresses the instruction there is in fiction, rather than its relaxation; but the same distrust is there. Both are unwilling to take it seriously, to appreciate the means as well as the ends; in a word, 'She'll do'.

The trouble with Waverley, as Scott himself confessed, is that, in the words of Byron's description of Marmion, he is 'not quite a Felon, yet but half a Knight'.[2] It is possible that, in creating him, Scott intended a gentlemanly tilt at Byron. There is no doubt at all that, by the time Savery wrote, the Byronic hero already existed to serve as the reason and excuse for much in both literature and life. According to Byron, in *Childe Harold's Pilgrimage*—itself an educational tour through experience, though a poem of 'morbid voluptuousness' in Lockhart's opinion[3]—the type had its origin in 'the self-torturing sophist, wild Rousseau'. He it was who knew 'how to make madness beautiful'.[4] Savery had the type in mind when fashioning his novel. He recognizes its interest, the interest of excess, and ascribes such excess to the waywardness his hero has been allowed to develop as a child; but he is unable to convince us of this excess because he is writing under constraint. It is not merely the constraint imposed by a system which, as Marcus Clarke and

[1] J. G. Lockhart, *Memoirs of the Life of Sir Walter Scott*, 7 vols., Edinburgh 1837-8, vol. I, 'Autobiography', p. 9.

[2] Lord Byron, *English Bards and Scotch Reviewers*.

[3] Op. cit., vol. III, p. 44.

[4] *Childe Harold's Pilgrimage*, Canto III, lxxvii.

'Price Warung' were to show later, was the very epitome of excess, the pains and pleasures of which imprisoned all who had anything to do with it. He is also constrained, and much more constantly than Scott in *Waverley*, by the code of a gentleman, or Gentleman, as Savery usually writes it, 'humane, benevolent, and mild';[1] in other words, one to whom excess is foreign. Quintus Servinton, as a convict, is moved by 'the word "Mr." . . . his spirits received a fillip';[2] we are repeatedly told with the warmth of self-justification that he 'had been born and educated a gentleman—who had preserved through thirty years, an irreproachable character'.[3] Like Waverley, such a man appreciates above all *Dulce Domum*: he was 'with all his faults . . . decidedly formed for domestic life';[4] there are few such men, it is said, 'who can turn their back upon their home and country, even under the expectation of a speedy return to them, who do not feel the separation acutely'.[3] Scott puts it another way in *The Lay of the Last Minstrel*, but without harping on the added claims to such feeling a gentleman might have:

> Breathes there a man with soul so dead,
> Who never to himself hath said,
> This is my own, my native land!
> Whose heart hath ne'er within him burn'd,
> As home his footsteps he hath turn'd,
> From wandering on a foreign strand!
> (Canto Sixth, i)

Scott thus offered a further attraction to anyone writing in or about early Australia: if this was how a Scotsman felt when returning home from England, how much more plangent would be the feelings of Australia's first unwilling immigrants.

Savery, however, does not use this particular poem; instead, he attaches to Chapter IV a motto taken from *Childe Harold's Pilgrimage*: 'My native land, good night'. From what follows in this chapter, what the whole novel is meant to convey, it is clear that Savery is intending Byron's line to support a sentiment in harmony with that of Scott's minstrel. Byron's complete verse reads:

> With thee, my bark, I'll swiftly go
> Athwart the foaming brine;

[1] *Q.S.*, p. 331. [2] Ibid., p. 295. [3] Ibid., p. 298.
[4] Ibid., p. 234.

Nor care what land thou bear'st me to,
  So not again to mine.
Welcome, welcome, ye dark-blue waves!
  And when you fail my sight,
Welcome, ye deserts, and ye caves!
  My native land—Good Night!
    (Canto First, 'Childe Harold's Good Night')

Nothing could be further from Savery's intention than this song of successful emigrants—like Voss, for instance, the latest of the Byronic heroes. At the same time, nothing could better illustrate the dual, often composite, influence of Scott and Byron on early Australian fiction. It is as though twelve thousand miles and an increasing number of years transformed Byron into a gentleman and Scott into a poet.

Despite, or perhaps because of, his imagination, Quintus Servinton is successful at school, becoming its captain. He is also successful in business and in love. In his social life, however, he does hear 'doctrines' that 'rather tended to ridicule and lessen, than to increase, the notions of reciprocal matrimonial devotion, which Quintus had ever been taught to consider inviolable, under any circumstances'.[1] There is a faint suggestion here of what Macaulay calls the 'moral depravity' associated with Byron's name and encouraged by his poetry; but Savery promptly kills any quickening interest in the character by returning to his concern to teach a moral: 'Not by this, is it meant to infer, that a general disregard of the marriage vow was sanctioned by such opinions as thus reached him; but, that attention to a wife's happiness, which rather bespeaks the lover, than the husband, was, by one and all too much treated with bantering levity.'[1] The gentlemanly code, though sometimes forgotten in the smoke-room, is never broken outside it. Nor is it in Australia: Quintus 'had sense and experience enough of life, to have resolved from the first, to adopt for his principle the seeking to acquire favour with his superiors, whoever they might be, by a strict observance of all established rules'.[2] For the Byronic hero, there were no superiors; and established rules existed only to be broken. From Rousseau's challenge, 'I say just what I think', had sprung the Byronic hero's practice of doing just what he wanted. As a convict in Australia, Quintus relies 'upon his uniform, previous

[1] Ibid., p. 167. [2] Ibid., p. 292.

good character—upon his offence having been a solitary blot on his escutcheon'.[1] This was so uniform that we learn towards the end of the novel that in their marriage, he and his wife 'never had had a single quarrel or disagreement', despite the contrary evidence when Quintus began dining out, and when he refused to confide in his wife either the details of his business or those of his crime.

Savery realizes that such uniform goodness makes dull reading, it appears; for, seemingly oblivious of any contradiction, he decks out his hero in the Byronic characteristics: 'he built his house upon the sand, choosing for its corner stones self-confidence, restless ambition, and wild speculation, rather than humility and a prudent ascent of the rugged path of wordly gains.'[2] While in Australia, 'He still clung to the gigantic nature of schemes', finding 'abundant opportunities of indulging that restless spirit, which had already proved his bane'.[3] Savery mentions a little later on 'the active restlessness of his mind, the towering grandeur of his projects'.[4] So much contradiction kills credibility; but this is a contradiction of influences. The constraint upon plausibility is imposed by an uncertainty about which 'mighty genius' offers the best guide to a budding author miles away from the society his future readers inhabit.

Plausibility is further impaired because we never learn what Servinton's trade was. In Defoe, where we are told the price of each roll of cloth or loaf of bread, the romance of trade has at least a secure basis in reality; but Defoe was writing at the beginning of a tradition, when attitudes had not set. Besides, Defoe, despite his Frenchified name, had no gentlemanly pretensions; but Savery was writing at a time when trade was no more respectable in literature than in life. Waverley was noble-born and inherited his riches, but Servinton is always on the edge of both: he acquires nobility and some wealth through marriage and through the author's late decision to supply the Servinton family with aristocratic relatives.

There is also another cause of constraint: Savery's need to justify himself, to assert that he was a good husband, with antecedents if no escutcheon, and that even when he betrayed them, there was something grand in the deed. We do not know how

[1] Q.S., p. 305. [2] Ibid., p. 158. [3] Ibid., p. 309.
[4] Ibid., p. 316.

strong this need was in Savery, and there is little use in surmise. We do know, however, that his wife came out from England and had her husband assigned to her as her convict servant; or, as Savery expresses it: 'it had long been the custom, when married men were joined by their wives, that the latter, in capacity of free settlers, claimed their husbands to be assigned to them, thus virtually removing many of the pains of transportation.'[1] The conclusion Savery draws is one point in the novel where we know fiction parts from fact; but of the usualness of the practice there need be no doubt.

What effects the practice has had on subsequent Australian society is now hard to say; yet no other society in recent times has placed so much authority in the hands of women. For if the convict servant of the wife—or mistress, for that matter, though Savery naturally does not mention it—displeased her, she could have him beaten by the 'Local Authorities', or replaced by another. The effect on literature of such a habit, however, can be seen as much in Lawson's stories about mates as in Marcus Clarke's dramatic use of it in *For the Term of his Natural Life*. But like the convict origins of Australia, the fact has so far been ignored by Australian critics for probably similar reasons; though it is easier for a man to acknowledge an ancestor transported for stealing a sheep than it is to admit that the old man's wife had her husband flogged whenever he failed her.

Mrs. Savery's arrival, her husband becoming her servant, did not remove 'many of the pains of transportation'. Certainly, she did not have him beaten for insubordination, nor did she return him to prison and take another; instead, she left for England, and remained there. In the novel, however, Mrs. Servinton returns to plead with the British Government for her husband's life. Not only did Mrs. Savery not do this; there would seem to have been good reasons why she could not. The British Government chose Australia as a prison because it was far away from England, chances of escape were minimal, and nobody worth worrying about lived there already. It could also be readily forgotten, and for fifty years more or less was. The notion that the fate of an insignificant convict called Henry Savery interrupted the British Government's worries with the French, with Revolution and Napoleon, with economic depression, with a mad king

1 Ibid., p. 334.

and his spendthrift heir, is implausible. But Quintus Servinton, Gentleman, is not quite Henry Savery, convict. Thus there is another reason for Savery to confer social significance upon his hero: the minister responsible for convict affairs was also a Gentleman. They shared a common code. Savery reduces the area of British government concern to the personal dimensions it had when Jeanie Deans appealed to John, Duke of Argyle, for her sister's life.

In *The Heart of Midlothian*, the relationship between Jeanie and Effie is one of sisterly love; Scott fails 'whenever he attempts to deal with romantic or sexual love'.[1] The reasons for this do not concern us here. What does concern us is to establish the ascendancy Scott's genteel heroines exercised over the minds of Australian novelists of the nineteenth century. The first of these fictional heroines was Rose Bradwardine in *Waverley*:

> Rose was indeed the very apple of her father's eye. Her constant liveliness, her attention to all those little observances most gratifying to those who would never think of exacting them, her beauty, in which he recalled the features of his beloved wife, her unfeigned piety, and the noble generosity of her disposition, would have justified the affection of the most doating father.[2]

We have no clear image in our minds of what Rose Bradwardine looked like or why we should admire her. We know only that she is good, beautiful, and a lady; and we are expected to respond appropriately to the description, much as a child responds to the image of Goodie Twoshoes. Eventually she marries the hero and lives happily ever after—at home. Home is the opposite pole to war in *Waverley*, the symbol of peace. Even Flora, Vich Ian Vohr's sister, is made to utter the same banalities, though banality is foreign to her nature:

> 'That man', said Flora, 'will find an inestimable treasure in the affections of Rose Bradwardine who shall be so fortunate as to become their object. Her very soul is in home, and in the discharge of all those quiet virtues of which home is in the centre. Her husband will be to her what her father now is—the object of all her care, solicitude, and affection. She will see nothing, and connect herself with nothing, but by him and through him.'[3]

[1] Walter Allen, *The English Novel*, Harmondsworth 1958, p. 121.
[2] *Waverley*, ch. xiv. [3] Ibid., ch. xxiii.

Marriage to such a woman would undoubtedly confer heroism on a man, no matter how devoid of it he was as a bachelor; and Mrs. Servinton is such a woman, though Mrs. Savery was not. Emily Servinton's satisfaction is to know 'through the remainder of her life, that the good work she had accomplished, was well requited; and she was permitted to feel that, notwithstanding all that had passed, her heart had not been bestowed unworthily'.[1] She brings her husband home—or 'Home', so to say.

This, then, is Savery's dream, founded on Scott, not on reality. It is a dream which haunted Australian fiction till it became a nightmare, when mateship briefly replaced it. In it, the woman is the man's spiritual superior, armed with beauty, piety, and goodness, though in fact she was often his physical superior, armed with all the appurtenances of legalized brutality. It is possible to suggest that Lawson's mateship, as it is expressed in his stories, was not merely the result of a predominantly masculine society finding homosexuality a ready alternative to heterosexuality, but rather of the undesirability of feminine company to men who, from reading or experience, associated women with the 'Local Authorities' or the 'home' in which ladies practised 'quiet virtues' under a husband's fatherly eye.

Less than a quarter of the novel is at all concerned with Australia; yet Savery's reading of Scott might have persuaded him that the unknown country would interest his English readers. In *Waverley*, Scott had already pointed the way for Fenimore Cooper: 'It seemed like a dream . . . that these deeds of violence should be familiar to men's minds, and currently talked of, as falling within the common order of things, and happening daily in the immediate vicinity, without his having crossed the seas. . . .'[2] And again:

> So little was the condition of the Highlands known at that late period, that the character and appearance of their population, while thus sallying forth as military adventurers, conveyed to the south-country Lowlanders as much surprise as if an invasion of African Negroes or Esquimaux Indians had issued forth from the northern mountains of their own native country.[3]

A Highlander's ease and ability to survive in his own bleak country is noted approvingly as he is seen 'crawling on all-fours

[1] *Q.S.*, p. 389. [2] Ch. xv. [3] Ibid., ch. xliv.

with the dexterity of an Indian, availing himself of every bush and inequality to escape observation, and never passing over the more exposed parts of his track until the sentinel's back was turned from him'.[1]

It has often been said that Scott, on a larger scale than Maria Edgeworth, encouraged in the metropolis an interest in its regions, thus laying some of the foundations for Hawthorne's and Melville's work; but the first of these passages from *Waverley* also indicates the interest violence has for those who imagine it a thing of the past; while the last two suggest that Scott, at least, would have liked to know something more about African Negroes or Esquimaux Indians. Australia provided at this time violence and a barely known native population in a country that was part of Britain's possessions; but none of this gets into Savery's novel. The fact is all the more surprising when we read early in the novel the passage dealing with Quintus's father's move from the country to the town:

> Shortly afterwards it was thought advisable that he should have a town establishment, and in this manner was the first step taken towards departing from the characteristics, that had for centuries marked the name of Servinton. Nor was it long ere it proceeded to others, tending in the end entirely to deprive it of what had so long constituted its pride and stability.[2]

Moving from his school in the country to business in town, Quintus is similarly undone. As Rousseau puts it: 'A man of good will finds it hard to satisfy his inclinations in the midst of towns, where he can find few but frauds and rogues to work for.'[3] At the risk of a simplification perhaps less than just to Rousseau, who advocated 'the patriarchal, rural life', it can be said that a town was an aspect of man's interference with God's handiwork; or as the first resounding sentence in *Émile* has it: 'God makes all things good; man meddles with them and they become evil.'[4]

It is not, however, what Horace, one of Rousseau's more important mentors, calls his 'hole in the wood, safe from surprise'[5] that consoles Servinton in Australia; for the briefly mentioned bush appears as a threatening punishment. He responds rather

[1] *Waverley*, ch. xxxviii.
[2] *Q.S.*, p. 10.
[3] Op. cit., p. 438.
[4] p. 5.
[5] *Satires* ii. 6. 115–16, transl. Dunsany and Oakley, London (Everyman) 1961.

to the civilized aspect of the place, to what most vividly reminds him of an English town:

Five and twenty years ago, New South Wales was not, what it has since become, an important English Colony, but partook more of the nature of a mere penal settlement for the reception of offenders, transported from the Mother Country, and was under a form of Government, precisely in keeping with this character. Still, some of the properties belonging to it, and which have subsequently served to exalt it to its present station, were known and appreciated . . .

. . . he found himself in the centre of a large, well laid out town. He had scarcely thought such a thing possible, considering the few years that had intervened, since the ground he now paced, had been an almost impenetrable forest . . . large, handsome buildings met his eye at every step—gardens, with a rich profusion of beautiful flowers and shrubs, enlivened the face of the town, and the carts, horses, and foot passengers, every where around, presented a scene which he had little anticipated.[1]

This is all that Savery tells us about Australia. There is no scene-painting of the kind later writers took over from Scott. In this first Australian novel, Australia as a geographical or topographical entity does not appear. What we find instead is Savery, surprised at the existence of buildings and gardens, responding to the beginnings of a city in a way we usually associate with Dickens. He forgets his earlier complaint about towns, which was based on his reading or his assumptions about gentlemen authors, and instead reacts as a nineteenth-century man, glad that Hell is a city much like London. As Asa Briggs remarks: 'The building of the cities was a characteristic Victorian achievement';[2] it can be added that a celebration of the *idea* of a city, despite the criticism of its actuality, was an equally characteristic Victorian achievement. In Australian fiction, however, this characteristic wanes after Kingsley, despite the existence of Australian cities, newspaper enthusiasm for them,[3] and the fact that an ever-increasing percentage of the population lived in them. One possible reason for this is suggested in Savery's brief encomium: they were built and sometimes planned by convicts; and 'the hand of convict labour is most efficacious . . . it is a lamentable truth, confirmed by the experience of many years, that a more than average share of talent is to be found in any

[1] *Q.S.*, pp. 305–8.
[2] *Victorian Cities*, London 1964, p. 16.
[3] Cf. ibid., ch. vii, 'Melbourne'.

given number of offenders against the laws of their country, compared to what is met with, in others.'[1] Just as Australian critics have tended to ignore the origins of their country, Australian writers have tended to ignore the material evidence of those origins, namely the cities of Sydney, Melbourne, and Perth. Where it has been at all possible for people to remove such evidence, as in the small town of Port Arthur in Tasmania, they have tried to do so. Over the years, the stones which the convicts cut and faced and dragged into position have been equally laboriously dragged to the harbour and pushed into the water. It is an act of considerable significance for Australian literature.

Although we are told so little about it in *Quintus Servinton*, Australia nevertheless assumes and fulfils a purpose. Not only does it receive convicts whom England wanted to ship out of her way; it also chastens and corrects: 'The stains that had marked him were removed by the discipline he had been made to endure.'[2] Australia as the austere and chastening land is an image that recurs in Australian literature, one that still has its appeal and usefulness today:

Yet there are some like me turn gladly home
From the lush jungle of modern thought, to find
The Arabian desert of the human mind,
Hoping, if still from the deserts the prophets come,

Such savage and scarlet as no green hills dare
Springs in that waste, some spirit which escapes
The learned doubt, the chatter of cultured apes
Which is called civilization over there.

'Australia'[3]

We read of the hero of *Voss* that 'deadly rocks, through some perversity, inspired him with fresh life'.[4] This is not the world of Rousseau, who says in *Émile*: 'Happy is the land . . . where one need not seek peace in the wilderness.'[5] A. D. Hope and Patrick White are using Australia's geography as the basis of their imagery, while Savery uses its history; but the effect of both geography and history is the same—to chasten, as Purgatory did, not to succour and reward, as Paradise did.

[1] *Q.S.*, p. 307.
[2] Ibid., p. 389.
[3] A. D., Hope, *Poems*, London 1960.
[4] Ed. cit., p. 18.
[5] p. 438.

2 Charles Rowcroft, *Tales of the Colonies* and *The Bushranger of Van Diemen's Land*

CHARLES ROWCROFT wrote more than a dozen novels but, apart from the disappointing exception of *The Confessions of an Etonian*,[1] most are retellings of two of his earliest novels, *Tales of the Colonies*[2] and *The Bushranger of Van Diemen's Land*.[3] It is proposed therefore to concentrate attention on these two.

Rowcroft was a free settler in what was to become Tasmania. He became a Justice of the Peace, made money, and left for South America, all in the years 1821 to 1824 or 1825.[4] His first novel, *Tales of the Colonies*, is the fictionalized account of these experiences, though its time span is encouragingly longer than his own brief stay, and the conclusion different.

Mr. Thornley and his family leave England in 1816, in his own opinion poor and in prospect poorer, because, it seems, of the Napoleonic wars. His search is for riches, not necessarily for himself, but rather that his children should enjoy the financial independence which he would have liked. Shortly after his arrival, he meets Samuel Crab, whose character of the typical disappointed settler, or 'moaning bloody Pommy', has received further emphasis by his having been robbed by bushrangers. With the help of Crab's experience, and the remains of a seemingly comfortable poverty, Thornley takes up land and prospers, despite the depredations of bushrangers and aborigines, who usually combine their forces as well as their distaste for that settled society which Thornley and his friends represent. Crab, although socially an inferior, remains with Thornley for reasons which often resemble those that vaguely define 'mateship'; and

[1] 3 vols., London 1852.

[2] *Tales of the Colonies, or The Adventures of an Emigrant. Ed. by a late Colonial Magistrate*, 3 vols., London 1843 (hereafter referred to as *Tales*).

[3] 3 vols., London 1845, (hereafter referred to as *The Bushranger*).

[4] H. M. Green, *A History of Australian Literature*, 2 vols., Sydney 1961, says Rowcroft left in 1825 (vol. 1, p. 87). Miller and Macartney say 1824 (p. 412).

he comes to assume the role of Thornley's superior, or spiritual protector. Their relationship is of experience on the one hand, and social position on the other; for Crab has had real farming experience both in Shropshire and more recently in Tasmania, whereas Thornley has merely dibbled in Surrey. To the point of obsession, Crab is aware of the difficulties of the 'new chum'. Swearing for thirty or forty years that he will catch the next boat home, he remains with Thornley, either because he thinks Thornley continues to need him, or because he by this time needs Thornley. Thornley, however, has a well-established family, even a wife who will help him make a success of the enterprise, though her young daughter wants the family to return to England, where ribbons are more available than in the Tasmanian bush. Rich and successful, Thornley eventually seals his determination to become an Australian by persuading an English friend to emigrate, becoming the first Australian in literature to 'Bring Out a Briton'. Crab dies, his work complete and even financially rewarding, despite his prophecies of doom; and he is buried in the land he spent his life vowing to leave.

Running through this account of successful settlement is the story of the escaped convict, Gypsey, who has been transported for the murder of one of his father's game-keepers in Yorkshire. He and his gang harass the countryside with the help of Musqueeto, a mainland aborigine whose life Gypsey has saved; because of the debt, they consider themselves as 'brothers'. Finally, of course, law and order prevail, and death overtakes them as surely as it overtook Dick Turpin, though not before they have been the cause of much adventure and some wise comment on the early settlement of Tasmania. It is this comment that justifies so much action in the novel, most of it of the cliff-hanging kind. Through such comment, it becomes apparent that the action of settlement cannot easily be separated from the reaction it provokes among convicts, bushrangers, and aborigines.

The settlers' attitude to Australia is early evident when Thornley says: 'I had reached the land of promise. I had taken possession of my land, and a noble domain it was.'[1] The remark is representative of an attitude that persists even today when Australians or those anxious to become such discuss Australia. Yet in this early novel, mostly devoted to putting the moneyed

[1] *Tales*, vol. 1, p. 106.

settler's point of view, there is also a sharp awareness that the attitude is questionable and relies on too many assumptions. One of these is that the settler, though poor, must have money in order to secure more, the possession of it being established in the world's eye, and the reader's, by the confidence and actions it permits. It permits Thornley, for instance, to assume the role of friend and benefactor to Crab and to invite him home; but, as Thornley comments, Crab, being without money, responds in a way that obliges Thornley to reconsider the man to whom he proffers friendship: 'When we got to the tents, he went, as a matter of course, to the men's sod-hut, where Bob did the honours; this relieved me from a little embarrassment, for I did not know on what footing to treat the stock-keeper.'[1] Thornley's difficulty is greater than Crab's, and also signifies much more. Thornley's response to Crab, who would be recognizably his social inferior in England, is complicated by his awareness that Crab knows more about farming, settlement, and Australia. The new land is thus exerting pressures which will alter the European values based on inherited wealth and position; instead, knowledge, of the bush, of the new land, is the new criterion. By going into the men's hut, however, Crab resists such pressures and the logic of his own position as the man of power: he responds in keeping with his Europeanness. In this brief incident is an insight comparable to Scott's when he says, in describing a Highland attack: 'The best-armed and best-born, for the words were synonymous, were placed in front of each of these irregular subdivisions.'[2] The best-born were those whose knowledge of the job in hand, namely fighting, was most complete: for they were the ones with the best weapons and the best training in how to use them. Rowcroft, however, having had his insight, which is based on the same logic as Scott's, refuses its conclusion; instead, he lets Crab go to the sod-hut.

Crab does not remain there; he rises till he is invited to share Thornley's home; and he dies there like some honest and valued retainer, except that he has made money as the result of a loan from Thornley. He is nevertheless content with this subservient position, despite the power his knowledge has conferred in the form of wealth. His situation is reminiscent of the position in

[1] Ibid., pp. 124–5.
[2] *Waverley*, ch. xlvii.

Australia of the 'little man', who increased his wealth only to the extent the squatter allowed. Russel Ward summarizes the reasons:

Australia is of roughly the same size and shape as the United States, but being nearer the equator and having much lower mountain chains, it is much more arid. As in the United States settlement proceeded inland from the eastern coastal plain, which, however, is much narrower in Australia. Crossing the Great Dividing Range, which corresponds roughly in height and position with the Appalachian Mountain system, Australian pioneers found the farther slopes rapidly merging into a region like the Great Plains beyond the ninety-eighth meridian in America, except that the Western plains in Australia were hotter and drier, and shaded off after a few hundred miles into desert too arid for even temporary pastoral occupation. On the coast and on the slopes of the Great Divide there is sufficient rainfall to sustain a rather sparse agricultural population, but even to-day the vast bulk of Australia's habitable land is fit only for pasturing sheep and beef-cattle . . . in the nineteenth century, with comparatively backward farming techniques, it was even more difficult for a small farmer to take root and survive in the Australian west . . . the effect of these geographical controls was accentuated by government land policies and legislation.[1]

One of Ward's important contributions is to have shown that the Frontier in Australia produced a very different kind of man and ethos from that which F. J. Turner, following de Tocqueville, suggested was produced by the American Frontier. Ward argues instead that the Australian Frontier conferred a power not on individuals, as in America, but on combinations of individuals; and, because the landless agricultural workers were numerous, and together powerful, they were able to consolidate the democracy which a few influential individuals were prepared to resist.

Ward's argument may be accepted; but, in literature at least, especially when set in Tasmania, a different premise is sometimes proposed. Instead of the class antagonism in society, there was the situation Rowcroft outlines, one which rests on an interdependence of interest between capital and knowledge. It is a British solution, apt for Tasmania, whose geography and climate most resemble those of Britain. The solution is an aspect

[1] *The Australian Legend*, p. 225.

of the Victorian Compromise, a shrewd, perhaps even wise avoidance of the revolution which so much of Europe experienced; and it is this spirit of Compromise which is found in literature about Australia.

Although for Thornley Australia is the land of promise—a promise it fulfilled—Crab's view is markedly different. When they first meet, Crab says to Thornley:

> '. . . A nice place, isn't it, for a gentleman to travel in?'
>
> 'But you can't expect,' said I, 'to find things in a new country all ready made to your hand; there must be a beginning to every thing.'
>
> 'Then why do you come to a new country? Why can't you wait till it's an old one, and fit for Christians to live in? Not that this place will ever be fit for anything to live in but a convict or a kangaroo.'[1]

Sociologically speaking, Crab's point is sound: in many ways it is preferable to live in an old country; newness cannot automatically be equated with a 'better life'. Rowcroft, however, by making Crab a source of humour in the novel diminishes the importance of the point of view; it is not an opinion he is anxious to forward. Crab is rather what his name suggests, 'testy, complaining, and pessimistic', as Cecil Hadgraft describes him;[2] but Hadgraft also remarks that he is 'a caricature in the manner of Dickens'. The opinion is evidently arrived at by way of Crab's name; but this is to omit the context in which he appears and to ignore his origins. His background is farming in Shropshire, a border county; farming on the border, between England and Wales, or England and Scotland, produces 'testy, complaining, and pessimistic' people:

> The sound of fight is silent long
> That began the ancient wrong;
> Long the voice of tears is still
> That wept of old the endless ill.
>
> In my heart it has not died,
> The war that sleeps on Severn side.[3]

[1] *Tales*, vol. 1, p. 98.

[2] *Australian Literature*, p. 14.

[3] A. E. Housman, *Collected Poems*, Harmondsworth 1956, 'The Welsh Marches', p. 56.

They are harassed by the weather, threatened and robbed by others keen to enslave them or set them free. They spend their lives among foreigners:

> When Severn down to Buildwas ran
> Coloured with the death of man,
> Couched upon her brother's grave
> The Saxon got me on the slave . . .

These uncertain conditions of the Border and the Marches, Rowcroft reproduces in Australia. Crab's literary antecedents are not in Dickens, the urban novelist, the poet of megalopolis, but in Scott. His original relationship to Thornley is the same as David Gellatley's to the Baron of Bradwardine, namely feudal: ' "He has made an interest with us," continued the Baron, "by saving Rose from a great danger with his own proper peril; and the roguish loon must therefore eat of our bread and drink of our cup, and do what he can, or what he will. . ." '[1] But the former relationship changes from the feudal one of service and responsibility to the capitalist one in which knowledge and effort are bought and sold. The earlier stage has its origin in literature, the latter in experience. Rowcroft is writing within the same tradition that produced Edie Ochiltree and Andrew Fairservice, a tradition which, taking war as its theme, proposed compromise as a preferable alternative.

There is one further important point in Crab's response to Australia: for him the country is fit only 'for a convict or a kangaroo'. Because Crab is often a source of humour, many of his views tend to pass as jokes; but just as there is shrewdness in his comparison of old and new countries, there is truth in his remark that Australia is the convicts' land. The truth is borne out later by a magistrate friend of Thornley's: 'it was the colonists who came to the convict country, and not the convicts who were imposed on the country of the colonists.'[2] The distinction, here so clearly marked, is one that not only the convict Savery acknowledged, but also one that a free settler like Rowcroft did not hesitate to make. Not to acknowledge it, as often happens in discussions of Australian literature, is rather like discussing American literature without referring to the Pilgrim Fathers.

[1] *Waverley*, ch. xii. [2] *Tales*, vol. 2, pp. 236–7.

Sometimes, however, Australia's origins are admitted:

> Some, rather fancifully, have traced the Australian passion for equality to the sense of community in worthlessness amongst the convicts, as though the convicts perceived darkly the spiritual truth that he that is down need fear no fall. Others, pointing to the great disproportion of males to females in the early days of New South Wales and Van Diemen's Land, have traced to the convicts the beginnings of a male-dominated society in Australia, from which developed the social habits of men and women collecting in different groups on social occasions and all the humiliations both great and small to which men subject women in Australia. Others have traced the attitude of defiance and hostility to the police back to the days when the police, who were often ex-convicts, taunted and mocked at the men in servitude. Others again have commented on the adverse effects on the large landowners of the use of convicts, to which they have traced the supercilious arrogance with which the upper classes have treated all members of the community. The use of convict labour, the same observers argued, began the alienation of the upper class of landowners from the rest of the community.[1]

The views so summarized are those of historians; and, except for perhaps the one about the results of the original disproportion of males to females, all suggest national self-justification and political bias. Early novelists like Rowcroft and Savery, while not free of their own prejudices and rationalizations, are yet free of these; and this is why their novels remain instructive and to that extent readable. For such writers, quite as much as for Governor Macquarie, Australia was the land of the convicts.

Not all of course were amenable to the reformation it offered. Some escaped and became bushrangers, providing the noble, not to say civilized, savagery which the aborigines could not provide. The first of these in literature is Rowcroft's Gypsey, though the description of his appearance suggests a long literary ancestry to which the reader is required to respond. Thornley says of him: 'He was one of the finest men I ever saw. Tall, broad-shouldered, and muscular, his whole form denoted great strength, combined with great activity. He stood a little in advance of his party, as cool as a cucumber, and quite regardless of the shots that flew about him.'[2] In appearance there is nothing to distinguish him from any other big, brave highwayman who

[1] Manning Clark, op. cit., pp. 117–18.

[2] *Tales*, vol. 1, p. 269.

'kills me some six or seven dozen of Scots at a breakfast, washes his hands, and says to his wife "Fie upon this quiet life. I want work".' Yet he is no mere Hotspur; an air of mystery surrounds him. His name is unusual, though only two years before the publication of Rowcroft's novel, George Borrow had established something of a gipsy fashion with *Zincali*.[1] Gypsey, however, is the man's name, not his race; but the name intimates mystery, of the kind Scott exploited in *The Heart of Midlothian*. He has also fathered a child during a marriage only lightly mentioned, the vagueness adding to the mystery, as does his fondness for the child. A doting father is unusual among highwaymen and was no commoner among bushrangers. He is finally shown to be a well-born younger son, transported for a crime he did not commit. Despite the respectability of his origins and of some of his behaviour, however, he does enough to justify the fear that surrounds his name. In suggesting the reasons for this, Rowcroft can provide a more substantial characterization than do the celebrants of Dick Turpin, Black Douglas, Macheath, or even Ned Kelly.

Gypsey is a convict, who breaks from gaol with thirteen others. Although Rowcroft was a magistrate after Macquarie's time, his comments on convict conditions and the reformatory aims of transportation belong to that earlier time. The increased severity that Macquarie's successor, Brisbane, introduced in 1821, he seems to have thought depressing to those Englishmen he wanted to encourage as immigrants. Yet he does say, in an aside, that all fourteen convicts were in chains. The fact is enough to convey the meaning of the system and thus help justify Gypsey's later excesses. It also elicits a display of comradeship which, granted Rowcroft's position, it seems at least tolerant of him to have particularized. Three of the fourteen could not rid themselves of their chains, but they were taken along by the others, ' "for we could not leave them" ', Gypsey says. The author's tolerance is deceptive. Far from suggesting that thieves do not always fall out, Rowcroft inserts the remark to heighten the loneliness of Gypsey's position. The three chained convicts are taken along because they may be useful, while left behind they could be dangerous. The same point of view is made more explicitly in a letter written to Gypsey

[1] *The Zincali, or an Account of the Gypsies in Spain*, London 1841.

by a friend involved in smuggling Gypsey's daughter out of the country: ' "there's no trusting one another in this country" ', a remark that chimes with Gypsey's fears of treachery and betrayal. Similar fears are prevalent in Marcus Clarke's and 'Price Warung's' accounts of the convict ethos; indeed, a great part of the tragedy in 'Warung's' stories is the result of just this inability of one man ever to trust another fully. Both writers were far more sympathetic than Rowcroft to the misfortunes of the convicts, but they agree with him on this point. Gypsey, like every other convict, has to contend with spiritual loneliness; and it becomes clearer why the Byronic hero should have an extended life in Australian fiction. Whether glanced at by Rowcroft, angrily explored by Marcus Clarke, or defined in tragedy by 'Warung', Australian convict conditions accounted for the loneliness of the individual who set his face against them long after the conditions which produced Byronic man in England had passed away.[1]

Naturally, with bushrangers causing so much exciting havoc in the novel, their former captors and opponents, the soldiers, are also present. Some twenty years before Kingsley introduced his Napoleonic veterans into Australian literature, Rowcroft establishes the military tradition. He does not do it as gaily as the sprightly crooked lads of the New South Wales Corps established it in Australia, but he does it firmly. A sergeant commanding a detachment sent to catch Gypsey and his gang proudly confesses that he is 'an old peninsular campaigner', though he is more aware than Kingsley's military heroes that such experience is insufficient to trap a bushranger. He adds that he has also 'had some experience in the bush with the Yankees', being therefore 'up to their manœuvres'.[2] He has no doubt about the treacherous nature of the enemy, who will readily break their oath, he says; and is proved right when, having given the signal for surrender, they then fire on him and his men.

A subtle response might be expected of men like Thornley when the new and strange confronts them. His rebuke to Crab on the nature of new countries encourages such expectations but,

[1] For a discussion of these conditions, see Benedetto Croce's *European Literature in the Nineteenth Century*, London 1924.

[2] *Tales*, vol. 2, p. 90.

in considering Australia's aborigines, Thornley shows himself limited:

I have often had occasion to observe the dull, listless, and almost idiotic appearance of the natives of Van Diemen's Land, when not excited by hunger or some passionate desire. It has struck me, that in this respect they much resemble the unthinking beasts of the field, so inanimate and log-like is their usual manner. The women will sometimes chatter a little, for it seems nature makes them all alike as to that matter, but the men have the most reserved and taciturn habit of any race of savages that I have known or read of.[1]

The final alternative, 'that I have known or read of', is included for its cadence, not for its truth. Thornley had no direct experience of any other 'race of savages'. What he is really referring to is his reading. To judge from the amount of dangerous adventure which the aborigines cause, he could be thinking of Fenimore Cooper, though his opinion of the aborigines appears rather to confide a regret that they are not more like American Indians. Or he could be thinking of that race of savages to which Crusoe's Man Friday belonged: there is much in the detailed information he offers future immigrants which recalls the more superficial aspects of Defoe's work. Or he could be thinking of that careful reader of *Robinson Crusoe*, Jean-Jacques Rousseau. Cooper, Defoe, and Rousseau constituted the intellectual apparatus, or vicarious experience, with which literate Englishmen armed themselves when they beheld the Australian native. It was not enough. The inadequacy is clear in a conversation Thornley has with a magistrate friend:

'It was only a few days ago', said the magistrate, 'that I was reading a specious argument of a French writer in favour of natural over civilised life; I am inclined to think that if the eloquent sophist had possessed the experience which we have of these savages—whose condition may be considered as the very perfection and model of the primitive state of society which the Genevese philosopher extolled—he would have modified his opinion.'

'The natives of Van Diemen's Land', said I, 'seem to be but one degree removed from the animal creation—a sort of connecting link between man and the brute. Having only one idea above the brute, and that is—to eat him! But they have only one brute to eat—to wit, the kangaroo. In my opinion, the degraded condition of the natives of this island may be ascribed in a great measure to the

[1] *Tales*, vol. 3, p. 163.

nature of the country itself. There is no fruit, herb, or root indigenous to the soil which is fit for the sustenance of man, and no animal, like an ox, a sheep, or a goat, capable of being domesticated so as to furnish a regular supply of food. The only animal fit to eat, apart from the opossum and such nasty things, is the kangaroo, and to catch the kangaroo the natives must be continually shifting their ground; consequently they are prevented from acquiring any fixed habitation, and are deprived of the advantage of those domestic habits which seem to form the first step in the progress of civilization.'[1]

Despite his recognition that the natives measure up neither to his dreams nor to his reading, Thornley, as a thinking man, does attempt to find an explanation; and he finds it by working back from the absence of any settled home, Scott's symbol of peace. He never questions whether it might not be preferable to live in Australia without a home, or to use one as a place in which to camp between work and play. It is sufficient that his experience should confound Rousseau, the 'sophist', which was also Byron's description of him.[2]

It is misleading, however, to equate Thornley with Rowcroft himself. Thornley's comments on what he observes help establish his character. When he says, 'The women sometimes chatter a little, for it seems nature makes them all alike as to that matter', he is reinforcing the tone heard in his much earlier comment on the men throwing the bones of their feast to the women: 'They don't seem to have much respect for the ladies.'[3] A certain kind of Englishman is being created through such comment, Savery's Gentleman, 'humane, benevolent, and mild'. Rowcroft, however, was a free man, not susceptible to the convict's inner pressures or external constraints. Consequently, his range of sympathies is greater than that of his main characters. During the settlers' preparations for battle with Musqueeto and his mob, one native complains while another, more friendly, interprets for him: 'He say you come take his country, and eat his kangaroo, and take his gins. He say you very bad white men.'[4] This is an opinion, simple, direct, and honest, which was not heard again in Australian literature till Eleanor Dark's *The Timeless Land*[5] almost a century later. Moreover, it is an opinion that has

[1] Ibid., pp. 186–7
[2] *Childe Harold's Pilgrimage*, Canto III, lxxvii.
[3] *Tales*, vol. 1, p. 75.
[4] Ibid., vol. 3, p. 201.
[5] Sydney, Toronto, London, New York 1941.

not so far been refuted or explained away, though Rowcroft offers a justification in *The Bushranger of Van Diemen's Land.* Further evidence of Rowcroft's sensibility to what colonization involves lies in the remark that Musqueeto is a mainland aborigine who leads a mob, not a tribe. Musqueeto is already one of the dispossessed, his followers in the process of becoming so as their land is taken from them.

Today it is easy to be impatient with Thornley's view of the aborigines and, attributing it to Rowcroft himself, to dismiss him and all his works; but there was another view, much more detestable and even today not without its adherents. Constable Scroggs expresses it most succinctly: ' "It's no use", said Scroggs, "to stand shilly-shallying; the best way is to shoot 'em down at once, and then you're sure they can't do you any harm. Never trust a native!" '[1] Compared to this, Thornley's attempt to understand the aborigines shines with enlightened generosity, especially when it is recalled that Scroggs's view was the one that prevailed in Australia. Rowcroft, the creator of both Thornley and Scroggs, consequently is revealed as a writer of broader intelligence and capable of discrimination.

In his discrimination, Rowcroft sometimes indulges in a refreshing irony. When Thornley and his party haggle with a group of natives over the price they are prepared to accept to track a flock of lost sheep, three bottles of rum change hands. One of the party, from New Norfolk—and thus perhaps an ex-convict from Norfolk Island—says he'll water it down, having earlier remarked, ' "It's astonishing how soon savages learn our Christian ways of doing nothing for nothing." '[2] He is being ironic about price, but behind his irony lies Rowcroft's comment on the ways of Christians. It is a complex irony; and in so far as irony is always defensive, the whole occasion illustrates at several levels the defensive nature of the white man's justification of his claim to Australia. There is a sense of unease about what is happening which owes nothing to Rousseau, Defoe, or Cooper, or even to the Bible from which Thornley takes his comparison of Australia and Paradise. The unease comes from what is evidently Rowcroft's experience: to a thoughtful man no action is entirely unambiguous, however inevitable it appears once it is done. In that no action is utterly complete, Rowcroft's outline of

[1] *Tales*, vol. 3, p. 194. [2] Ibid., vol. 1, p. 78.

Australian settlement continues in its problematical form to the present day, haunting writers as different as Xavier Herbert and Randolph Stow. What such writers undoubtedly feel, inhabiting Australia's wastelands, is that something of value was lost when the aborigines became the concern of the Department of Native Affairs, instead of remaining a people who had 'developed a culture but not a civilization of their own'.[1] Rowcroft also seems to have felt it:

> 'There are no natives now', said Betsey, 'to fire the country; they have all been removed these many years.'
>
> 'Have they? [Crab asks] Ah! I remember something about those sweeping expeditions, and what fun it was! making a line across the country, and the natives behind us all the while wondering what we were after!'[2]

Crab is referring to the Black Line of 1830, when the settlers of Van Diemen's Land, transforming their island into Tasmania, swept across the country in a line. The purpose was to round up all the aborigines that remained; and the total catch was one woman and a boy. Crab is doing more than indulge an old man's nostalgia for his youth. His remark conveys what experience had made obvious: that the natives were at home in Australia. They understood the country, could live in it, and disappear in it. Despite the white man's final success in changing some of the country to suit his needs, he cannot change his needs to suit the country. There is a sense of lost opportunity, a feeling that perhaps the aborigines could have shown him how to live at peace with himself in a hard land. It is a theme which Patrick White and Randolph Stow, among others, have continued to develop.

The title of *The Bushranger of Van Diemen's Land* exhibits a different emphasis, though the ingredients are much the same as in *Tales of the Colonies*. Instructing the emigrant gives way to the telling of an adventure story, but of a special kind. It is not entirely the result of Rowcroft's Australian experience.

Mark Brandon, like Gypsey, escapes from gaol with some companions. He is the intellectual force of the group, their leader by nature, his origins mysterious, his crime a mere smuggling in England. By impersonating the pilot, he with two others captures the brig in which Major Horton, his daughters Helen and Louise, and their factotum Mr. Silliman, have just sighted

[1] Manning Clark, op cit., p. 14.

[2] *Tales*, vol. 3, pp. 281–2.

Van Diemen's Land, their voyage from England complete. Brandon's followers, while trusting his intellect to provide escape from the island, distrust its subtlety. They are justifiably afraid that he will use them and abandon them, which is what happens when the convicts who have remained in the bush are told to meet Brandon and the other two. They are captured as they gather at the appointed spot. It is a prospect that Grough, now Brandon's only 'mate', also fears, again with cause. Brandon wants and perhaps eventually loves Helen Horton, their remaining hostage. Grough is jealous, as was Sewell, their other companion whom Brandon shot rather than accept the luck of the draw for Helen. Similarly, Brandon fears betrayal for the price on his head. This too occurs, though it is not immediately fatal; it allows Helen to escape, but only to be captured by the aborigines who already hold Mr. Silliman prisoner. Fortunately, the Governor's soldiers, among whom is the intrepid Ensign, Mr. Trevor—who loves her from old times in England—and the Major himself rescue her. Brandon, wounded, alone, surrounded by aborigines, exhausted, and attacked by eagles, is carried over a precipice into a raging bush-fire. His apparently all-Australian demise is spectacular by any standards.

Interspersed throughout the novel is comment on the bush, the aborigines, those aspects of Australia obviously foreign to an English reader; but the information is less than the spectacle.

Besides the information from foreign parts, the novel offers an instructive moral. Hadgraft summarizes it by saying that Rowcroft wrote the book 'to show that transportation to the penal colonies was not at all pleasant'.[1] He then quotes the following passage from the introductory pages:

> the circulation of the history, inculcating the certain punishment and remorse which follow crime, may assist in repressing that morbid craving after notoriety which of late years has increased with such lamentable rapidity.

Hadgraft's comment is '*Plus ça change* . . .' But he omits Rowcroft's next sentence which reads:

> With respect to the curious psychological phenomena developed by the peculiar condition of solitude to which the modern Cain, of which

[1] *Australian Literature*, p. 15.

this history treats, was exposed, they cannot fail to interest deeply all those who think that

'The noblest study of mankind is Man'.[1]

Rowcroft's reference is to Byron, 'the modern Cain' personified, and personified most completely, in *Cain: a Mystery*. Apart from Scott, to whom it was dedicated, and Shelley, whose *Prometheus Unbound* it complements, most misunderstood Byron's *Cain*, complaining quite as loudly as Rowcroft. E. H. Coleridge in his Introduction to *The Poetical Works of Lord Byron* quotes Byron himself as saying: 'Parsons preached at it from Kentish Town to Pisa.'[2] Twenty years after the drama's publication in 1821, the thunder was still echoing among the more distant ranges. It was this mildly disturbed atmosphere that produced *The Bushranger of Van Diemen's Land*. Rowcroft is of course at some pains to ensure his villain gets his just deserts, though no more vindictive than the author of Genesis; yet he is still responding to Byron's fascination, to 'the curious psychological phenomena' of the modern Cain. Though he attributes these to 'the peculiar condition of solitude' encountered in Australia, there is no further trace of them. His villain is an orthodox example of Byronic man, his outline more firmly drawn than in *Tales of the Colonies*; but still only an outline: the name Mark Brandon, recalling the mark branded on Cain by the angel of the Lord; the spectacular death of the villain, consumed by fire and torn by eagles, though these suggest a confusion of Shelley's Promethean vision with Rowcroft's failing memory of the Byronic convention.

If we remember that the convention was European, we are saved from considering the novel as an essay in Australian realism, of 'adventures among dangers, of which the chief, in ascending order, appear to be spiders, scorpions, snakes and aborigines'.[3] We are also saved from attributing un-Australian prejudices to Rowcroft: most of this 'ascending order' of danger is in Eve's great curse on Cain:

May all the curses
Of life be on him! and his agonies
Drive him forth o'er the wilderness, like us

[1] *The Bushranger*, vol. 1, p. 2.

[2] *The Poetical Works of Lord Byron*, ed. E. H. Coleridge, London 1905, Introduction, p. xli.

[3] C. Hadgraft, *Australian Literature*, p. 15.

From Eden, till his children do by him
As he did by his brother! May the swords
And wings of fiery Cherubim pursue him
By day and night—snakes spring up in his path—
Earth's fruits be ashes in his mouth—the leaves
On which he lays his head to sleep be strewed
With scorpions! May his dreams be of his victim!
His waking a continual dread of Death!
May the clear rivers turn to blood as he
Stoops down to stain them with his raging lip!
May every element shun or change to him!
May he live in the pangs which others die with!
And Death itself wax something worse than Death
To him who first acquainted him with man!
Hence, fratricide! henceforth that word is *Cain*
Through all the coming myriads of mankind,
Who shall abhor thee, though thou wert their sire!
May the grass wither from thy feet! the woods
Deny thee shelter! earth a home! the dust
A grave! the sun his light! and heaven her God![1]

Thus Brandon's death—a death 'something worse than Death' —in a war against man, the elements, the birds, beasts, and insects of the wilderness, is not necessarily or even specifically Australian. Only the presence of the aborigines distinguishes it from Cain's fate; but there is nothing in their final appearance around the 'wall of eagle-baffling mountain'[2] to distinguish even them from Shelley's Furies: 'Horrible forms . . . execrable shapes' that 'track all things that weep, and bleed, and live'.[3]

One result of Rowcroft's following Byron is that, because Cain is driven off into the wilderness, Tasmania becomes in the novel rather more a wilderness than it was in fact. The details of its wildness are no more definite than they are in Eve's curse. Rowcroft relies instead on general descriptions of the effects a wilderness can have on a man: 'if the many crimes which he had committed could be atoned for by any earthly torture, that which [Brandon] suffered in the wilds of the bush might be considered a sufficient punishment.'[4] Such moral earnestness adds nothing to our understanding of either the wilderness or Brandon.

[1] *Cain: A Mystery*, act 3, scene 1, lines 421–3.
[2] *Prometheus Unbound*, act 1, scene 1, line 20.
[3] Ibid., lines 445–6.
[4] *The Bushranger*, vol. 3, p. 208.

Occasionally Rowcroft's two aims of providing information encouraging to English emigrants and moral instruction to others conflict sharply:

> they beheld a wild and uncultivated country, presenting an appearance of the most romantic beauty. Green hill and green dale, for it was the spring-time of the year, the only season in which the dusky brown aspect of an Australian landscape is divested of its usual autumnal tint, met the eye on every side. Stately trees, mingling their fresh green leaves with their brown and yellow winter foliage interspersed with pink, and but sparingly scattered over a magnificent plain, gave to the scenery a magnificent park-like air, which induced the spectator to expect that there must be some princely mansion near to correspond with the vastness of the unenclosed lands around; while the want of farm-houses or cottages, and the feeling of the absence of any inhabitant of these fertile spots, inspired a sensation of regret that such valuable domains should remain uncultivated and useless, and almost unknown, while there were so many able and willing hands in England whose labour would soon turn the melancholy waste of the wilderness into smiling corn-fields, and thriving villages.[1]

What begins as 'park-like' ends as 'the melancholy waste of the wilderness'. Tasmania possesses scenery of both kinds, though they remain as clearly differentiated as they do anywhere else in the world. Rowcroft's confusion of the two arises perhaps not only from his wish to inform and at the same time to tell the tale of modern Cain, but also from a confusion of literary precedents. Rowcroft justifies his tale with Pope's line, 'The proper study of mankind is man', an odd justification for a study of excess of the kind Rowcroft appears to link with Byron's name. A similar oddity is apparent in the extract quoted above: it begins like Pope's appreciation of Cobham's work at Stowe and ends in a wilderness such as Byron used in *Cain*. Rowcroft's description, however, 'the melancholy waste of the wilderness', is reminiscent rather of Milton's line, 'The dismal situation waste and wilde'. As it was for Thomson a hundred years earlier in *The Seasons*, when he attempted the Miltonic, 'savage Rosa' is also Rowcroft's securest point of reference: 'The spot . . . was one of the most romantic of that beautiful island, abounding, as it does, in varied and romantic scenery. It was a spot worthy of the

[1] Ibid., pp. 167–8.

pencil of Salvator Rosa. Nothing could exceed the gloomy grandeur of the scene, and the lights and shadows cast by the fires around added to the solemn beauty of the picture.'[1] Yet it would be unhelpful to say that Rowcroft's attitude to the Australian bush is unsympathetic, or his description unrealistic. More obviously than most, Rowcroft is looking at the new land through eyes exercised by literature. The fact that this literature is European does not make him less of an 'Australian' novelist, any more than Furphy's wider reading, also of European literature, makes him more of an 'Australian'. It would be surprising to find any novelist's view of landscape unaffected by his reading. But Rowcroft as a reader did not have the perception to distinguish between a convention and a tradition, and this helps to make him a poor novelist. What can be made of the Australian landscape with the help of intelligent reading, of the Gospels for instance, is best illustrated in Patrick White's *Voss*. Rowcroft, however, not only sees the bush in terms of a European convention, he also wants to change it till it resembles more exactly the English landscape out of which that convention grew. He does not see, as Scott did, what a wilderness can mean for a writer to whom it is no longer alien:

> O Caledonia! stern and wild,
> Meet nurse for a poetic child!
> Land of brown heath and shaggy wood,
> Land of the mountain and the flood,
> Land of my sires![2]

This awareness is perhaps one reason why Scott admitted himself so 'partial' to *Cain*; and why he so happily made the mistake of believing Byron had 'certainly matched Milton on his own ground'.[3]

Even for Rowcroft, the wilderness has its possibilities: 'Major Horton had resolved to mend his broken fortunes in a new world, where there was verge and scope enough for enterprise and exertion.'[4] Like Thornley, he is another land-taker. He is less of a family man, his wife having died, but his two daughters are

[1] *The Bushranger*, vol. 1, p. 193.
[2] *The Lay of the Last Minstrel*, Canto VI, ii.
[3] *The Poetical Works of Lord Byron*, p. 625: Scott's letter to Murray, 4 December 1821, accepting dedication.
[4] *The Bushranger*, vol. 1, p. 4.

destined to be ladies, and he has the same need for a competency. His martial background emphasizes the qualities he is likely to show in acquiring it. Besides his two intrepid daughters, he has with him Mr. Jerry Silliman, a Cockney whose name suggests he is a fool about most things, particularly Australia. He is the only member of the party who expects the country to be a sylvan paradise, but snakes, scorpions, spiders, and soldiers' tales of them, make him quickly change his mind. Occasionally, when with his adored but unrequiting Helen, he relapses into what would seem to be the proverbial city-dweller's idea of the proverbial country. Even when hiding from the aborigines, he comforts Helen thus:

'Think only of the agreeables . . . I have been thinking how happy two people might live together, in a beautiful cave like this—loving one another! and listening to the birds, and gazing at the cockatoos as they fly about; eating the wild fruits of the earth, and drinking the water from the spring . . . all love! . . . and a little bottled porter.'[1]

Unlike the Major and his daughters, Jerry is not prepared to face paradise without the civilized comfort of porter. Unlike Crab, in *Tales of the Colonies*, he does not know that Van Diemen's Land has no 'wild fruits of the earth', at least of a kind palatable to white men. Unlike anybody else, he is in love, hopelessly.

A factotum, Jerry Silliman's social position resembles Crab's; like Crab, he is also a source of humour; but there the resemblance ends. His literary function is quite different from Crab's; and the difference comes from their different English origins. Crab is a countryman, cantankerous and dissatisfied in a countryman's way, but no fool; Thornley depends on his greater experience and ingenuity. He is shrewd, hard-working, and possesses a reassuring awareness of the social hierarchy and his place in it. Scott, not Dickens, is his progenitor. That Dickens is not, would seem to be emphasized by Rowcroft's portrayal of the typical Cockney. Silliman, like so many of Dickens's Cockneys, thinks of the countryside as the mythical home of goodness and contentment, 'a green and pleasant land'. He has never been there, but believes in its existence as unquestioningly as Joe, or 'Toughy' in *Bleak House* believes. In Dickens, this ignorance, or

[1] Ibid., p. 274.

faith, is touching, is the cause of compassion in both author and reader. Such believers may not be right, but they have been dispossessed, not only of the countryside, but also of the chance of testing their belief in its goodness. Rowcroft, however, allows Silliman none of this. Instead, his naïvety is foolish and laughable.

Another name for such naïvety is 'Rousseauism', of the kind Rowcroft condemned in *Tales of the Colonies.* Even there it is vague, and has little to do with anything Rousseau actually wrote. Rowcroft disapproves of it because he imagines it was vague in the first place, an airy-fairy theory, having nothing to do with the facts of life as Major Horton experiences them in Australia. Yet the society Rowcroft envisages as possible in Australia, where the 'wilderness' gives way to 'smiling cornfields' and 'thriving villages', is precisely the kind which Rousseau approved. Such villages would be based on a contented peasantry, for 'a society made up of peasant families would be a virtuous and contented Society. This Arcadian dream already lies at the core of the *Discours des Sciences et des Arts.*'[1]

As in *Tales of the Colonies,* so in *The Bushranger of Van Diemen's Land* the aborigine conflicts with what Rowcroft believed to be the idea of the Noble Savage. Yet, again, he is just in his analysis:

> Now it is to be borne in mind, that the natives of Van Diemen's Land had been gradually expelled, by the immigration of the white people, from some of the most fertile spots on the island; that is to say, where the grass land was favourable to the increase of the kangaroo, and the peppermint trees to the opossum. These successive usurpations compelled the tribes of natives who were dispossessed of their hunting-grounds to fall back on the hunting-grounds of other tribes; and the disputes to which these collisions gave rise were the cause of constant fights between the conflicting parties.
>
> The natives, therefore, regarded the white people as most unjust and cruel oppressors; and there was a mischief attendant on the encroachments of the Europeans in this country, greater than usually attends their usurpation of the lands of savage regions.
>
> The native of Van Diemen's Land, the lowest in the scale of human beings, unlike the rudest of the most ignorant of other savages, had no fixed place of residence; he neither planted, nor sowed, nor built a dwelling.

[1] Bertrand de Juvenel, 'Jean-Jacques Rousseau' in *Encounter*, December 1962, p. 38.

The country being destitute of indigenous fruits or roots on which man could subsist, his only resource for food were the wild animals which the island afforded, and the gum of the trees similar to those from which the well-known gum-arabic is produced. To these aliments were added snakes, occasionally locusts, large caterpillars found in the resinous blue-gum-tree, and a few other delicacies of a like nature; which, however, were considered rather in the light of a relish than as a substantial food.

Their principal sustenance, therefore, being wild game, it was necessary for them to have a wide range of country at their command, in order to afford them the means of subsistence; and this led to the division of the country into different districts, in each of which a particular tribe reigned paramount, jealously resisting the intrusion of neighbouring tribes; which was in fact doing no more than defending the circuit of country from which they derived their means of living, from the invasion of parties who had no right to trespass on them.

It may be said that the necessity of traversing over a large space of country to procure subsistence, and the remarkable absence of anything like a permanent dwelling-house, had a reciprocal action on the habits of the native of Van Diemen's Land. Having no house, he had no home; and he had no tie to bind him to a particular spot; and having the habit of roaming over the country for food, he felt the less necessity for a fixed dwelling-place, and therefore was less solicitous about erecting one.

Thus he ever remained, so far as his history can be ascertained, the only being in the human form without a roof of some sort wherewith to shelter himself from the inclemencies of the weather.

It is to be observed also, in explanation of the peculiar habits of those aboriginals, that the country produces no wild seed similar to any grain, such as wheat, barley, or Indian corn: they had no bulbous root, nothing like the yam, or the banana or the bread-fruit. Neither have they any nutritive fruit in the whole of Australia.

This singular denial of Nature in these countries of the food necessary for the sustenance of man in the shape of grain, fruit, herbs, or vegetables, is of a piece with the other singularities of those primitive regions. There the trees are all evergreens, and shed not their leaves annually, but their bark; almost all that grows there is, in some respects, different from all that grows in the rest of the known globe; and all the animals, and even some of the fishes, possess an organic peculiarity of formation, in the false belly, or pouch, which is different from that of the animals in all other countries.

It is to be observed that the natives of Van Diemen's Land are now to be spoken of in the past tense, for none exist at present in the colony; the remnants of the surviving tribes having been removed to an island, which they have to themselves, under the care of the government; but these records of their customs and habits refer also, mainly, to all the known existing tribes of the continental island of Australia still existing, but fast disappearing before the exterminating approaches of the white people.

The absence of any grain indigenous to the country, deprived the native of Van Diemen's Land of the opportunity of cultivating the arts of agriculture even in their rudest form; for there was no material on which he could exercise his industry, or which could be the means of developing his ingenuity.

Neither was there any animal which could be domesticated. The kangaroo is the only animal fit for food, so far as has yet been discovered, in all Australia; and this creature is peculiarly unfitted for domestication; and all the arts of the settlers in the various Australian colonies have failed to do more than to tame it in a certain degree; and in that semi-domesticated state it seldom lives long; for such is the fondness of this strange and uncouth animal for liberty, or such is its necessity, that it soon pines away and dies when deprived of its free range of forest pasture.

Thus the native of Van Diemen's Land was compelled by necessity to be what he was, and what he is in other parts of Australia, a mere wandering savage, without a home, and without those arts, contrivances, and tendency to intellectual development and progress, which the possession and the love of home engender.

It is remarkable also, that the native of Van Diemen's Land had not arrived even at that degree of human progress, which consists of feeling the necessity of some sort of clothing, for decency's sake, or even for the purpose of warmth in the cold season of the year, which in that latitude is sometimes, in the early morning, very severe.

Thus they were mere savages, having only one thought, that of obtaining the day's subsistence, for they never provided for the morrow; and of preserving for their own use—that is, each tribe its own district—the extent of country which formed their hunting-ground.

It is not to be wondered at, therefore, that they regarded the white people, from the first, with suspicion and distrust, and that having been already driven from the lands of which they had from time immemorial retained possession, they were exceedingly jealous of the intrusion of strangers on the portions which remained to them; and that they were ready to resist such aggressions by all the means in their power.[1]

[1] *The Bushranger*, vol. 2, pp. 90–6.

Hadgraft calls the novel 'a Southern instead of a Western thriller, with black Australians replacing Red Indians'. He also says of Rowcroft's attitude towards the aborigines: 'Though Rowcroft does put the case for them, on the whole he appears to regard them as an inferior and dangerous species, probably human, to be placated if possible, but likely to attack at any moment, and therefore to be fired on eventually.'[1] There are several objections to this view of the novel, some of which, if sustained, affect not only our understanding of nineteenth-century Australian literature, but the impressive novels of the mid-twentieth century.

The passage represents Rowcroft's own view. On the whole it is shared by the officer class in the novel: which is to say that the causes of aboriginal discontent and anger are understood and accepted. At least to such people the aborigines are not a 'dangerous species', but a race with a just grievance. On the other hand Rowcroft, through one of his minor characters, a corporal, expresses the objection to acting on a basis of such understanding: ' ". . . but I don't see, your Honour, what right any set of men have, let them be black or white, to prevent others from cultivating the lands which they don't use themselves. It's like the dog in the manger to my mind." '[2] The corporal does not realize that an agricultural economy will destroy the aboriginal economy based on hunting; but, as the earlier extended passage shows, Rowcroft realizes it. Historically, the corporal's view prevailed; but it is worth noticing that the corporal specifically says that no men, 'black or white', have the right to adopt a dog-in-the-manger attitude to settlement. The view was popular among Japanese corporals in 1942; though they were defeated, their argument has never been refuted. Instead of argument, Australia has relied on the racialist doctrine enshrined in the unofficial 'White Australia Policy'—'a lesson in international good manners', as W. K. Hancock called it.[3] Australia has thus denied the conclusion that follows from the premise by which Australia was settled: dogs should not use mangers. Rowcroft

[1] Op. cit., pp. 15–16.

[2] *The Bushranger*, vol. 2, p. 186.

[3] W. K. Hancock, *Australia*, London 1930. O. H. K. Spate in *Australia* (London 1968) ends a paragraph of difficult explication of this unofficial policy: 'Yet it cannot be denied that there were ugly racist tones in its enunciation' (p. 68). Its operation was uglier still.

did not share this denial, any more than Patrick White and Randolph Stow share it today.

The second objection to Hadgraft's view is related to his mistaken opinion of Rowcroft's reaction to the aborigines. If they are not a 'dangerous species' likely to attack at any moment merely because *by nature* they are belligerent, then they cannot be equated with the Red Indians. If they are also 'inferior' and only 'probably human', the equation becomes even more difficult to establish. As any reading of 'Western thrillers' should show, from Fenimore Cooper to the most recent, most colourful defence of the Alamo, the American Indians—or at least some of them, like the Cherokee and Iroquois peoples—were considered as exciting literary material as Scott's Highlanders, precisely because they were thought to be rather splendidly human, naturally warlike, in many ways superior to their white adversaries. In literature their noble savagery was often defined by the nobility with which they bore savagery. They provided western man with western thrillers in English, German, and Italian, and western children with endless games; they bequeathed to their more successful conquerors the hammock, the moccasin, even the game of lacrosse now played in the better-class English public schools for young ladies. The aborigine, 'without a home, and without those arts, contrivances, and tendencies to intellectual development and progress, which the possession and love of home engender', had nothing to give, save his land—and the sometimes haunting memory of the injustice done to him.

The third objection to Hadgraft's view follows from the other two: he appears to accept, however loosely, the analogy of Australian and American settlement, and to regard the Frontier as producing the same kind of results in the literatures of the two countries. This analogy is confusing, even where it is not false. It is particularly confusing when early Australian literature is considered, and the confusion spreads into a consideration of later Australian literature.

One reason why the Byronic hero has continued to live on in Australian literature long after he died or was transformed in European literature is that the conditions of Australian settlement favoured his continued existence. Although opinions might differ about the 'bush', some considering it a paradise, others a wilderness, there was no doubt that beyond the boundaries of settlement lay the desert. Some dreamed of crossing it and finding fertile plains; those who tested their dreams came back with the truth or died as witnesses to its harshness. The frontier in Australia was not an ever-moving line to the ocean, as it was in America. Consequently, we look in vain among novels about Australia for a sentence that can match Huck Finn's 'I got to light out for the Territory ahead of the rest'. Beyond the Australian line of settlement lay the dead heart, an image that has impressed itself on Australian poets as firmly as it has on Australian explorers. As A. D. Hope reminds us in 'Australia', prophets may arise there; or, as Patrick White suggests in *Voss* and Christopher Brennan in 'The Wanderer',[1] the *Übermensch* may die there, humbled into a final momentary saintliness. All are aspects of the 'blinding images' Randolph Stow records in 'Ishmael', taken from the desert where

> The hawks wheel in the dawnlight, the dawn breeze blows
> from the heart of drought, from the hungry waiting country.[2]

The literary convention in which prophets, *Übermenschen*, and spiritual exiles meet is the Byronic hero, particularly in the character of Cain.

Like Cain, Brandon is 'wandering about in the bush . . . exposed to betrayal . . . every day and every hour, waking or sleeping . . . alone—exposed to all the horrors of the terrible solitude of the bush'.[3] Like the hero of *Lara*, Brandon the bush-ranger would

> do what few or none would do beside;
> And this same impulse would, in tempting time,
> Mislead his spirit equally to crime;
> So much he soar'd beyond, or sunk beneath,
> The men with whom he felt condemn'd to breathe,
> And long'd by good or ill to separate
> Himself from all who shared his mortal state.[4]

Brandon, however, has begun his Australian career as a convicted criminal. Thus in the association of Byronism and crime,

[1] Christopher Brennan, *Poems*, Sydney (title-page dated 1913, published 1919).

[2] *Australian Poetry 1964*, selected by Randolph Stow, Sydney, Melbourne, London 1964.

[3] *The Bushranger*, vol. 1, p. 120.

[4] *Lara*, Canto I, xviii.

we see another reason why the Byronic hero should attract nineteenth-century Australian authors, or those since who have written about nineteenth-century Australia. Their country was founded by men whose spirits had been misled to crime; and, as Savery is at pains to point out, they had rather more than their share of talent and endurance.

Tracing the ancestry of the Byronic hero back to Mrs. Radcliffe's Schedoni, in *The Italian, or the Confessional of the Black Penitents*, Mario Praz remarks about Schedoni: 'Certain qualities can be noticed here which were destined to recur insistently in the Fatal Men of the Romantics: mysterious (but conjectured to be exalted) origin, traces of burnt-out passions, suspicion of a ghastly guilt, melancholy habits, pale face, unforgettable eyes.'[1] Brandon more or less conforms to the pattern. His origins are mysterious and turn out to be exalted; he is 'As clean-made and good-looking a fellow as ever you set eyes on . . . broad-shouldered; waist slim; foot small . . . his hands rather white and delicate.'[2] He is also 'the most carneying devil that ever came over a woman'.[3] So complete is his later passion for Helen Horton, 'he lost sight of his usual habits of caution, and was ready to risk life and liberty to regain possession of her', though normally

> coldly passing all that pass'd below,
> His blood in temperate seeming now would flow.[4]

Even when they were not convicts, such men often found Australia briefly congenial. Just as Schiller's *Räuber* and Milton's Satan had their counterparts in the world of actuality, so also did the Byronic hero. Not the least influential example of social anachronism was Lord Byron himself, inheriting an ancient title and pride to match, but without the money to justify either. During the nineteenth century, Australia attracted such people with the promise of land and gold, and unmortgaged opportunity. The younger sons of younger sons who would normally have gone into the army, emigrated instead because 'there was no sign of either of the two great wars which were about to call forth the strength of English arms'.[5] Some established

[1] Mario Praz, op. cit., p. 79.
[2] *The Bushranger*, vol. 1, p. 47.
[3] Ibid., p. 49.
[4] *Lara*, Canto I, xviii.
[5] Marcus Clarke's 'Preface', p. v, to *Poems*, Adam Lindsay Gordon, London 1905.

themselves, their army interests and training reinforcing Australia's tradition of organized violence which reached its brave apotheosis at Gallipoli. Others, like Adam Lindsay Gordon himself, jumped well-bred horses over and through a variety of fences in determined attempts to prove their relevance to the Australian social scene. Such men as Gordon were Byron's descendants in more than their hectic ennui. The reason is evident in Marcus Clarke's Preface to Gordon's poems: 'The phantasmagoria of that wild dreamland termed the Bush interprets itself, and the Poet of our desolation begins to comprehend why free Esau loved his heritage of desert sand better than all the beautiful richness of Egypt.'[1] This is the authentic voice of Byron. Cain too accepted the wilderness:

> Eastward from Eden will we take our way;
> 'Tis the most desolate, and suits my steps.[2]

Mark Brandon does not: the wilderness terrifies him. The difference is due to Rowcroft's moral intentions, not to his nationality. He disapproves of Brandon, not of Australia.

[1] Ibid., p. xi. [2] *Cain*, act 3, scene 1, lines 552–3.

3 Thomas McCombie, *Arabin*

SAVERY was a convict, and so had to stay in Australia; Rowcroft was a brief but successful settler; Thomas McCombie provides a third type, a man who went and stayed, from choice, even becoming a member of government. Despite Disraeli, no politician has yet written a great novel in English although the politician's world of power and influence, and personal tragedy, seem to be the ingredients out of which one might be made. McCombie does not disturb the generalization. It is because he does not, and because he was a permanent free settler, that a brief study of one of his novels is enlightening. Like Savery and Rowcroft, he drew on Scott and Byron for his ideas of what a novel should be. He was himself a Scot, a member of a race whom necessity, fortitude, and an often oppressive rectitude, have made successful immigrants. An appreciation of all three qualities is evident in his novel *Arabin, or The Adventures of a Colonist in New South Wales.*[1]

The novel is what it says it is, much interspersed with advice and comment on life in the Colonies and life in general. Godfrey Arabin, a melancholy enthusiast, grows up in Scotland, becomes a misanthropic medical student and, later, doctor, who emigrates to Australia, where he practises in the bush. Despite his longing to return Home, after being lost in the bush and dealing with his equally melancholic acquaintance, Willis, he marries Martha Waller, the sister of a squatter's wife. He takes up land and sheep himself. He is ill immediately after the wedding, but under his wife's influence and that of his sickness, he is purged of melancholy. He settles down to becoming a rich Australian.

Willis, on the other hand, who also loves Martha, goes mad, from drink or inherent causes, and is eventually murdered. Before he dies, however, it is discovered that he is the second son of a noble family. He at last inherits the title but, before he can claim it, death claims him.

Despite their similar personalities, there is an opposition

[1] London, Edinburgh, Aberdeen 1845.

intended in the characters of Arabin and Willis. Unlike Willis, Arabin began with little money and no favour, but triumphed by keeping honour bright. In literary terms, there is an opposition in the novel between the influences of Scott and Byron; and the terms are specified.

We learn that in Scotland 'many of the lower orders are passionately attached to the literature of their country . . . the schoolboy would often spend the winter evenings with some one who would talk over the adventures of Ivanhoe'.[1] Later, Godfrey Arabin reads Scott for himself; but McCombie's Scotland and Scott's Scotland are worlds apart. In Scott many of the lower orders cannot read or write. The adventures which his characters talk over belong to the oral, not the literary, tradition of their country. These adventures were history, tales, and songs that linked the past with the present. In the Scotland McCombie describes, it is the novel which has least of all to do with Scotland that forms the subject of talk. Perhaps McCombie is right: many of the lower orders were in his youth perhaps content to discuss the worst of Scott's novels, and the one furthest removed from their experience. What we should notice, however, is the way in which this same habit infects McCombie's own novel, so that his experience of Australia and men and women, is moulded by literature in a way that Scott's was not.

At the beginning of the novel, McCombie writes:

> Here we may remark, that many may observe in Arabin some resemblance to the character of Waverley; we firmly assert, however, that we have not copied from the great work of the 'Wizard of the North;' indeed, it is because the character is founded upon truth and *permanent* that it *must* resemble. The future career of Arabin will have no affinity with 'the fortunes of Waverley,' for, from the peculiar constitution of society in the present day, there are many Waverleys and Arabins.[2]

It might be inferred that McCombie's remarks about 'the peculiar constitution of society in the present day' are merely the complaints of an elderly snob: that he regretted the 1832 Reform Bill as he says he regrets Australia's convict origins. Reading on, however, we find that he is complaining about the effects of literature; and, when we realize how seriously he took these

[1] *Arabin*, p. 6. [2] Ibid., p. 8.

effects, we can understand the reason for his own high moral tone. He writes of Arabin at eighteen:

> Even at this period the same feature of melancholy marked his character; the translations from the German writers, which were just then becoming the rage, were eagerly devoured by him, and their dreary metaphysics pleased him, and increased the flame of melancholy which glowed in his heart, engendered by solitary habits and the Byronian style of fictitious literature. This morbid misanthropy bid fair at one time to nip the flower in the morning of life, for he would crouch about without enjoying the pleasures of nature. . . . In plain words, Arabin was a melancholy enthusiast. Have we overdrawn the character? or, on the contrary, might it not be found to assimilate with that of many young men of the present day, even among the classes known as tradesmen? We have observed in the world too great an anxiety to ape the misanthropy in which the Byron school of poets have so completely enveloped their heroes.[1]

McCombie confirms what was tentatively suggested in an earlier chapter: that the Byronic type had close affinities with Waverley; but Waverley, like Arabin, is educated out of his Byronism by experience. The one character in *Waverley* who is not is Vich Ian Vohr, of whom his sister Flora finally says: 'Oh that I could recollect that I had but once said to him, "He that striketh with the sword shall die by the sword"; that I had but once said, Remain at home; reserve yourself, your vassals, your life, for enterprises within the reach of man.'[2] This is the Overreacher, distant cousin to Marlowe's Faustus and Milton's Satan; but just as Milton's Satan can be seen as a figure compiled in part from disruptive political views of the seventeenth century, so Vich Ian Vohr can be seen as the personification, far more than is the Young Pretender, of the real political elements of the Stuart cause. Yet literature, as well as

[1] *Arabin*, pp. 9–10. McCombie is here reproducing the penultimate paragraph of Macaulay's 1831 essay on Byron: 'The number of hopeful undergraduates and medical students who became things of dark imaginings, on whom the freshness of the heart ceased to fall like dew, whose passions had consumed themselves to dust, and to whom the relief of tears was denied, passes all calculation. This was not the worst. There was created in the minds of many of these enthusiasts a pernicious and absurd association between intellectual power and moral depravity. From the poetry of Lord Byron they drew a system of ethics, compounded of misanthropy and voluptuousness, a system in which the two great commandments were, to hate your neighbour, and to love your neighbour's wife' (*Edinburgh Review*, liii, June).

[2] Ch. lxviii.

history, suggested to Scott the form such a character might take. He is to be found in translations from the German writers, such as that of *Götz von Berlichingen* which Scott himself did.

The political implications of Byronism, fascinating though they are, do not disturb McCombie. What he regrets is, as Martha Waller says to Arabin, the fact 'that Byron was a licentious man'.[1] His influence was especially pernicious because 'the beauty and power which break out everywhere fascinate the mind'.[1] Licentious here means excess of any kind; and it is Willis whose fate is as rigorously instructive as Vich Ian Vohr's. 'He could not live without excitement.'[2] He suffered from 'The melancholy which preyed upon his mind',[3] a hint of that quality particulary associated with Byron; though, as Macaulay writes in explaining its attraction, 'this faint image of sorrow has in all ages been considered by young gentlemen as an agreeable excitement'. Willis was also 'reared in affluence, and had mixed with the nobles of England: a family quarrel was the reason of his forced exile, and his own unfortunate temper, which preyed upon itself and scorched up the purer affections. It is more than likely . . . that he had an hereditary taint.'[3] Because of the influence McCombie believes literature can have, he is obliged to limit Willis's Byronism to the sad but at least mentionable sin of alcoholism. In a way worthy of a Presbyterian divine, and utterly alien to Scott, McCombie pushes home his moral: 'We have seen several dying from the effects of intoxication, and we can only compare their state of mind to those who are shut out from hope or pardon.'[4] Thus is the Byronic hero's Satanic ancestry established: from drink to damnation. McCombie reads this lesson from Willis's death: 'This was the end of an unfortunate man, who had every advantage in respect to birth and education. Instead of having his remains interred in some noble vault, with a magnificent mausoleum in some public place to his memory, he rests in the wilderness.'[5] The wilderness, like God, claims its own; and this is all McCombie says of the wilderness, or the bush. For him, it was merely the absence of a noble vault—which, even in the negative terms he proposes, is not a detailed visualization of the bush. He does not disapprove of it; he is

[1] *Arabin*, p. 118.
[2] Ibid., p. 199.
[3] Ibid., p. 217.
[4] Ibid., p. 223.
[5] Ibid., p. 224.

happy enough to leave Arabin there once he is morally recovered. McCombie is responding to it, not as a Scotsman, or an Australian, but as an ambitious politician, for whom power, influence, and personal tragedy are best symbolized by a magnificent mausoleum.

There is a further example of the way in which two useful influences are so misused in this novel as to seem foolish in themselves. During his life, Willis continues to haunt Martha Waller's mind, even after her marriage to Arabin. He appeared to her 'always as a dark phantom, such a figure as Salvator Rosa would have delighted to paint'.[1] Salvator Rosa's influence in English literature was long and various, until Ruskin scorned him; but Scott, not unwilling to be influenced by him when painting a scene, is a useful reminder that not everyone believed the influence entirely beneficial. He appeals instead to experience, to actuality. Writing of Donald Bane Lane in *Waverley*, he says:

> The profession which he followed—the wilderness in which he dwelt—the wild warrior-forms that surrounded him, were all calculated to inspire terror. From such accompaniments, Waverley prepared himself to meet a stern, gigantic, ferocious figure, such as Salvator would have chosen to be the central object of a group of banditti. Donald Bane Lane was the very reverse of all these.[2]

McCombie, however, intending an effect 'calculated to inspire terror', relies on a mere mention of Rosa's name to do it for him, not realizing that in a novel such a gesture is inadequate, and that this particular gesture had become as empty as magnificent mausoleums.

The novel's minor characters, who play no part in the moral tale, are nevertheless also seen through the uneven glass of literature. Arabin visits a small-town theatre, for instance, and comments on his fellows in the audience, all of them young squatters:

> In their manners they were boisterous and abrupt; they assimilated pretty closely to the young squires of Osbaldiston—Messrs. Thorncliff, Richard, John, and Wilfred Osbaldiston, although the eye wandered in vain for a Die Vernon to brighten the picture. Not even a figure met his eye which bore the least resemblance to his old favourite Archie

[1] *Arabin*, p. 216. [2] Ch. xvii.

Fairservice, and to look for the Baillie in Australia would have been too absurd.[1]

Although McCombie is so often hampered in his response to Australia by his very literariness, which provides him with precedents that condition his attitudes to people and things, he does respond in an original way to Australia's vastness. He was without a literary precedent that referred to a continent's extent: the European literature with which he was familiar was all written long after Europe's extent had ceased to surprise. Australia's size is perhaps its most obvious quality; but McCombie was the first to note it in a novel:

There is, however, a grandeur present in the scene—a magnificence derived from its vast proportions: compared with it, the scenery of Britain is tame; its tiny parks and its pretty forests, its mimic mountains and brawling rivulets, are all insignificant. In an Australian scene you have Nature in her grandest aspect and most gigantic proportions; you gaze around, and the heart thrills, because you feel you are nothing when alone with your Maker.[2]

It is in this one instance of original appreciation that McCombie's character does not interfere with his response: one cannot easily formulate a moral approach to a geographical land mass, though this does not prevent McCombie from trying in a way Burke would have approved. At the same time he is helped to his appreciation by his Scottishness, by his joyful need to 'do down the English at their own game', to talk to them as though it was they who inhabited a small outcrop of rock in the North Sea. He is also helped by the confidence that comes from an awareness of the basis of power. His humble tone is that of a Christian before the magnificence of God; but his pride is that of a politician surveying a nation's future which he will be glad to prepare. It is a tone that does not occur again in Australian fiction until Furphy's *Such is Life*.

[1] *Arabin*, p. 111. [2] Ibid., p. 30.

4 James Tucker, *Ralph Rashleigh*

JAMES TUCKER's novel, *Ralph Rashleigh*,[1] divides into four parts: experience in England, convict life, adventures with bushrangers, and adventures among aborigines. There is no plot; the four parts are held together by the presence of the hero, whose name, Rashleigh, summarizes his character in the way that Roderick Random's does in Smollett's novel. Of Smollett's novel, *The Oxford Companion to English Literature* says: 'Much of the story is repulsive'; and the same can be said of Tucker's. This is not its only interest, but it is an important one. It deals with a repulsive period in Australia's history; but, unlike Caroline Leakey's *The Broad Arrow*[2] or John Lang's *The Forger's Wife*,[3] it deals with that period as though it mattered.

Ralph Rashleigh begins life in England as an apprentice cobbler. He quickly tires of this, and takes to thieving and coining, even contriving a grand tour as a gentleman's companion. He is charged, condemned, imprisoned in the hulks, transported, and begins his Australian life as a convict at Emu Plains in New South Wales. From there he is assigned as a farm labourer to a man he quarrels with, who is only prevented from giving him in charge by Rashleigh's having already reported to the police to lodge his own complaint. While he is in custody, the bushranger Foxley appears, burns the place down, and takes Rashleigh with him as an unwilling member of the gang. They are eventually caught; despite his plea of extenuating circumstances, based on the inactive nature of his participation, Rashleigh is sentenced to the coal mines and finally the limestone quarries, places where the sordidness of the work is matched only by the brutality of man. He discovers a boat, and with some

[1] *Ralph Rashleigh*, ed. Colin Roderick, Sydney 1952, London 1962, (hereafter referred to as *R.R.*). Some still choose to dispute Tucker's authorship. See Roderick's Introduction.

[2] Caroline Leakey ('Oliné Keese'), *The Broad Arrow: Being Passages from the History of Maida Gwynnham, a Lifer*, 2 vols., London 1859.

[3] *The Forger's Wife, or Emily Orford*, London 1855. There is another London edition of this work, which is undated and called *Assigned to his Wife*; and an Australian edition, also undated, called *The Convict's Wife: A True Tale of Early Australia*.

others escapes in it under the navigation of Roberts, a man transported for industrial rioting. Finding themselves followed, they sink the boat and retire inland, returning when they think it safe; but the boat is gone. After a quarrel among themselves and a fight with the aborigines, only Rashleigh and Roberts remain. They camp on an island, which a flood submerges, leaving Rashleigh as the sole survivor and the captive of the aborigines, who treat him well, initiate him into the tribe and even stain him black. When his especial protector dies, however—the tribe's *carandjie*, or medicine-man—the tribe withdraws its favour, obliging him to fight for his native wives. Though one of them is killed defending him, he leaves with the other two to wander along the eastern coast, passing himself off to other tribes as a *carandjie*, in the hope that he can somehow escape from Australia. He finds a wrecked ship and two women survivors with a child. They are ladies, and instinctively Rashleigh becomes their protector, as he hopes they will be his, should they be saved. A boat picks them up and returns them to Sydney, where Rashleigh is indeed made a free man in a country he has been at liberty to explore only as a captive. He is at last killed fighting the aborigines, whose colour and ways he had for so many years assumed; but not before 'The sufferings of his early career in the Colony produced such an effect of reformation in his mind that he was for ever after respected as a man of scrupulous integrity by all that knew him'.[1]

Despite Colin Roderick's painstaking work, very little is known of Tucker's early life, and some of what is known appears unaccountable. Roderick says that Tucker was educated at Stonyhurst College in Lancashire, at that time recently come from Bruges with its Jesuit staff. There were several colleges nearer Bristol, one of which, Downside, also recently come from abroad, offered the Catholic instruction which Tucker experienced at Stonyhurst. Yet we do not even know that Tucker was a Catholic, although his understanding of Ireland's plight appears from the novel to be greater than that of most Protestant Englishmen of the time. There seems to be a similar discrepancy between the education he would have received at Stonyhurst—'a thorough training in English composition and in French and Latin'[2] and the employment he eventually undertook, which

[1] *R.R.*, pp. 302–3. [1] Ibid., Foreword, p. vii.

Roderick describes as that of a clerk and shopman. There is, however, nothing surprising about his being unemployed in 1826; many were in the same condition in the aftermath of the Napoleonic wars. Tucker helped support his mother by working on a cousin's farm until they quarrelled, and he tried to blackmail the cousin with a charge of unnatural crime, an attempt for which he was transported.

The form of the novel is eighteenth-century picaresque, its emblem the open road. It has the restless quality of *Moll Flanders*, the isolated adventures of *Tom Jones*, the episodic nature of *Gil Blas*; and nothing at all in common with the work of Dickens, Thackeray, or Lytton. There are several possible reasons for this. Early Australia was in much the same condition as England often appeared to be to the educated metropolitan in the eighteenth century. Beyond the roads and tracks there was little but trees, hills, scrub, and the fear that accompanies the unknown. A further reason for the similarity between eighteenth-century novels and Tucker's is his wish to tell his English readers, even those few who were members of the Port Macquarie Literary Club to whom Tucker read his manuscript, of the variety of Australian conditions. Obviously, one of the best ways was to move his hero around the continent and allow him to comment, the author correcting or supporting where necessary. The only disadvantage to the form was the difficulty in keeping the hero alive long enough to cover the course. Coincidence was the method, and implausibility often the result. Because Tucker was not alone in recognizing the form's advantages for his purpose, or in his ways of overcoming its difficulties, we are left with the interesting speculation that the demands of English readers helped create the Australian myth of the invincible bushman of the outback. The myth has been well sustained since by Australian readers in the mainland's five capital cities.

One result of Tucker's following the earlier novel form—or one reason why he did so—is that much of *Ralph Rashleigh* is 'realistic'; it has a tone of plain speaking as well as the completeness of actuality. The tone is quickly evident: 'One day three of the patients died, and as deceased convicts were then usually buried in a graveyard near a number of ruined buildings on the Gosport side which were among the prisoners called

"Rats' Castle", some of the convalescent patients, of whom Rashleigh was one, were selected to go there and dig the graves.'[1] The phrase, 'Rats' Castle' is the idiom of the people, to whom death came frequently, brutally, and early. Only to the well-to-do observer, or those whom bereavement surprised, could death be a 'sleep so beautiful and calm, so free from trace of pain, so fair to look upon'.[2] The poor were obliged to rely on a grim merriment of the kind that describes a chief constable as one 'who had formerly been a member of that fraternity, so useful to anatomical science, yclept *stiff-hunters*, or body-snatchers'.[3]

Some of the merriment comes from the juxtaposition of such an idiom with an inflated style; but it is safe to say that Tucker shares this view of the world because he has been compelled by experience. It enables him later to describe a scene of brutality that is almost devoid of authorial comment even in the form of imagery; but, because we are accustomed to his tone, the comment is implied in the accurate details:

> Foxley sprang upon the wounded wretch with his knife and stabbed him repeatedly until the yells of the dying man, which had at first rung though the forest, died away in inarticulate sobs, whereupon McCoy, who had stood threateningly over the prostrate wretch with the broken musket barrel but feared to strike while Foxley was engaged in his brutal work, now rained a shower of blows upon the victim's skull until it was actually smashed into a shapeless pulp of hair and brains. Both bodies were now stripped and hauled to a deep waterhole close by, into which they were finally thrown and a number of large loose masses of stone piled on them.[4]

For such a visualized description of killing we must return to Smollett in the eighteenth century or Nashe in the sixteenth; for in the nineteenth, hair, brains, and the pulp of a crushed skull had become merely 'gore', and no man died inarticulately sobbing. Similarly absent from almost all nineteenth-century literature is this willingness of Tucker to allow the action to speak for itself, unaided by the author's or the hero's apologies, encouragement, or even delight. Its presence in *Ralph Rashleigh* is one reason why the novel is important. Like *Wuthering Heights*, *Ralph Rashleigh* reasserts a literary tradition which itself is

[1] *R.R.*, p. 52.
[2] *The Old Curiosity Shop*, ch. lxxi.
[3] *R.R.*, p. 71.
[4] Ibid., p. 162.

based on life, of which death forms a part, death of a kind that nothing can excuse.

On those occasions, however, when Tucker considers the quality of the action not sufficiently evident in its description, he directs our attention to it with comment, italics, or an inflated style. Like some master of ceremonies at a music-hall, he invites his audience to hiss and cheer; but it is never quite clear who it is that he considers villainous and who virtuous. This unpredictability is a further attraction. It suggests an author who to some extent shared that 'negative capability' which has been taken as one of the marks of the great novelist; but it also suggests one who, at the same time, was often constrained by circumstance to observe a literary convention which experience had taught him to question. The constraint is similar to Savery's, though not as pressing: *Ralph Rashleigh* was not published till long after Tucker's death. Obviously, he did not fear a charge of libel, even in a society where it was easy for a convict to be so charged. The constraint is rather that of a man unsure of where literature ends and life begins. He is sure in his scorn for hypocrisy, vindictiveness, and brutality, but is aware that even the most unreasonable action is not without its cause. The strain is evident in his habit of completing the life-stories of even the most minor characters, no matter how much implausibility and coincidence this involves, and how much it disfigures the shape of his novel. He remains true to the poor man's conviction that only death makes life whole, and therefore explicable. It is the dilemma of the realist writer.

The dilemma has as source the contradiction inherent in the realist's situation: as a novelist, he must select; and selection is determined by matters that have little or nothing to do with the desire to record the wholeness of experience. All the novelists so far considered have been more or less anxious to convey as much as they can of the new country; yet the aim of each is compromised by personal motives or ideas of what form a novel should usefully take. Tucker's situation is slightly different in that he abandons plot; but his success is greater because, coming later than the others, he can assume so much more in his readers. He does not have to explain why Australia became a convict settlement, or what bushrangers are, or comment on the antagonisms of the aborigines to white settlement. By his time these are known; he takes them for granted and uses convicts, bushrangers, and aborigines as the conventional ingredients by which even a realistic novel is recognized as Australian. Far from cramping him, the assumption leaves him free to exercise the realist's conviction that there is more in heaven and earth than this world dreams of. The result in Tucker is symbolism.

This large vision is evident in the motto to the chapter on Rashleigh's arrival in Australia:

> The band of Romulus, it is most certain,
> Were ruffian stabbers and vile cutpurse knaves;
> Yet did this outcast scum of all the earth
> Lay the foundations of the Eternal City.[1]

Despite their hopefulness, the lines oversimplify in that they accept a view which Savery, for instance, could not: that Australia's convicts were all 'outcast scum'. He knew that there were men of talent, as well as birth and honour, among the convicts; but like him, and like Rowcroft too, Tucker does accept that Australia was established by convicts, and by the soldiers who were their guards.

The simplistic comment of the motto is continued in the narrative:

> The town at that time contained but two classes, one comprising the high government officers and a very few large merchants, who formed at that period the aristocracy of Australia. The other was composed of men who, like Ralph, either were or had been convicts, or, to use the milder colonial phrase, 'prisoners of the Crown'. Many of the last, who were now free, had become very wealthy; but Heaven knows, they formed no exception to the description given by Pope of those on whom riches are generally bestowed, they being, he says,
>
> Given to the fool, the vain, the mad, the evil,
> To Ward, to Waters, Chartres, and the Devil.
>
> And surely, the men among the freed convicts of New South Wales who had acquired riches offered abundant evidence of the truth of the above couplet, the nucleus of their gains having been acquired either by the exercise of every art of fraud, or at least by chicanery, and in some cases by pandering to the grossest vices of their fellow-convicts, whose chief luxuries, and in fact the grand *prima mobile* or *summa bona*

[1] *R.R.*, p. 68.

of whose existence were *rum* and *tobacco*, to wallow in beastly drunkenness being to them the very acme of earthly bliss![1]

This is a keen and total condemnation, its severity perhaps to some extent accounted for by the fact that Tucker himself wallowed and ultimately drowned in 'beastly drunkenness'. Yet a little later we find a totally approving description of Robert Marshall and his wife, both of them freed convicts who have prospered as small farmers. Their ordered, hard-working lives are the touchstone for all others in the novel.

Tucker takes a similarly large view of the military, the other half of Australia's founding fathers:

when one of these ministers of torture did not appear to please this *humane* man of power in the vigour with which he dealt out the lash, the 'Captain' rushed upon him and belaboured the scourger himself with a cane, bidding him at the same time, 'Go on, sir! Go on!!' And every stroke the scourger applied to the back of the culprit was accompanied by one upon his own shoulders from the commandant's cane, with a loud shout from the latter, 'Harder yet, sir! Harder yet!!' until at last the weapon flew into fragments in the hands of this *splendid specimen* of a British officer![2]

Again the contempt is total, though again the author's scorn frames the action; it does not intrude and diminish its immediacy. Yet further down the same page an important correction is added:

Lest this picture should appear overcharged respecting the partiality of this officer for flogging those under his sway, the reader is requested to remember that corporal punishment was of almost daily occurrence in the British Navy, as well as the Army, twenty-five years ago; and it is very probable the *gallant* captain in question had been selected for his present command to control upwards of two thousand lawless desperadoes from his known severity in his military capacity. And he might have considered that nothing short of absolutely breaking down the bodies as well as the minds of the ruffians—for such no doubt they were for the most part—could either sufficiently punish them for their past crimes or prevent them from committing further atrocities in the exile to which they were doomed.[2]

Historical perspective and an understanding of men as well as authority combine to adjust the earlier scorn; and the balance

[1] *R.R.*, p. 71. [2] Ibid., p. 227.

maintained is keen. But, having achieved this, Tucker does more. By way of a further reference to his experience of actuality, he affirms that such treatment, combined with hunger, was successful in achieving what it was intended to achieve. It even brutalized those who were not 'ruffians', thereby confirming the brutality of the gaoler. Only Marcus Clarke and 'Price Warung' have been as conscious of the implications of the brutality in which Australia was born.

Finally, lest there be any doubt about his objective appraisal of the behaviour of the military, Tucker shows that on the two occasions when Rashleigh experiences a kindness, he receives it at the instigation of army officers, one of whom is honest enough as a magistrate to believe his story and doubt his gaoler's, the other of whom is grateful enough to help him obtain his freedom.

Tucker relies on the convention of the bushranger to provide much of the novel's adventure. His description of Foxley, the suggestively named bushranger, is also conventional: he 'shot forth a glance of sarcastic contempt, twisting his naturally coarse features into a truly Satanic as well as sardonic grin',[1] and 'no tiger was ever more pitiless to his prey than the fiend in human shape'.[2] Apart from these slight gestures to the Satanic ancestry of the Byronic bushranger, there is little else in Foxley's character to emphasize the convention. Instead of being a well-born younger son, dark-haired, pale-skinned, possessing 'eyes That sparkling blazed', Foxley is a shaggy, red-headed Irishman 'talking to his nearest mate' McCoy, with O'Leary and Shanavan as the other 'companions of his fall'; and it is McGuffin, an Irish overseer, who finally kills him. In a curious way, Tucker's novel anticipates the story of Ned Kelly, the final incarnation in Australia of a literary convention; for Kelly, Joe Byrne, and Steve Hart were hunted by Lonigan, Kennedy, Wheelan, O'Connor, Fitzpatrick, and O'Day, all policemen and as Irish as the Kellys. This did not prevent Ned, in his Jerilderie Letter, explaining that his anger had been first aroused by what England had done to Old Erin. Foxley, though demented, offers a similar explanation to William Allen, whose name he has just asked:

'You lie, blast you!' roared the querist; 'for you are long Hempenstall,

[1] Ibid., p. 168. [2] Ibid., p. 169.

that used to hang the rebels long ago in Ireland'. . . I have heard my father talk about you when I was little, how you used to go about with ropes, and when the soldiers would catch a couple of rebels, they would tie them together by the neck and throw them over your shoulder so that they was choked!'[1]

Tucker's anticipation of the Kelly affair is established by a reference to historical circumstance, in the same way that Scott attempts to understand the present by an imaginative recreation of the past. And, because the historical circumstances to which Tucker refers so resemble those of the past Scott recreated (Scott's own acknowledged indebtedness to Maria Edgeworth underlines the resemblance), we can recognize a further reason why Scott's work could remain, if not an influence, then at least a useful example to anyone wishing to turn Australia into fiction. As Frank Hardy shows in *Power without Glory*, the Irish in Australia continue to live out what Manning Clark calls their 'melancholy history'.

One of the difficulties about bushrangers in Australian fiction is that, though their exploits are many without being varied, their motives are almost entirely unmentioned. This is the result, as in Rowcroft, of using a literary convention's surface characteristics without indicating its historical origins—historical in social or literary terms. Rowcroft's readers could of course rely for both on their reading of Scott's translations from the German or his novels, or, if they were old enough, rely as Scott did on recollection of history. In reading Tucker, however, the difficulty is absent, not only because his bushranger is an Irishman whose racial history is still very much a part of him. Tucker also makes clear that Foxley is motivated by revenge, a characteristic of course of the Byronic hero:

> If we do but watch the hour
> There never yet was human power
> Which could evade, if unforgiven,
> The patient search and vigil long
> Of him who treasures up a wrong.[3]

Though there is some doubt about the motives of Milton's Satan, there is none at all about Scott's Bertram in *Rokeby*, who is like Foxley another shaggy outlaw of the hills. Nor does Scott fail to emphasize his hero's Satanic ancestry:

[1] *R.R.*, p. 202. [2] Op. cit., p. 82. [3] Lord Byron, *Mazeppa.*

Here stood a wretch, prepared to change
His soul's redemption for revenge![1]

Scott's footnote is instructive: 'It is agreed by all the writers upon magic and witchcraft, that revenge was the most common motive for the pretended compact between Satan and his vassals.'[2] It seems permissible to suggest, therefore, that the bushranger's Satanism, such as it is in this novel, comes from Scott and the old tradition of witchcraft, and not from Byron and the Christian tradition which Milton made so influential. And indeed mottoes to three of Tucker's five chapters concerning Foxley do in fact come from *Rokeby*. The last perhaps also explains where Foxley acquired his not particularly Irish name:

He took a hundred mortal wounds;
As mute as fox mid mangling hounds.
And when he died, his parting groan
Had more of laughter than of moan![3]

More important than this influence, however, is the way Tucker's reference to actuality makes Foxley's desire for revenge plausible. The details of the gratuitous brutality of the convict system, as Tucker describes it, justify Foxley's explanations of revenge and the brutal form that revenge can take. The following passage, about the gang's indictment of overseer Huggins, is a useful illustration:

'Ah,' resumed McCoy, 'You know me too well! It is not twelve months ago since I was under you in your infernal gang, and one day when I wanted to go and see the doctor, you put me in the lock-up. You left me there thirty-six hours, handcuffed over a beam, both wrists twisted above my head, all my weight hanging on my hands, and my toes only resting on the ground. You delighted in nothing but tyranny, as long as you had the power. But now, *our turn* is come; and you may say your prayers, for you are standing on your own grave!'

'Oh', remarked Foxley. 'That tricing men up to a beam is a very common trick of his. Why, not a month ago one of the deputy overseers was tried for killing a poor devil of a crawler who was very sick and wanted to go to hospital; but Mr Huggins ordered him to be triced up, and the other obeyed him, and handcuffed the man over a pole for two days and a night. The first night the deputy was told

[1] *Rokeby*, Canto III, ix. [2] Ibid., Note 28.
[3] Ibid., Canto VI, xxxiii.

the man was dying; but he only answered, "Let him die and be damned, there's too many of his sort in the country." So the next night, when the doctor came at last to see him, the poor fellow was dead and stiff. That scoundrel, though he was committed, managed to pull through it. *He* made shift to escape from the *law*. But I'll take rattling good care *you* don't escape from *justice*, my fine fellow, for I'm judge in this here Court, and I never acquitted a tyrant like you in my life.'[1]

This is the kind of suffering which we have already seen Ralph Rashleigh experience in the earlier part of the novel. Foxley's restatement confirms it, reinforcing the prevailing tone of the book: a connection is established between the convict, bush-ranger, and aborigine sections. At the same time Foxley's explanation of his proposed revenge on Huggins also goes some way towards explaining the brutality inflicted on the aborigines. Where the law is contemptuous and brutal, contempt and brutality become the law. A kind of chain-reaction is set up in the novel; and because no one doubts Tucker's general historical accuracy—or, to put it another way, his claim to be a realist writer—it is possible to say that the chain is even today not broken. In terms of literature, the 'crucifixion' of Mordecai Himmelfarb in Patrick White's *Riders in the Chariot* by drunken ex-soldiers has its connection with the death of Huggins in *Ralph Rashleigh*. Because of historical circumstance, Australian society, as it is reflected in literature, permits, even encourages, a measure of brutality, often disguised as playfulness, that is not found, say, in Canadian literature.

If play is thought of as a concentration on the means, not the ends, of an action, it is possible to see this connection more clearly. Mock crucifixion is a clumsy way of embarrassing a man, quite as clumsy as tying a can to a dog's tail in order to get rid of it, as happens in Lawson's 'Loaded Dog',[2] or chasing Chinese with hounds in order to give them a fright, as happens in Boldrewood's *The Miner's Right*.[3] The means are similarly excessive when Foxley and his gang decide to kill Huggins. The description, one of the best-known in the novel, shows the absurd exaggeration of the process. The details of the preparation

[1] *R.R.*, pp. 169–70.

[2] *Prose Works of Henry Lawson*, Sydney, London 1948.

[3] *The Miner's Right: A Tale of the Australian Goldfields*, 3 vols., London 1890.

invest the action with an element of playfulness, which here, because the ends are intended to be fatal, in turn heightens by contrast the shock the description creates:

> Huggins was now hurled again on the ant-bed, from whence he had so nearly escaped, and the top of which having been flattened down, a slight trench had been made in it to receive the luckless wretch. The insects, angered into madness at the injuries inflicted on their storehouse, were swarming in thousands around it; but the moment the fresh shock was felt from the fall of Huggins's body, they all rushed to the spot and he was completely covered with them directly afterwards. The bushrangers, being thus relieved from the attacks of the furious ants, now coolly set to work, and tied the wretched sufferer fast down with several cords passing over his thighs and body, two to each arm and leg, and two crossing his neck. The ends of the cords were secured to the pegs cut by Foxley, which were now driven tight into the ground in a sloping direction the better to retain them. The struggles of the wretched victim to escape from these bonds, which were at length so numerous as to form a complete network over him, were further rendered nugatory by logs that were piled upon the cords, between his body and the pins on every side, so that they were tightened until they cut into the flesh.
>
> All these dire arrangements were completed before Huggins had recovered from the effects of that fatal blow which had caused his recapture. When he again became conscious, the convulsive throes of agony that heaved the mass of flesh, cord and logs were so appalling that a sensation of dizzy sickness came across the brain of Rashleigh, who fell to the earth and cut his head severely.[1]

John Barnes has said of this description that 'incidents like this are not marked by any particular literary skill'.[2] The point which was raised earlier about such descriptions is, therefore, worth repeating: comment is absent and the immediacy of the action enhanced. Moreover, Foxley's justification for such bestiality, his desire for revenge, has its echo in the response of the ants: they are 'angered into madness at the injuries inflicted', they destroy Huggins out of revenge, their natural bestiality paralleling the unnaturalness of Foxley's. The parallel acquires added point when the contemptuous attitude of the System towards the convicts is recalled; having escaped Rats' Castle, they

[1] *R.R.*, p. 172.

[2] *The Literature of Australia*, ed. Geoffrey Dutton, Ringwood, Australia 1964, p. 145.

die like flies because they are treated as less than human; while those that live show themselves, like Foxley, as less than human in their revenge. Even the absurd punctiliousness of their revenge follows the pattern of their own suffering as convicts:

> Shortly afterwards, the names of all the men being read over, each shouldered his implement of labour, and the gangs began to move off; but for Rashleigh's part, the overseer Joe called him and ordered him to take up a rope that lay near, and bring it along. Ralph looked at the rope, which appeared heavy enough to load a horse, it being nearly as thick as a cable and of great length. He attempted to lift it, but finding it far beyond his strength, he was fain to desist. He then received a volley of oaths from the little Jew, and two men being called, they placed the rope on his back. It was as much as he could stagger under, and finding it impossible to walk steadily, he ran a few paces, when his foot caught something, and he fell beneath his load, cutting his shin upon a root, so that it bled profusely. But the inflexible Joe directed the rope to be replaced on his back, which was done, and although he repeatedly fell down, it was as repeatedly again hoisted on his back, until at length, trembling in every limb from the intensity of this over-exertion, Ralph reached the scene of their appointed labour.[1]

Rope, the symbol of servitude, and wounds, the signs of suffering, are common to both passages; though it is Rashleigh who is treated like an animal, it is Foxley, an ex-convict and fellow sufferer, who revenges himself like an animal. But more interesting are the parallels of excess: to net a man in rope over an ant-hill is not the quickest way of killing him, but to burden a man like a horse is not the quickest way of shifting rope. Indignity and pain are the intentions behind such actions. The manner in which they suffuse the whole novel suggests Tucker was a finer writer than anybody has so far given him credit for.

It will be recalled that Foxley concludes his justification of revenge by saying of Huggins: '*He* made shift to escape from the *law*. But I'll take rattling good care *you* don't escape from *justice*, my fine fellow, for I'm judge in this here Court, and I never acquitted a tyrant like you in my life.' Later he says he'll be 'revenged on all such bloody tyrants. . .'.[2] It is clear that revenge moves from the personal level to the social, where tyranny in any form becomes the object. Again it is prophetic of Kelly's

[1] *R.R.*, p. 76. [2] Ibid., p. 171.

threat in the Jerilderie Letter that 'it will pay Government to give those people who are suffering, innocence, justice and liberty'.[1] The transformation from bushranger hunted by the law into the opponent of injustice parallels the development in European literature of the Byronic hero into the apostle of Good. Byron had already anticipated as much in a distinction which Foxley echoes:

> There are things
> Which make revenge a virtue by reflection,
> And not an impulse of mere anger; though
> The law sleeps, justice wakes, and injur'd souls
> Oft do a public right with private wrong,
> And justify their deeds unto themselves.[2]

There is a logic in Tucker's analysis that encourages the belief that he has exhausted the subject of revenge; but he concludes by returning to his premise and questioning it. Tyrant, he observes, 'is the term used by all the convicts of New South Wales to designate any person, whether magistrate, overseer or constable, who may perform his duty more strictly than is agreeable to the exalted notions these worthies entertain of the deference and consideration with which they ought to be treated'.[3] It is not a pleasant point of view; taken in isolation, it lacks charity. Yet there is no reason why it should be taken in isolation. In the whole context the view is made tenable by Tucker's understanding of the brutal and brutalizing System, of which his novel remains the earliest intelligent record. Conversely, its conclusion, where Rashleigh is restored to freedom by the interest and gratitude of Colonel Woodville, the father of one of the women Rashleigh has rescued, is not 'conventional' as John Barnes appears to suggest.[4] Rather, it is the final illustration of an opinion that attempts throughout the novel to correct the easy but mistaken view that the convicts were all saints and their captors all sinners. We are offered instead the irony that Byron defined when he wrote: 'There is no freedom, even for masters, in the midst of slaves.'[5] This was the essential irony of Australia's foundation.

[1] Max Brown, *Australian Son, The Story of Ned Kelly*, Melbourne 1956, p. 276.

[2] Lord Byron, *Marino Faliero*, act 4, scene 2, lines 102–7.

[3] *R.R.*, p. 173.

[4] Op. cit., p. 145.

[5] *Byron: Selections from Poetry, Letters and Journals*, ed. Peter Quennell, London 1949, p. 830.

A similarly balanced view is evident in the fourth and final part of the book, which deals with the aborigines; but it is not as keenly balanced as the earlier sections. One reason is the change Rashleigh undergoes as the result of his Australian experiences. Another is that Tucker appears to be here more affected by the opinion of his time that the aborigines were a lesser breed without the law. When, for example, Ralph Rashleigh's protector has died and he is told he must fight to retain his wives,

> the manner of the claimant indicated a kind of contemptuous superiority which Ralph had no notion of, seeing that he well knew his own muscular strength was greater than that of any warrior in the tribe. In fact, he had in sport wrestled with two of them at once, whom he overcame without much difficulty, because, though they look large in many instances, yet the aborigines of Australia are physically very weak.[1]

The obvious retort is that any people which manages to live in Australia by hunting game across the continent cannot be so physically weak; but it is better to consider Tucker's remark as undeveloped and therefore meaningless, for the judgement he offers is based on a comparison of physical strength as impossible as that between an Olympic runner and a wrestler. Occasionally, of course, he prevents such consideration by saying, as he does of a battle between white men and aborigines: 'The white man's superior stamina at length prevailed.'[2] In such battles the white man usually did prevail, but whether because of his superior stamina it is impossible to say. Even without his rifles and poison, he was well armed with disease and rum. Tucker, however, knows the answer no more exactly than we. He accords the victory to physical superiority, as his contemporaries did, and in a brief and muddled way he was probably right. At least he did not ascribe it to the white man's superior intelligence, a view which has inspired much of the social legislation in Australia aimed at discriminating against the aborigine.

Tucker extends the notion of white supremacy when he records Rashleigh's response to the burial of his friend, protector, and teacher, the *carandjie*. He 'viewed this whole ceremony with much the same degree of melancholy feelings that are apt to im-

[1] *R.R.*, p. 272. [2] Ibid., p. 245.

press themselves on the minds of men when they are bereaved of some such humble friend as a dog or horse they value . . .'.[1] This is the language of Rowcroft's narrator and the reasoning is also his: '. . . in spite of the service rendered to him by the old carandjie, who doubtless had saved his life, yet the form of this disgusting specimen of antiquity was so very revolting that our exile had much ado to consider him as being at all human.'[1] On the other hand, the force that honesty exerts in trying to break through a response that convention has moulded is particularly noticeable in the sentence immediately following:

And yet it was no very long time before Rashleigh found that in him he had sustained the loss of a most powerful friend, who had hitherto controlled the savage humours of the males belonging to the tribe, who of themselves would have been now ready enough to mark their hatred of one every way so much superior to any of them. . . .[1]

The excitement of Rashleigh's struggle with the aborigines is to some extent sustained by Tucker's struggle to understand them. Although he is as sceptical of their magic as Scott was of miracles, he is aware of what Australian experience had taught him and his novel inexorably shows: that to exist at all in Australia, the white man must first become a black man. As the history of Australian exploration vividly illustrates, without the aborigines' knowledge of the bush, more than one white hero has come to unheroic grief. Tucker's struggle to understand and to be just is still going on in the last chapter, where the inadequate response to an alien society, of which Tucker can rightly be suspected, is specifically condemned. On seeing Rashleigh, still disguised as an aborigine, Colonel Woodville's

female servants, who were not long in the Colony . . . appeared to consider a native black of Australia as only a higher sort of brute; and they were consequently much astonished to observe that Ralph knew the usages of civilized life, until he told them he had been bred in a white family, when their exclamations of surprise at his having again taken to the bush almost deafened him.[2]

This conclusion has a further interest. Tucker is suggesting that a bush life is preferable to the society of foolish female servants. It will be recalled that Rashleigh does indeed 'take to the bush again' and dies there, though as a white man. This is perhaps

[1] Ibid., p. 272. [2] *R.R.*, pp. 296–7.

the earliest serious passage in a novel about Australia where bush life is acclaimed as superior to urban settlement, or at least that kind of urban settlement represented by foolish female servants.

Elsewhere in the novel only the silence and the loneliness of the bush are mentioned, while there is implied the fear of bushrangers, aborigines, and the unknown, to which the silence and loneliness give rise; in fact in a novel which moves, like Australian civilization itself, from urban England to the 'suburban' settlement at Emu Plains, and from there to the bush, there is very little mention of that bush which is the setting for one half of the story. Even in a passage like the following, it is not the bush that especially interests Tucker, but the social implications of its tenure. He regrets its aspects not as a solitary, but as a social man:

> After he had passed the river and its clustering settlers, he journeyed through bypaths across the bush and was soon deeply immersed in the almost twilight gloom of an Australian forest, where the deepest silence ever prevails. No warbling choristers here greet the merry morn with jocund flights of song. No lowing of herds or bleating of flocks awakes the slumbering echoes. The feathered tribes are here entirely mute or only utter either discordant screams or brief harsh twittering. The solitary bell-bird chiefly, whose voice may be heard sometimes, disturbs the primeval solitude with its single sharp note, which resounds through the grove with so great a resemblance to a sheep bell that it requires a practised ear to detect the difference between the bird and the reality.
>
> Animated nature here appears to slumber, for not a single living thing can be seen, except at rare intervals, when a gaudily-marbled goanna of great size may perhaps hurry on his spiral route up a tree to avoid the approaching foot of man, or perchance, a snake may glide hastily across his path, the glittering colours of its skin, in its convolutions, chiefly attracting the eye by their brilliant contrast with the faded dull brown herbage or the dead leaves among which it rustles in its sinuous way. No kangaroo, emu or other larger fowl or animal may be seen; 'tis too near the busy haunts of man, while on the other hand, the domesticated quadrupeds are not found, because this forms part of a large settler's grant. He has got no stock in this neighbourhood; yet he will not allow his poorer neighbour's single cow to subsist upon the grass, which annually springs, comes to maturity, is parched to dust by the winds of summer and blown away by the breath of autumn.[1]

[1] *R.R.*, pp. 115–16.

Tucker is regretting the antagonism between the squatter and his poorer neighbour, a source of drama which Trollope recognized before Lawson and Steele Rudd saw it as a source of doubtful humour. Tucker is also, however, lamenting the difference between Australia and England, although, curiously, not the England which Rashleigh has left. His farewell to Home is cool and brief, his welcome to Australia correspondingly warm:

> The misery of his abode, he being thus overwrought and rather more than half starved all day, and being devoured by myriads of vermin all night, made Ralph long for the arrival of the vessel which was to remove him to New South Wales. . . .[1]
>
> Ralph had little to do with either leave-taking or bargaining. His slender store of money was soon expended in purchasing a little tea and sugar, with a few other trifling comforts, for his long voyage; and it was with no very poignant feelings of regret that he saw the anchor weighed and the sails loosed which were to waft him away from the land of his birth.[2]

This is the England of Rashleigh's experience. In the passage previously quoted, the equally real Australia of lizards and snakes is in part a reflection of the real meanness of outback society as it was experienced by the wealthy squatter's poor neighbour. The England which is implied in the rhetorical figures of antithesis and periphrasis, and the heightened prose of 'No warbling choristers here greet the merry morn with jocund flights of song', is the England of pastoral poetry. It is possible to hear in Tucker's phrase 'the busy haunts of men' a distant echo of Milton's 'the busy hum of men'. Tucker's whole description is indeed not far removed from Goldsmith's, when in *The Deserted Village* he considers the nature of those 'distant climes' to which dispossessed peasants have emigrated:

> Those matted woods, where birds forget to sing,
> But silent bats in drowsy clusters cling;
> Those poisonous fields with rank luxuriance crowned,
> Where the dark scorpion gathers death around;
> Where at each step the stranger fears to wake
> The rattling terrors of the vengeful snake.

Pastoralism in fiction, however, encourages, even requires, a relaxation of intelligence.

[1] Ibid., pp. 51–2. [2] Ibid., p. 61.

Tucker must have known that it was a fifty-year old commonplace that Australia had no blackbirds and thrushes, just as he knows, and mentions, that the country had no gardens where they could warble. He certainly assumes that jackasses need no introduction to the reader: he refers to them as 'laughing jackasses—certain birds so called'.[1] Either he imagines his reader has heard of them before, or that they are unimportant. He nevertheless persists in mentioning the absence of the jocund feathered tribe because it provides him with an occasion for pastoralism. Tucker employs the picaresque form because, as William Empson says of Gay's *The Beggar's Opera*, 'its casualness and inclusiveness allow it to collect into it things that had been floating in tradition.'[2]

Kingsley, in *The Recollections of Geoffry Hamlyn*,[3] seems to have the same attitude to pastoralism and for the same reason. He, however, discovers that the morning warble of Australian magpies is a good substitute for the absent merle and mavis. The discovery is no more useful to the novel than is Tucker's lament to his; but it does show that, whatever an author's opinion on Australian flora and fauna, pastoralism is the means chosen to express it. It can thus be suggested that the argument that went on, or was assumed, in nineteenth-century Australian fiction was determined by a literary convention: if pastoralism was a necessary ingredient of a novel, then an author was bound to commit himself on the subject of blackbirds and gum-trees. After all, the actual appearance of the country—or that part of it which the argument was about, the bush (which could mean Tucker's forests or Furphy's Wimmera)—was unimportant to the narrative, to the novel's instructive element, and to Australia's present and future settlers. As any reading of nineteenth-century English fiction makes clear, most Englishmen would have been hard pressed to tell the difference between a mavis and either variety of the Australian magpie. For them, 'the crow doth sing as sweetly as the lark, when neither is attended'. The convention, of course, which Australian writers are following is from Scott, a countryman, one of the few novelists in English who were.

[1] *R.R.*, p. 141.

[2] *Some Versions of Pastoral*, London 1935, Harmondsworth 1966, p. 159.

[3] Henry Kingsley, *The Recollections of Geoffry Hamlyn*, 3 vols., Cambridge, London 1859.

Tucker refers to a host of literary celebrities, many of them, like Mrs. Barbauld and Robert Bloomfield, now considerably less celebrated than they once were. In referring to Trapbois, however, and using his phrase, 'a fair con-sid-e-ra-tion', Tucker needs to mention neither the character's creator, Scott, nor the novel in which he appears, *The Fortunes of Nigel*. The character, the phrase, even its typography, are evidently known exactly to Tucker and his audience. This provides a further indication of how completely Scott had permeated the English-speaking world; it is also a useful corrective to today's dismissal not merely of Scott but also of his influence. It is when passages like the following are read in the novel—realistic though it often is—that we recognize the extension of pastoralism, namely the set scene, set of course for the painter, not the narrative. Scott is the source of both. The following occurs when Ralph is still with the bushrangers:

> Their provisions again began to grow short, when, on the fourth morning from the death of O'Leary, a few hours after they had quitted the spot of their past night's sojurn, they came to the summit of a lofty range, where a prospect equally unexpected as it was beautiful and varied burst upon the sight of the enraptured Rashleigh, whose tormenting feelings, induced by the fear of what fate might have in reserve for him as punishment of his involuntary association with the desperate and bloodstained ruffians who now formed at once his guard and his masters, all gave way before the majesty of nature, and he drank in large draughts of delight in contemplating the lovely scene now expanded before him.
>
> Immediately in front of his present position was a precipice some hundred feet in height, whose ragged breast sank sheer down to the broad expanse of the low country; but immediately at its base the Nepean river, here narrowed to about the distance of a hundred yards between its banks, rushed with tumultuous force around the greater part of the hill on which they stood, from which immense masses of rock had apparently been detached by some long past convulsion of nature, and now lay in the bed of the torrent, causing the rapid waters to flash around them in sheets of snowy foam. Far to the right and left the winding convolutions of the stream might be seen at intervals appearing through the foliage, here in magnificent sheets of water, and anon, beyond a projecting promontory forming a low range of hills, the river seemed contracted into the semblance of a dazzling silvery riband that sparkled in the beams of the morning sun.

In the background rose the lofty heights of gloomy mountains, whose variously undulating sides were chiefly clad with the dark evergreen foliage of New Holland, though here and there might be seen upreared the giant form of some rude and fantastically shaped peak or rifted cliff whose grey bosoms were boldly exposed in naked sublimity. As far as the eye could reach in front was an expanse of nearly level woodland, broken here and there by cultivated patches of a greater or less extent, and thinly studded with solitary farm-houses, cots and one or two hamlets with their churches.[1]

Descriptions such as this, like pastoralism, add nothing to the narrative, and apart from 'the dark evergreen foliage of New Holland' do not tell the reader anything about Australia. Such passages in nineteenth-century Australian novels—and there are many—could have come only from Scott:

the view extended beyond them down a wooded glen, where the small river was sometimes visible, sometimes hidden in copse. The eye might be delayed by a desire to rest on the rocks, which here and there rose from the dell with massive or spiry fronts, or it might dwell on the noble, though ruined tower, which was here beheld in all its dignity, frowning from a promontory over the river. To the left were seen two or three cottages, a part of the village; the brow of the hill concealed the others. The glen, or dell, was terminated by a sheet of water, called Loch-Veolan, into which the brook discharged itself, and which now glistened in the western sun. The distant country seemed open and varied in surface, though not wooded; and there was nothing to interrupt the view until the scene was bounded by a ridge of distant and blue hills, which formed the southern boundary of the strath or valley.[2]

Such scenes bear no distinctive characteristics, which is why it is a mistake to say of authors, like Tucker, that they saw Australia through English eyes. Except for Europe's 'ruined tower', there is nothing especially English, Scottish, or Australian about such scenes. They were determined not by nationalism but by literary requirement. When embryonic writers decided what form their novel was to take, they referred to Scott for guidance, which explains Tucker's otherwise inexplicable habit of referring to the 'potato bogle' as the Scotch equivalent of the English 'scarecrow';[3] or the following remark: 'The Scottish language has at this day a word expressive of the

[1] *R.R.*, pp. 166–7. [2] *Waverley*, ch. xiii. [3] *R.R.*, p. 76.

national belief in such a doctrine. It is *fey*, and is used to designate the conduct of a man who rushes, as it were, upon destruction . . .'[1] Scott's influence is evident even in the final mention of 'solitary farm-houses, cots, and one or two hamlets with their churches'. The vocabulary is English, though the scene could be Australian; yet such characteristics are unimportant when compared with the necessity Tucker apparently felt to include such a final picture of settlement and domesticity in a description which emphasizes sublime solitariness. Settlement, by which is meant a home, completes the picture, just as the restoration of Tully-Veolan, the Baron of Bradwardine's home, completes *Waverley*. Unlike Scott's hero, Ralph Rashleigh has no share in the settlement. He is an onlooker, among the outlaws on a peak of rock. His final preference for the bush is therefore plausible, but his admiration is no less than Kingsley's for the 'abundant proofs of the wonted energy of the Anglo-Saxon race, who speedily rescue the most untamed soils from the barbarism of nature and bid the busy sounds of industry and art awaken the silent echoes of every primeval forest in which they are placed'.[2] Such a victory was represented most completely in *Waverley*, in which the Anglo-Saxon race under their German king triumph over the Scottish outlaws and their French Prince.

The argument, however, has one weakness: the admiration of the Anglo-Saxon race is in fact Tucker's, not Rashleigh's. To what extent the two can be separated is sometimes difficult to say, and it is further complicated by the changes that Rashleigh's character undergoes. In the first, English section, he is a petty thief who, in his rise from rags to riches, acquires a shrewd resourcefulness but no courage. In the second section, when he is a convict, courage is not a quality that would have had much use, even if he had possessed it. He suffers; there is no possibility of a different response. At the same time he is critical of his gaolers and of the brutality they inflict on and encourage in their captives. In the third section, he secretly helps those he can among the victims of the bushrangers, but obviously lacks responsibility, cunning, and bravery to escape from his companions; and they tell him so. Of the fourth section, however, in which it can be said that Tucker's view of the aborigines is the conventional one of the time, it can also be said

[1] Ibid., p. 198. [2] Ibid., p. 68.

that Rashleigh's physical superiority, his resourcefulness, and his ability to bear deprivation are the results of his experiences in the earlier parts of the book. We are left in no doubt that he has learnt all the old *carandjie's* magic, which Tucker dismisses as tricks. Similarly, when Rashleigh builds a raft, he does it in the way he has seen Foxley do it; and when he navigates it, he is relying on the example of Roberts, the convict with whom he finally escaped. It might be said sceptically, that any man who had withstood as many rigours as Rashleigh was virtually indestructible. Yet this is precisely what some of the convicts were. What is important here is that Rashleigh is the foundation of a legend as well as a fictional example of what in fact did happen. He is the forerunner of Judd, the convict in Patrick White's *Voss*, or of those latter-day Australians of whom A. D. Hope says:

> In them at last the ultimate men arrive
> Whose boast is not: 'we live' but 'we survive',
> A type who will inhabit the dying earth.
>
> 'Australia'

They possess what D. H. Lawrence called in *Kangaroo* 'the strange Australian power of enduring—enduring suffering or opposition or difficulty—just blank enduring'.[1] Rashleigh is the product not only of his own experiences, but those of his nation. In order to survive, he assimilates the knowledge of thief, convict, bushranger, and aborigine. Unlike the free settlers of fiction, or often those of history, he survives even to die in Australia, all thought of escape abandoned. On a factual level, his being dyed black and his removal of the dye is implausible; but on a symbolic level, in the history of Australia they signify as much as Crusoe's friendship with Friday does in the history of Europe:

> it was fully a week before his person had resumed its former appearance, when the newly-formed cuticle, though extremely tender at first, appeared to him much more delicate and pure than ever he could recollect it to have been before; and it produced such a youthful effect in his appearance as quite surprised him when he looked at his face in a mirror.[2]

Pink purity which is the result of the removal of the black man;

[1] Op. cit., p. 339. [2] *R.R.*, p. 301.

the continuing emphasis on youthfulness in a young society already nearly 200 years old; and the mirror of engrossed self-approval—these are some recognizable Australian characteristics. To have expressed them so early and so completely in a novel of realism is Tucker's claim to our attention as Australia's first symbolist.

5 Henry Kingsley, *The Recollections of Geoffry Hamlyn*

OF Henry Kingsley's nineteen books of fiction only two, *The Recollections of Geoffrey Hamlyn*[1] and *The Hillyars and the Burtons*,[2] refer to Australia at all extensively; in a third, *Ravenshoe*,[3] set in England, a Moravian missionary with Australian experience appears briefly; and in a fourth, *The Boy in Grey*,[4] Australia is the conclusion to a political allegory involving a world-journey. In *Reginald Hetherege*,[5] and the story, 'The Two Cadets', which is included in *Hetty and Other Stories*,[6] Australian material is used for a scene or an incident—old material reworked to support failing creative powers. Despite the slightness of reference to Australia, Kingsley's name remains in any list of Australian novelists; not as high as such earlier admirers as Boldrewood placed it, but nevertheless there, in spite of Joseph Furphy's scorn. On the other hand, Anthony Trollope's is not, and never has been, although his long short-story *Harry Heathcote of Gangoil*,[7] which is set entirely in Australia, and his novel *John Caldigate*,[8] half of which is set there, make far more intelligent use of the Australian experience than Kingsley's work does. Admittedly, the percentage these works represent of each author's total production is different. There is, however, another reason for Kingsley's name appearing on any Australian list, and it can best be discovered by concentrating where attention has already mainly been concentrated, on *The Recollections of Geoffry Hamlyn*, though it is not as interesting to a contemporary reader as *The Hillyars and the Burtons*.

Geoffry Hamlyn concerns the fortunes of two aristocratic but impoverished Devon families, the Buckleys and the Brentwoods, and the disruptive effect of a misalliance between two

[1] 3 vols., Cambridge, London 1859.
[2] *The Hillyars and the Burtons: A Story of Two Families*, 3 vols., London 1865.
[3] 3 vols., Cambridge, London 1862.
[4] London 1871.
[5] 3 vols., London 1874.
[6] London 1871.
[7] *Harry Heathcote of Gangoil: A Tale of Australian Bush Life*, London 1874.
[8] 3 vols., London 1879.

lesser families, the Thorntons and the Hawkers. Major Buckley and his wife Agnes sell their ancestral home in England and, with their child Sam, sail to recover their fortunes in Australia. Their friend and neighbour, the widowed Captain Brentwood, whose life Buckley saved at Waterloo, accompanies them with his daughter Alice. Together, they represent all that is good, or 'noble' as Kingsley insists; for most readers today, they perhaps resemble more nearly the 'unco' guid.'

Having brought her father's grey hairs to the grave because of her marriage to George Hawker, who has been transported for coining, Mary Hawker, the wilful daughter of the local vicar of Drumston, accompanies them with her small son. They are all, good and not so good, encouraged to emigrate by reports sent back by their Drumston friends, James Stockbridge and the narrator of the tale, Geoffry Hamlyn. Also of the 'Buckley society', as Kingsley calls the party, is Doctor Mulhaus, a German exile in Drumston since the Napoleonic wars. Unlike the others, he goes for friendship's sake, not to make money. Mary Hawker goes to forget the social disaster of her marriage, James Stockbridge to forget Mary, whom he loves, Tom Troubridge to farm with his friends Stockbridge and Hamlyn. Yet for all of them money is the antidote to pain as well as poverty. Mulhaus is the exception.

Having made their money, they return to England, more exalted among the county than when they left. Doctor Mulhaus is shown to be Baron von Landstein disguised, a hero of the fight against Napoleon; he returns to the family *Schloss*, of which his brother had cheated him along with his good name. George Hawker, the transported coiner who became an Australian bushranger, has been killed, leaving Mary free to marry her business partner, Tom Troubridge. The only other casualties are her son by Hawker, who is shot by his father unknowingly in the final battle; and James Stockbridge, who is killed by the aborigines, but not before he is cured of his love for Mary. Everyone affected, however remotely, by Mary's passionate nature is removed.

Hamlyn expresses Kingsley's purpose:

> This narrative which I am now writing is neither more nor less than an account of what befell certain of my acquaintances during a period extending over nearly, or quite, twenty years, interspersed, and let us

hope embellished, with descriptions of the country in which these circumstances took place, and illustrated by conversations well known to me by frequent repetition, selected as throwing light upon the characters of the persons concerned. Episodes there are, too, which I have thought it worth while to introduce as being more or less interesting as bearing on the manners of a country but little known, out of which materials it is difficult to select those most proper to make my tale coherent. . . .[1]

The vague chronology—'nearly, or quite, twenty years'—is matched by the divided intention—'neither more nor less than an account . . . interspersed, and . . . embellished, with descriptions of the country', plus episodes 'bearing on the manners of a country but little known'. Together, they account for much of the novel's humbugging tone.

The 'narrative' to which Hamlyn here refers concerns only the years in Australia; the extract quoted appears at the opening of the second of the original three volumes. The novel begins in England at the time of the Napoleonic wars and ends in England at the time of the Crimean War. Between are the years of getting and forgetting, disturbed only by tales of battles in India and the threats of bushrangers. The feeling of isolated nationalism shared by all, with the notable exception of Mulhaus, the novel's one 'foreigner', is largely that of an embattled England. The years of peaceful Australian money-making between 1814 and 1854 were those in which England garnered her harvest in preparation for the years of famine which to some seemed introduced by the reforms of 1832, to others by the hungry Forties, to some by the revolutionary threats of 1848, and to all by the outbreak of war in 1854. The fact that Edmund Gosse's father and mother interrupted breakfast to sink 'on their knees in front of their tea and bread-and-butter' to give 'thanks to the God of Battles' for the victory at Alma does suggest 'the strain of national anxiety'.[2] It can, of course, be said, as his son was the first to say, of Gosse senior, Charles Kingsley's friend, 'there existed in Great Britain no more thorough "Jingo" than he'; but it cannot easily be said of his wife, whose Christian tract 'The Guardsman of the Alma'

[1] Henry Kingsley, *The Recollections of Geoffry Hamlyn*, 3 vols., London 1859; The World's Classics, London 1924 (hereafter referred to as *Hamlyn*), p. 201.

[2] Edmund Gosse, *Father and Son*, London 1907, p. 31.

circulated in more than half a million copies, urging not the joys of battle but those of conversion and faith.

The forty years of external peace between the two wars were not at the time felt to represent the prevailing condition of national life. As Thomas Hardy recalls in *The Trumpet-Major*:

> When lawyers strive to heal a breach
> And parsons practise what they preach;
> Then little Boney he'll pounce down,
> And march his men on London town.

The fear of Boney lived on long after his death, and not merely in soldier's songs and children's rhymes. There was also immense social unrest during these forty years, for which a foreign war might offer a temporary cure by providing an excuse for halting, even reversing, social reform; and of course by removing overseas all those who disturbed the peace. Emigration, forced or free, was another possible solution. Kingsley, however, discovers a further argument in its favour. Not only does he remove all passion to Australia, where one way or another it grows cold, he also uses Australia as the source of renewal for those impoverished by war. When foreign war begins again, they return to England rich enough, and opportunely enough, to re-establish themselves as members of the ruling group. The difficulty of 'these times' is the cause of Sam Buckley being characterized as the man he is:

> we will if you please appoint him hero, with all the honours and emoluments thereunto pertaining. Perhaps when I have finished, you will think him not so much of a hero after all. But at all events you shall see how he is an honest upright gentleman, and in these times, perhaps such a character is preferable to a hero.[1]

In objecting to Sam's puerile nature, Joseph Furphy in *Such is Life*[2] is questioning only Sam's credibility as a successful squatter and his Tory sympathies. What he ignores is Kingsley's analogy, which the opening and the conclusion make clear, between the Napoleonic and the Crimean wars. Sam's idyllic life in Australia is the counterpart of England's peaceful idyll.

[1] *Hamlyn*, p. 13.

[2] Joseph Furphy, *Such is Life: Being Certain Extracts from the Diary of Tom Collins*, Sydney 1903.

The analogy, long since shown to be false, was nevertheless accepted by many among all classes, much as today most people would accept the analogy of the First and Second World Wars. Kingsley's objection to a hero was that heroes disturb the peace, just as Napoleon did or George Hawker the bushranger. Hawker is ambitious and feels himself above the law. As the upright Sam says of savagery: 'All men who act entirely without any law . . . arrive at much the same degree, whether white or black.'[1] The perspicuity which insists that it is possible for men to be as savage while acting entirely within the law is a quality Kingsley lacks; and it is more useful in an understanding of Australian literature to admit this than to spend much time blaming him for it.

Kingsley's difficulties in making the 'tale coherent' arise from his divided intention to say what happened to certain acquaintances and at the same time to tell readers about Australia. These acquaintances are so surpassingly 'noble', enjoying an idyllic existence, that their experiences are unlikely to represent anything other than nobility. That the Australian experiences, besides being profitable, are also idyllic should not be in doubt. Not only is the whole Buckley 'society' noble—with the exception of the Hawker connection; its peacefulness also extends to its relations with nature. There are of course bushfires, storms, even an earthquake, but the society survives them without loss of life or property. Of Sam Buckley for instance, we learn that 'Never a dog but wagged his tail when he caught Sam's eye'.[2] He and his horse are described thus: 'Now in holiday clothes and in holiday mind, the two noble animals cross the paddock. . . .'[3] Both quotations come from the chapter called 'The Golden Vineyard', when Sam meets Alice Brentwood for the first time and falls in love. The whole chapter, from its descriptions of the tame animals that hop round the Brentwood's place, to the Captain's remark on seeing Alice and Sam gathering fruit that it is a scene from *Paradise Lost*, establishes the idyllic nature of young love in a young country. The chapter, placed centrally, is the substance of the novel's idyllic aspect. The Napoleonic

[1] *Hamlyn*, p. 312.
[2] Ibid., p. 275.
[3] Ibid., p. 278.

disturbances, the shortage of cash, the abandonment of position, the labouring for a competence, all lead up to it. After it come rivalry in love, the child lost in the bush, storms, earthquakes, bushrangers, death, and the Crimean War. How Major Buckley saved Captain Brentwood, how the Donovans drove off the aborigines, 'an old gold-laced cap' on the wall, and the book of pictures of 'the conquest of an empire greater than Haroun Al Raschid's' which Sam and Alice look at—these are the echoes of actuality, reminders of permanence. The chapter is followed by one called 'The Gentleman from the Wars', describing Lieutenant Halbert as he recovers in Australia from blighted love and the rigours of distant Indian campaigns. His name is a reminder of his martial affinities with the Buckleys.

The method by which Kingsley establishes the omnipresence of his idyll is to impute the same noble characteristics that the protagonists possess to everything else. Of a jug of claret on the table in the Brentwoods's house, he says it was 'standing, with freezing politeness, upright, his hand on his hip, waiting to be poured. In the centre, the grandfather of watermelons. . . '.[1] Cecil Hadgraft misses the point when he calls the following passage 'ambiguous for a moment if the reader is not alert':[2] 'With broad intelligent forehead, with large loving hazel eyes, with a frill like Queen Elizabeth, with a brush like a fox; deep in the brisket, perfect in . . .'[3] The description is of Sam's dog Rover; Hadgraft is suggesting the unwary reader might be misled into thinking the description is of a person. But the similarity, the common nobility, is precisely what Kingsley wishes to suggest. The passage continues: 'perfect in markings of black, white, and tan; in sagacity a Pitt, in courage an Anglesey, Rover stands first on my list, and claims to be king of Collie-dogs. In politics I should say Conservative of the high Protectionist sort.' The dog is neither more nor less aristocratic than the claret jug, or Sam's horse Widderin, whose granddam was owned by Sheik Abdullah and whose sire belonged to the Duke of C—; or Alice Brentwood, possessed of 'A Norman style of beauty . . . and high-bred grace in every limb and every motion'.[4] As Hadgraft says, 'they are fine animals', even the claret jug; but this is the idyll, told by an old

[1] Ibid., p. 288.
[2] *Australian Literature*, p. 44.
[3] *Hamlyn*, p. 214.
[4] Ibid., p. 283.

man. And for the same reason they are all tame. The ambiguity Hadgraft notes is really anthropomorphism. The lion lies down with the lamb; one is noble and probably a gentleman, and the other a Christian. Such a view of nature's common nobility was perhaps more necessary in the year Charles Darwin published *The Origin of Species* than it is today.

There are other possible reasons for this anthropomorphic view of life, such as the one F. H. Mares[1] suggests in discussing Kingsley's strange work *The Boy in Grey*. Mares hints at Kingsley's possible psychological difficulties, but is unfortunately unable to do more than hint because so little is known about them, despite S. M. Ellis's *Henry Kingsley, 1830–1876: Towards a Vindication*.[2] An explanation along these lines is inviting, especially for the chapter called 'How the Child Was Lost'. This is one of those 'episodes' Kingsley promises in the earlier pages, an episode often used since in Australian fiction and film—mainly, of course, because it is unhappily frequent in Australia. It is the story of a child lost in the bush, whose body is found by Sam Buckley and his friend and rival, Cecil Mayford. Joseph Furphy, who used the same episode in *Such is Life*, has the child lose itself in searching for its father. In Kingsley's account, family is forgotten; it was never important in the first place. The child goes in search of what he imagines are white playmates—of 'society', it might be said—in the wood across the river. The shadows he has seen turn out to be kangaroos, harmless, but not as friendly as the shell-parrots which 'twittered and ran to and fro quite busily, as though they said to him, "We don't mind you, my dear; you are quite one of us" '.[3] This is another example of the habit of using anthropomorphism to establish an idyll which fate destroys. Here, it is perhaps more easily acceptable because our ideas of childhood are less precise than our experiences of young adulthood. But Kingsley, significantly it seems, goes out of his way to explain the habit by making his elderly narrator say: 'Depend on it, a man never experiences such pleasure or grief after fourteen as he does before, unless in some cases in his first love-making, when the sensation is new to him'.[3] In other

[1] *The Literature of Australia*, p. 248.
[2] London 1931.
[3] *Hamlyn*, p. 327.

words, Sam Buckley courting Alice Brentwood is reliving the pleasure of childhood. It is a questionable view, although the addled age of the narrator might answer our questions; so too the apparently total absence of success of any kind in Kingsley's life up to this time, which later years seem to have left harshly unrelieved. The effect of such a view, however, is that, in so far as Sam Buckley is the 'hero', his experiences set the tone. This is why the Australian section can be called an idyll, and why so many have found it puerile.

It is more important, however, to notice how the idyll conflicts with the reality of Australia. The discovery of gold, for instance, is one of the promised 'Episodes . . . more or less interesting as bearing on the manners of a country but little known . . .'; it was also one of which Kingsley himself had first-hand experience, having originally gone to Australia as a digger. Yet in writing about gold, he says: 'the knowledge of its existence was confined to very few, and those well-educated men, who never guessed (how could they without considerable workings?) how abundant it was. As for the stories of shepherds finding gold and selling it to the Jews in Sydney, they are very mythical, and I for one entirely disbelieve them.'[1] Who first found gold in Australia is uncertain: James McBrien, a surveyor, is the first who recorded his find near the Fish River in New South Wales in 1823. The occasions on which Kingsley's episode seems to be based are Count Strzelecki's discovery near Hartley in 1839 and the Rev. W. B. Clarke's near Bathurst in 1841. These discoveries were kept secret at the behest of Governor Gipps, who gave his name to the area in which Kingsley sets his novel. The discoveries that began the first rush were those of Edward Hargreaves, a grazier, and John Lister and James Tom, two bushmen. None of them was well-educated, but Hargreaves had been to California, recognized the auriferous country as resembling the Bathurst district, and tested his experience when in 1851 he returned to Australia: 'considerable workings' were not necessary merely to 'guess'. Compared experience, of Californian strata with Australian, was enough. This is the version of discovery Furphy prefers when he pours scorn on Kingsley's tale. Kingsley must have known all about this; he was in Australia as a digger in 1853.

[1] Ibid., p. 241.

The peculiar terms of his idyll, however, oblige him to discount a probability which was based on known facts, namely that shepherds found gold and sold it.

Sometimes the idyll conflicts with the reality even as it is acknowledged in the novel. On several occasions Kingsley mentions that an 'Australian' or 'working men in Australia' never touch their hat in greeting because the convicts were forced to do it. Yet Lee, an ex-convict in Mary Hawker's employment, makes a point of doing so; or Kingsley makes the point of saying that he did so. Again, the idyll is preserved.

Similarly, Frank Maberly, the Reverend Thornton's muscular successor as vicar of Drumston, translated to an Australian deanery, finds his way to his Devon friends, and decides to visit the men in an outlying hut. They have already been lamented as hopeless cases by all who know them, yet Maberly preaches to them on the text, 'Servants, obey your masters'. As though this is not implausible enough, Kingsley records that the sermon was 'homely, plain, sensible, and interesting, and had succeeded in awakening the whole attention and interest of the three who were listening . . .'.[1] The social comment is accurate. Why should men employed as shepherds—possibly the loneliest job in the last century, attracting only those for whom nothing else offered, as Trollope reminds us in *John Caldigate*—listen to the voice of a noble's Lord? And in Australia, 'that working man's paradise',[2] as Kingsley calls it? Yet he contradicts the social comment with an individual example, solely in order that the idyll, in which that individual represents organized religion, should prevail.

Outside the idyll which is the heart of the novel, Kingsley's attitude to Australia is similarly mixed. He begins by saying that 'all creation is new and strange', and continues the image of the Promised Land when describing the Buckley society—even tribe—establishing themselves in Gippsland: 'the scene so venerable and ancient, so seldom seen in the Old World—the patriarchs moving into the desert with all their wealth, to find new pasture-ground.'[3] This is 'the first and simplest act of colonization'. The statement is perhaps just true enough in

[1] *Hamlyn*, p. 271.
[2] Ibid., p. 63.
[3] Ibid., p. 173.

general, but it is certainly not true of Australia's first settlement, as Bill Lee's and George Hawker's presence in Australia constantly reminds us.

Kingsley is, however, accurate in another way: although his story is a bush idyll, he takes a Dickensian delight in the existence of urban Australia:

> I never stood in Venice contemplating the decay of the grand palaces of her old merchant princes, whose time has gone by for ever. I never watched the slow downfall of a great commercial city; but I have seen what to him who thinks aright is an equally grand subject of contemplation—the rapid rise of one. I have seen what but a small moiety of the world, even in these days, has seen, and what, save in this generation, has never been seen before, and will, I think, never be seen again. I have seen Melbourne. Five years in succession did I visit that city, and watch each year how it spread and grew until it was beyond recognition. Every year the press became denser, and the roar of the congregated thousands grew louder, till at last the scream of the flying engine rose above the hubbub of the streets, and two thousand miles of electric wire began to move the clicking needles with ceaseless intelligence.[1]

Writing of Dickens's originality, John Holloway has recently said it 'was in part that he responded adequately, in both his vision and his technique, to the extraordinary fact of Victorian London: recorded, for the first time in English, the Life of Megalopolis'.[2] In the passage from Kingsley, which moves untrammelled by the necessities of idyll, the author responds to the equally extraordinary fact of nineteenth-century Melbourne, 'the Paris of the Antipodes', 'the Chicago of the South', 'marvellous Melbourne', as visitors as well as locals called it.[3] It is a pity Kingsley so seldom allows himself to respond in this way: but when he does, he is far removed from what is later recognizable as the Australian pastoral tradition of literature. He is closer to the English tradition which Dickens, Thackeray, and Mrs. Gaskell were at this time establishing.

A comparison of attitudes apparent in Kingsley's use of the phrase 'these days', in this passage and the earlier one suggesting upright gentlemen as preferable to heroes, illustrates the same Victorian conflict. Delight in material progress and frank

[1] Ibid., pp. 256–7. [2] *The Novelist as Innovator*, London 1965, p. 48.
[3] Asa Briggs, op. cit., chapter vii, 'Melbourne'.

unease at its possible political and spiritual consequences are as evident in the two uses as they are in Dickens. By the time Kingsley wrote *The Hillyars and the Burtons*, Dickens had established in readers' minds the expectancy of an analysis of the conflict; and Kingsley obliged, though in crude metropolitan terms of the English versus the Irish, whose representatives are in the main 'lifted' from a source Boldrewood used, namely Charles Lever. Kingsley fails to recognize the political problem in its distinctive Australian terms, as Trollope for instance, in *Harry Heathcote of Gangoil*, does not. The basis of the problem was land use and ownership; its protagonists, as Trollope realized in literature years before the Sydney *Bulletin*, were the squatter and the free-selector.

Kingsley's peroration in praise of Melbourne ends in a final flutter of honesty: 'Unromantic enough, but beyond all conception wonderful.' It is a conclusion to which we will return.

If this passage expressed the whole of Kingsley's attitude to Australia, the fact that the Buckley society returns to England would lack the credibility or literary convenience that even Kingsley acknowledges. He therefore tempers his vision of Australia's future and enhances the nobility of England's past. After Doctor Mulhaus, for instance, has prophesied a 'peopled landscape' of peace and prosperity, he continues:

> 'I see . . . a vision of a nation, the colony of the greatest race on the earth, who began their career with more advantages than ever fell to the lot of a young nation yet. War never looked on them. Not theirs was the lot to fight, like the Americans, through bankruptcy and inexperience towards freedom and honour. No. Freedom came to them. Heaven-sent, red-tape-bound, straight from Downing-Street. Millions of fertile acres, gold in bushels were theirs, and yet—'
>
> 'Go on,' said the Major.
>
> 'I see a vision of broken railway arches and ruined farms. I see a vision of a people surfeited with prosperity and freedom grown factious, so that now one party must command a strong majority ere they can pass a law the goodness of which no one denies. I see a bankrupt exchequer, a drunken Governor, an Irish ministry, a—'
>
> 'Come down out of that,' roared the Major, 'before I pull you down.'[1]

As in the England of Dickens in *Hard Times* and in Boldrewood's Australia, the threat to peaceful progress comes from

[1] *Hamlyn*, pp. 409–10.

democracy, from the determined wish of the many to define and to share in that progress. We see why it is preferable 'in these times' to have honest upright gentlemen and not heroes at the centre of affairs, a preference which nearly every Victorian novelist shares.

Earlier in the novel, Frank Maberly condemns the choice made by the small freeholder when he leaves England for Australia: he gives up 'an old, well-ordered society, the ordinances of religion, the various give-and-take relations between rank and rank, which make up the sum of English life, for independence, godlessness, and rum! He gains, say you! Yes, he gains meat for his dinner every day, and *voilà tout!*'[1] Major Buckley's analysis, despite his rejection of Mulhaus's final 'vision', is fundamentally the same: 'There is no social influence in the settled districts; there are too many men without masters.'[2]

In refurbishing England's image, which has been discoloured by comparative poverty and vice in order to get the 'society' off to Australia, Kingsley is again careful not to inflict too great an implausibility on the novel. Thus it is young Sam Buckley and his wife who return first; only when they are there does the older generation respond to family ties. It is not family, however, that persuades Sam and his wife:

> 'What honours, what society, has this little colony to give, compared to those open to a fourth-rate gentleman in England? I want to be a real Englishman, not half a one. I want to throw in my lot heart and hand with the greatest nation in the world. I don't want to be young Sam Buckley of Baroona. I want to be the Buckley of Clere. Is not that a noble ambition?'[3]

This is a mixture of motives, though the strongest appeal is of a nation where 'social influence' ensures that there are not 'too many men without masters'.

Alice Buckley has much earlier committed herself. She says of England:

> 'A glorious country . . . what would I give to see it?—so ancient and venerable, and yet so amazingly young and vigorous. It seems like a waste of existence for a man to stay here tending sheep, when his birthright is that of an Englishman: the right to move among his

[1] Ibid., p. 261. [2] Ibid., p. 262. [3] Ibid., p. 506.

peers, and find his fit place in the greatest empire in the world. Never had any woman such a noble destiny before her as this young lady who has just ascended the throne.'[1]

The return of the Buckley society to England coincides with the first external threat to that still comparatively young lady's throne, thus continuing the parallel of England threatened by Napoleon, which opens the novel. The two events were at the time thought to have more in common than later commentary suggests. According to G. M. Trevelyan, one of the justifications for an attack on Russia was the belief that it would guarantee the 'independence of Germany',[2] a cause for which Doctor Mulhaus, as well as Major Buckley and Captain Brentwood, had fought at Waterloo. It was a cause Kingsley himself later espoused, when as a newspaper correspondent with the German army he reported Napoleon III's 'threat' to German independence.

The theme of Britain's wars, obvious at the opening and conclusion of the novel, is sustained in its middle sections. Lieutenant Halbert is introduced from India into the Buckley society—halberd is matched with buckler. Kingsley also recalls the theme when describing the attack by Hawker's bushrangers: 'I remark that the Lucknow and Cawnpore men don't much like talking about the affairs of that terrible six weeks; much for the same reason, I suspect, as we, going over our old recollections, always omit the occurrences of this lamentable spring.'[3] Earlier, in examining the Limestone Gates where Hawker makes his last stand, Sam Buckley suggests 'that a few determined men with rifles, posted among those fern-trees, could make a stand against almost any force'.[4] This is what happens, although Jim Brentwood, later known as the 'Inkermann pet', anticipates the manner of their defeat when he says: 'they might be cut up by cavalry. Horses could travel right up the face of the slope there. Now, suppose a gang of bushrangers in that fern-scrub; do you think an equal number of police could not turn them out of it?'[4] Of this same threat to peace, Sam confides the tactics likely to be used by Desborough, the Anglo-Irish chief of police: 'I heard him say, myself, that the best way was to tempt

[1] *Hamlyn*, p. 291.

[2] G. M. Trevelyan, *History of England*, London 1928, 3rd edn. reissued 1952, p. 650.

[3] *Hamlyn*, p. 423.

[4] Ibid., p. 300.

them to stay and show fight, by taking a small force against them, as our admirals used to do to the French, in the war.'[1] This suggestion of threatened peace is constant. The threat may come from other nations, or bushrangers, or hot-headed democrats out for their rights, or even aborigines, though these last are infinitely trifling, despite their killing James Stockbridge. Being so constant, it gives the novel a tone unique in English fiction of the time. Apart from Dickens's *Tale of Two Cities*, published the same year as *Geoffry Hamlyn*, no novel so persistently expresses its conflict in terms of martial violence. It does not reappear until Henley, Henty, and Kipling. One reason may well be that Kingsley was alone among novelists of the time in having known at first hand the actual process of colonization, part of the imperial basis on which that prosperity and personal degradation explored by others was based. Like Kipling much later—and Scott much earlier—he responded to the romance of the process.

Kingsley's importance in the history of Australian literature is that he extends the meaning, the implications, of that lawful violence in which Australia was conceived. It forms the staple of Clarke and Boldrewood as much as it does of Leonard Mann's *Flesh in Armour*,[2] published half a century later. As Patrick White remarks in *Happy Valley*: 'there was an underlying bitterness that had been scored deep and deep by time, with a furrow here and there and pockmarks in the face of black stone. Over everything there was a hot air of dormant passion, of inner war, that nobody seemed to be conscious of.'[3] In America, such inner war has always been acknowledged: the Constitution allows every man to carry a gun. In Australia, it has always been unconscious, undefined, accepted as a law of nature, as the violence of Australia's origins were and are. Such origins go far towards explaining the sometimes fortunate welcome Australian governments and people have always given to war, against the Boers, the Germans, the Japanese, the Koreans, and now the Vietnamese. A tradition of fear and of fear overcome breeds enemies as well as courage.

In Sam Buckley's wish to be known as 'the Buckley of Clere', there is an indication of the tradition to which Kingsley is reverting. Clere is in Devon, we are told, but the designation

[1] Ibid., p. 312. [2] Melbourne 1932. [3] London 1939, p. 19.

of a man by his home is Scottish. To say 'the Douglas of Douglas', 'the Mac-Ivor of Glennaquoich', 'the Graham of Montrose', even 'the Cambell of Argyll', signifies not merely that such men are notable among the county. Much more, the habit indicates that they are men whose home is a defence against a threatening world, if not literally a castle.[1] They are each leaders of their own society, or clan, to whom blood and fealty matter more than progress or political rights. It is to this world of Scott's works that the Buckley society belongs, in England or Australia. The idyll Kingsley describes, the distillation of the whole novel, is feudalism extended to include the birds and the beasts; and he got the idea from his superficial reading of Scott. As much as Fenimore Cooper, he recognized that the new country had more in common with Scotland than with England: a sparse population that lived off the land or one another. And what Australia lacked, he provided from his reading.

Not to appreciate Scott's influence on Kingsley induces a mistaken appreciation of his response to Australia, as occurs for instance when F. H. Mares says of him: 'He has an eye for scenery in any continent, but seems to be particularly moved by the high forest scenery of Australia, as in the description of the meeting of Hamlyn with Major Buckley's pioneering party, or George Hawker's desperate flight over the watershed between the Snowy and the Gates of the Murray after the defeat of the bushrangers.'[2] If we examine these passages, and others like them, we discover Kingsley responding not to the forests or the Australian Alps, but to the 'romance' of such scenery. He likens Buckley's party to the 'patriarchs of the desert', a particularly inappropriate comparison, since the party did not come from a desert and is not crossing one; but even the scenery as Kingsley describes it shows little response in the onlooker to those features that distinguish it as 'a new heaven and a new earth'. The passage continues:

Tier beyond tier, height above height, the great wooded ranges go

[1] Cf. *Waverley*, ch. xv: 'And did you ever see this Mr. MacIvor, if that be his name, Miss Bradwardine?' 'No, that is not his name; and he would consider *master* as a sort of affront, only that you are an Englishman, and know no better. But the Lowlanders call him, like other gentlemen, by the name of his estate, Glennaquoich; and the Highlanders call him Vich Ian Vohr, that is, the son of John the Great; and we upon the braes here call him by both names indifferently.'

[2] *The Literature of Australia*, p. 251.

rolling away westward, till on the lofty sky-line they are crowned with a gleam of everlasting snow. To the eastward they sink down, breaking into isolated forests, fringed peaks, and rock-crowned eminences, till with rapidly straightening lines they disappear gradually into broad grey plains, beyond which the Southern Ocean is visible by the white reflection cast upon the sky.

All creation is new and strange. The trees, surpassing in size the largest English oaks, are of a species we have never seen before. The graceful shrubs, the bright-coloured flowers, ay, the very grass itself, are of species unknown in Europe; while flaming lories and brilliant parroquets fly whistling, not unmusically, through the gloomy forest, and over head in the higher fields of air, still lit up by the last rays of the sun, countless cockatoos wheel and scream in noisy joy, as we may see the gulls do about an English headland.[1]

The extract is picture-painting: it moves in lines from the foreground to the background. Once the outline is complete, the interesting features are put in: trees, flowers, birds, to lighten the 'gloomy forest'. Kingsley continues: 'To the northward a great glen', and we recognize the original by Salvator Rosa done into English by Walter Scott.

Similarly, in describing George Hawker's flight over the snow-bound mountains Kingsley responds not to snow in Australia, something which still amazes most Englishmen, but to the terrible loneliness of nature matching the loneliness of the hunted brigand chief. That Kingsley was not the first to recognize a Scottish likeness is indicated in the earlier name given to Gippsland in 1838: Australia Caledonia. Angus McMillan, who discovered and named the area, was himself a Scot; but Kingsley, who calls one of the mountains Aberdeen, was not. He had never been to Scotland. Just as Hazlitt tells how impossible it was for him to look at a sunset after once sharing such a scene with Wordsworth, so it was impossible for the literate Englishman to see a mountain without recalling Scott, especially if he was telling an adventurous tale. This is why Kingsley concludes his panegyric on 'marvellous Melbourne': 'Unromantic enough, but beyond all conception wonderful.' His main concern is with what is 'romantic'.

Douglas Grant[2] quotes the following suggestive passage from

[1] *Hamlyn*, pp. 170–1.

[2] 'Sir Walter Scott and Nathaniel Hawthorne', *University of Leeds Review*, 1962, pp. 35–41.

George Woodberry's study of Hawthorne: 'something of Scott is to be found permanently in his work . . . in the oddities of character humorously treated, and especially in the set scenes individually elaborated to give the high lights and to advance the story.' Grant adds a further comparison, from *Peveril of the Peak*, of 'Julian Peveril's meeting with Alice Bridgenorth under the stone at Goddard Crovan on the Isle of Man: a "tall, shapeless, solitary rock, frowning, like a shrouded giant, over the brawling of the small rivulet which watered the ravine" '. Grant concludes that this 'was just such a rendezvous as Hawthorne preferred for the solitary interviews of his lovers'. Kingsley, dealing with the adventures of phlegmatic English gentlemen—'gloomy', as he calls them—does not expose their courtship to such natural rigours. Illicit love, like that between the young Mary Thornton and George Hawker, is thought the only kind that favours the dark outdoors. The 'tall, shapeless, solitary rock' is nevertheless always at hand to offer its contrast to the settled life lived in its shadow. We learn from Desborough that the Organ Hill behind Buckleys' place was 'not unlike Staffa'.[1] Although it can be argued that Gippsland has many such rocks, they are not compared by Anglo-Irishmen like Desborough to Staffa, a place whose fame Mendelssohn emphasized precisely because he had read Scott. Desborough is painting a picture of it: we learn that the rock usually appeared 'a dim mass of pearly grey, but tonight, in the clear frosty air, it was of a rich purple, shining on the most prominent angles with a dull golden light'. The night is that before the final battle with the bushrangers, in the chapter called 'Before the Storm'. It is what Woodberry calls one of those 'set scenes, individually elaborated to give the highlights and to advance the story'. The fact that Desborough is painting the scene also recalls Scott in a way reminiscent of the earlier passage describing the 'patriarchs of the desert' in the forest. J. L. Adolphus[2] points out how Scott's descriptions of nature were in themselves like framed pictures, rather than representations of actuality. He adds that few of his 'poetical descriptions . . . do not owe part of their beauty to the distribution of light and shade'. Adolphus calls it 'Chiaroscuro'; Kingsley would have called it 'romantic'.

Similarly the 'tall pinnacle of rock' at the Limestone Gates:

[1] *Hamlyn*, p. 444. [2] *Letters to Richard Heber*, London 1821, pp. 156–7.

although he likens it to 'one of the same kind in Dovedale', it is approached via 'one of the most abrupt and romantic gullies'.[1] The Australian 'gully', however, immediately becomes a 'glen', when one might have expected a Devon man to call it a combe or at least a valley.

Mary Hawker's station is backed by 'a picturesque little granite cap';[2] the child loses itself on 'a lofty bare knoll';[3] George Hawker is dramatically sighted at 'a thin wall of granite, like a vast buttress . . . pierced by a great arch'.[4] All may be real enough; but they are selected either for their picturesque or dramatic possibilities.

The result of this habit is for a contradiction to become apparent in Kingsley's picture of Australia. Gippsland is in fact a very fertile area, as appears from the ease with which the Buckley society replenish their war-emptied coffers; but because of the emphasis on adventure in the novel, and the consequent necessity for a bleak backdrop, Australia is often shown as an inhospitable place. This aspect of Kingsley's picture has possibly helped to stamp the novel as 'offensively English', with of course its 'conscious Tory principles reflected in incidental comments which oppose democracy and praise the values of aristocracy'.[5]

In an interesting passage early in the novel, Devon too is transformed into a picture of which Scott could have approved:

> Those who only know the river Taw as he goes sweeping, clear and full, past orchards and farm-houses, by woods and parks, and through long green meadows, after he has left Dartmoor, have little idea of the magnificent scene which rewards the perseverance of anyone who has the curiosity to follow him up to his granite cradle between the two loftiest eminences in the West of England.
>
> On the left, Great Cawsand heaves up, down beyond down, a vast sheet of purple heath and golden whin, while on the right the lofty serrated ridge of Yestor starts boldly up, black against the western sky, throwing a long shadow over the wild waste of barren stone at his feet.
>
> Some Scotchmen, perhaps, may smile at my applying the word 'magnificent' to heights of only 2,100 feet . . .
>
> It is an evil, depressing place. Far as the eye can reach up the glen and to the right it is one horrid waste of grey granite . . . But on

[1] *Hamlyn*, p. 298. [2] Ibid., p. 221. [3] Ibid., p. 326. [4] Ibid., p. 382

[5] Thomas Crawford, *Scott*, Edinburgh, London 1965, pp. 52–3, on *Woodstock*.

a wild winter's evening, when day is fast giving place to night, and the mist shrouds the hill, and the wild wind is rushing hoarse through tor and crag, it becomes awful and terrible in the extreme.[1]

Again, there is the 'glen', and the Scottish 'whin' for the English 'gorse' or even King Alfred's West Saxon 'furze'. Such 'an evil, depressing place' is not for English gentlemen, however; it is the backdrop to George Hawker's illicit rendezvous with Bill Lee, the ex-convict who returns to his native Devon, comparable with the following passage from *The Heart of Midlothian*:

It was a wild and very sequestered dell in Tweeddale, surrounded by high hills, and far remote from human habitation. A small river, or rather a mountain torrent, called the Talla, breaks down the glen with great fury, dashing successively over a number of small cascades, which has procured the spot the name of Talla Linns. Here the leaders among the scattered adherents to the Covenant, men who, in their banishment from human society, and in the recollection of the severities to which they had been exposed, had become at once sullen in their tempers . . . met with arms in their hands, and by the side of the torrent discussed, with a turbulence which the noise of the stream could not drown, points of controversy . . .[2]

Comparison of the passage from Kingsley with the scene where Magwitch meets Pip, in *Great Expectations*, published a year later than *Geoffry Hamlyn*, reveals a change, a move from the hitherto fashionably eerie highlands of literature to the terrible lowlands of actuality observed. Kingsley marks a fraction of that change; in his role of elderly English gentleman he disapproves of such high places, reserving them for battles, clandestine love-affairs, or plans for blackmail and murder. In daylight, they form part of the scene-painting; and one feels as Carlyle felt about Scott's originals when he said that 'scarcely the Author of Waverley himself can tempt you not to skip.'[3]

Cecil Hadgraft, speaking of Crab in Charles Rowcroft's *Tales of the Colonies*, calls him 'a caricature in the manner of Dickens'. He continues the analogy when discussing *Geoffry Hamlyn*. He says: 'Kingsley's resemblance to Dickens appears in the crowd of characters, with individual and family stories that interact.'[4]

[1] *Hamlyn*, pp. 24–5. [2] Ch. xviii.
[3] 'Characteristics', *Edinburgh Review*, liv, December 1831.
[4] *Australian Literature*, p. 44.

This is also misleading. The Buckley society are English gentlemen with strong literary affinities with clans like the Campbells, who saw themselves as less bigoted Caledonians than their neighbours. The minor characters in Kingsley's novel certainly take their origin from Scott. Hawker's mother, for instance, the gipsy 'Madge the witch', 'at least six feet high', is a descendant of Madge Wildfire, Scott's 'stout Amazon'. The repetitive, Old Testament, non-conformist quality of the conversation of an unnamed shepherd, a teller of ghostly tales, is from a reading of Scott as well as from an observation of Scotsmen: 'Oh, ay! Ye're Hamlyn and Stockbridge! I ken ye well; I kenned yer partner: a good man—a very good man, a man o' ten thousand. He was put down up north. A bad job—a very bad job! Ye gat terrible vengeance, though. Ye hewed Agag in pieces! . . . It were the sword of the Lord and of Gideon that ye fought with!'[1] The same is true of another shepherd, Macdonald, 'one of the Macdonalds of Skye', that is, related to Flora Macdonald. As he says, 'I am cousin to my lord.' Burnside, another Scot, is a gossip, a braggart, like the others an object of English irony and German scepticism. Yet their interest in other people's affairs is of the same kind that unites the Buckley society from Devon. Scott suggests a reason:

> There are . . . more associations common to the inhabitants of a rude and wild, than of a well cultivated and fertile, country; their ancestors have more seldom changed their place of residence; their mutual recollection of remarkable objects is more accurate; the high and the low are more interested in each other's welfare; the feelings of kindred and relationship are more widely extended. . . .[2]

This tendency in Kingsley is not merely evidence of what George Woodberry calls 'the oddities of character humorously treated' as in Scott; nor does it mean only that Kingsley, seeing Australia as Cooper and Hawthorne saw America, or as Scott saw Scotland, namely as England's poor relation, wished therefore to correct an opinion. It is useful to the novel in introducing by means of Madge's prophecies, Burnside's tales, and the shepherds' ghost stories, an element of fancy that relieves the dullness of so much English 'nobility' which justifies its existence by hunting the peace-breakers. Such fancy has its origin

[1] *Hamlyn*, p. 414. [2] *The Heart of Midlothian*, ch. xxxviii.

in the speech patterns of Scott's Highlanders, who 'when familiar and facetious . . . used the Lowland Scottish dialect,—when serious and impassioned, their thoughts arranged themselves in the idiom of their native language; and in the latter case, as they uttered the corresponding ideas in English, the expressions sounded wild, elevated, and poetical'.[1]

The novel also contains two direct references to Scott. The first occurs when a lubbra is upbraiding in her own language a small boy who has upset her canoe. A visitor to the Buckleys, Harding, ironically remarks on the 'sweet song that old girl is singing!' saying he must write it down 'from dictation, and translate it, as Walter Scott used to do with the old wives' ballads in Scotland'.[2] Although one intention seems to be to diminish the aborigines by comparison, the irony boomerangs. Others have since done what Harding suggests. As so often, Kingsley has a genuine insight but then refuses its significance with a chuckle. One reason appears to be that he misunderstood his model. Behind Harding's irony lies the suggestion that Scott shared the same attitude, a suggestion that could only be the result of a superficial reading—or, it might be said, an English reading. As Scott says in *The Heart of Midlothian*, when introducing the passage already quoted, 'Perhaps one ought to be actually a Scotsman to conceive how ardently, under all distinctions of rank and situation, they feel their mutual connection with each other as natives of the same country'.[3]

The second reference to Scott is when Mrs. Mayford, on the eve of her son's death, insists that he should not read *Waverley* aloud that night, but rather 'a chapter out of the Bible'.[4] The change in practice marks the evening's ominousness; it also suggests the favour in which Scott's work continued to be held in Australia at a time when Englishmen were reading Dickens aloud. The time to which Kingsley was referring was, of course, closer to Scott than to Dickens: the time between Cecil Mayfords' death and the return to England is certainly vague. And books from England took a long time to travel to Australia, therefore colonial fashions in reading as in dress were likely to lag a little behind those in England. On the other hand, the

[1] Sir Walter Scott, *Rob Roy*, ch. xxxv.
[2] *Hamlyn*, p. 193.
[3] *The Heart of Midlothian*, ch. xxxviii.
[4] *Hamlyn*, p. 456.

evidence of Scott's influence on Australian writing and reading habits can only be accounted for by a reference to the kind of small agricultural society Australia so long remained, and continued to imagine itself to be, even when it was one no longer. This is why Donald Horne can today write, in *The Lucky Country*: 'Almost all Australian writers—whatever their politics—are reactionaries whose attitude to the massive diversities of suburban life is to ignore it or condemn it rather than discover what it is.'[1] Horne may be complaining of Australian writers' attitudes to the massive *diversities* of suburban life but his use of the word 'it' suggests that 'suburban life' is the antecedent; and it is this that Australian writers condemn or ignore. It was condemned or ignored by English writers until Dickens replaced Scott as the writer to whom readers went to see themselves as they thought they were, and feared they might be.

According to Mark Twain, Scott was also widely read in the Southern States of America; and his effect was bad: Scott 'created rank and caste down there, also reverence for rank and caste, and pride and pleasure in them'.[2] Twain concludes: 'Enough is laid on slavery, without fathering upon it these creations and contributions of Sir Walter Scott.' This may be true; but slavery and caste seem to be different aspects of the same hierarchical attitude of mind. A slave society would appear more likely to reverence rank and caste than one which, for whatever reasons, is without slaves. Similarly, the more pride and pleasure a society takes in class, the more likely it is to attempt to secure that class structure by instituting a slave group. In *Geoffry Hamlyn*, Kingsley was writing of an Australia that still used convicts as slaves; an important difference, of course, between Australia and the Southern States was that no one was born into the convict condition. Nor was there anything about the children of convict parents, such as their colour, to mark their descent. For ex-convicts, however, life was less forgiving. As Trollope, in *Harry Heathcote of Gangoil*, says of old Brownbie: 'Everyone knew that he had been a convict; and even had he become a man of high principle—a condition which he certainly never achieved—he could hardly have escaped altogether from the thraldom of his degradation.'[3] Trollope

[1] Ringwood 1964, p. 22. [2] *Life on the Mississippi*, ch. xlvi.
[3] Ed. Marcie Muir, Melbourne 1963, p. 75.

also substantiates Kingsley's view of a class-conscious Australia. In the same novel a recent arrival in Australia compares the class system there with that of distant England: 'Classes hang together just in the same way; only I think there's a little more exclusiveness here than there was there.'[1] Dymphna Cusack's novel, *The Sun is Not Enough*, suggests Kingsley's picture of Australian society has not changed in this respect. We learn that in Burfield, a Sydney suburb of the sixties, 'under the superficial egalitarianism that made friendly contact possible between shopper and shopkeeper over the counter, invisible grid-irons of caste divided the wives and the homes from any closer contact'.[2] Kingsley's portrayal is often uncertain, but it is not wholly inaccurate. This is why his acceptance of a slave-group as the logical result of the class-system is disturbing. In what passes for a joke, he suggests that only one thing was wanting to make Captain Brentwood's verandah perfect,

> and that was niggers. To the winds with *Uncle Tom's Cabin*, and *Dred* after it, in a hot wind! What can an active-minded, self-helpful lady like Mrs. Stowe, freezing up there in Connecticut, obliged to do something to keep herself warm,—what can she, I ask, know about the requirements of a southern gentleman when the thermometer stands at 125° in the shade? Pish! Does she know the exertion required for cutting up a pipe of tobacco in a hot north wind? No! Does she know the amount of perspiration and anger superinduced by knocking the head off a bottle of Bass in January? Does she know the physical prostration which is caused by breaking up two lumps of hard white sugar in a pawnee before a thunderstorm? No, she doesn't, or she would cry out for niggers with the best of us! When the thermometer gets over 100° in the shade, all men would have slaves if they were allowed. An Anglo-Saxon conscience will not, save in rare instances, bear a higher average heat than 95°.[3]

From the sixties of the last century until Federation, this same argument was used to justify the introduction of Kanaka labour on the Queensland sugar plantations, and in the nineties the South Australian demand for 'Indian coolies'; while in the name of 'the tribunal of civilization' Sir Henry Parkes con-

[1] *Harry Heathcote of Gangoil*, Ed. Marcie Muir, Melbourne 1963, p. 98.
[2] Dymphna Cusack, *The Sun is not Enough*, London 1967, p. 29.
[3] *Hamlyn*, p. 502.

demned a 'slavery' that introduced 'into Australia inferior and unprivileged races of men'.[1] Yet Kingsley, in commenting on Major Buckley's dismissal of his convict servants, has already provided one reason against having such a group: it was inefficient, and, by constituting a separate society, was a threat to the greater it was supposed to serve. A second reason is inherent in the novel: such a class would threaten what Sir Henry Parkes, several times Premier of New South Wales, called 'the British character of the colonies'.[2] What in fact removed the Kanakas and has ever since kept coloured people from settling in Australia was that they were thought likely to take the jobs of white men. A consideration of the first two reasons shows Kingsley aware of the dangers in a situation he later appears to welcome, however humorously; but again he refuses his own insights. A consideration of the last shows him incapable of imagining a country, desperately short of people, ever rejecting anyone.

F. H. Mares has suggested Kingsley saw Australia's influence as mainly regenerative, but the suggestion is only partially true. It is that part of the truth which later Australians have embraced: the belief that everybody who goes to Australia goes for a greater freedom, wealth, or health than Europe offers. It is of course regretted that some, like the Buckleys, are mean enough to leave and take their fortunes with them. The comfort, for Furphy, is in knowing them to be fools anyway. This, however, is only half the truth, as it is only half the novel. For half its history, Australia was a prison; and George Hawker's fate illustrates what could happen to those for whom Australia's effect was only briefly intended to be regenerative. The novel is not merely about exile. Byron said, 'My native land—Good-night!', but this novel, in the terms so far used, is about the death of the Byronic hero at the hands of English gentlemen.

George Hawker is not nobly born, but he is surrounded by the 'romance' of illegitimacy and gipsy descent, his mother being 'of one of the best families'.[3] He is the offspring of passionate love, which, like high mountains, is in Kingsley 'romantic' but distrusted. Apart from his complexion, which is

[1] *Fifty Years in the Making of Australian History*, London 1892, p. 576.
[2] Quoted by Douglas Pike, *Australia: The Quiet Continent*, p. 122.
[3] *Hamlyn*, p. 39.

ruddier than is usual with the Byronic hero, his physique is Byronic:

As the light from the candles fell upon his figure while he stood in the doorway, any man or woman who saw it would have exclaimed immediately, 'What a handsome fellow!' and with justice; for if perfectly regular features, splendid red and brown complexion, faultless white teeth, and the finest head of curling black hair I ever saw, could make him handsome, handsome he was without doubt.[1]

Lest he be mistaken for one of the other 'noble animals', however, Kingsley immediately readjusts his description:

And yet the more you looked at him the less you liked him, and the more inclined you felt to pick a quarrel with him. The thin lips, the everlasting smile, the quick suspicious glance, so rapidly shot out from under the overhanging eyebrows, and as quickly withdrawn, were fearfully repulsive, as well as a trick he had of always clearing his throat before he spoke, as if to gain time to frame a lie. But, perhaps, the strangest thing about him was the shape of his head, which, I believe, a child would have observed. We young fellows in those times knew little enough about phrenology. I doubt, indeed, if I had ever heard the word, and yet among the village lads that man went by the name of 'flat-headed George.' The forehead was both low and narrow, sloping a great way back, while the larger part of the skull lay low down behind the ears. All this was made the more visible by the short curling hair which covered his head.[2]

Clearly, the man is both a handsome fellow and an ugly brute, depending on the point of view. Or on the model:

His countenance was decidedly Scottish, with all the peculiarities of the northern physiognomy, but yet had so little of its harshness and exaggeration, that it would have been pronounced in any country extremely handsome. The martial air of the bonnet, with a single eagle's feather as a distinction, added much to the manly appearance of his head, which was besides ornamented with a far more natural and graceful cluster of close black curls than ever were exposed to sale in Bond Street.

An air of openness and affability increased the favourable impression derived from this handsome and dignified exterior. Yet a skilful physiognomist would have been less satisfied with the countenance on the second than on the first view. The eyebrow and upper lip bespoke something of the habit of peremptory command and decisive

[1] *Hamlyn*, p. 16. [2] Ibid., pp. 16–17.

superiority. Even his courtesy, though open, frank, and unconstrained, seemed to indicate a sense of personal importance; and, upon any check or accidental excitation, a sudden, though transient, lour of the eye, showed a hasty, haughty, and vindictive temper, not less to be dreaded because it seemed much under its owner's command. In short, the countenance of the Chieftain resembled a smiling summer's day, in which, notwithstanding, we are made sensible by certain, though slight, signs, that it may thunder and lighten before the close of evening.[1]

The description is of Edward Waverley's first impression of Fergus MacIvor; but Scott is suggesting the man is attractive partly because he is unpredictable, representative of the gaiety and harshness of the Jacobite cause; from this gaiety Scott creates the romance of *Waverley* in order to condemn the cause. It was an attractive cause but politically useless to Scotland precisely because it was unpredictable, and so often unsuccessful and discredited. For Kingsley, however, George Hawker's ugliness is indicative of the moral rottenness which is felt to be the inevitable concomitant of Byronic beauty. Scott's attitude is political: he favours peace yet responds to the colour of war. His concern is with the actuality of history, whereas Kingsley's is with a literary type, which, though unrepresentative of anything in actuality, must yet instruct while it delights.

There is no doubt that Kingsley is imitating Scott here, even to small details, whose significance eludes him. The reason for George Hawker's visit to the Thornton household in Devon is to see Mary, but he has also brought some snipe he has shot for her father. The father says merely that they are not as plentiful as they were, and that his sight is fading anyway. The snipe are then forgotten. In introducing Fergus MacIvor, Scott writes: 'His page, as we have said, carried his claymore; and the fowling-piece, which he held in his hand, seemed only designed for sport. He had shot in the course of his walk some young wild ducks, as, though *close-time* was then unknown, the broods of grouse were yet too young for the sportsman.'[1] A detail, true, but one that points the novel's themes. That the gun 'seemed only designed for sport' anticipates the use to which such guns were put in 1745; that '*close-time*' was then unknown establishes the freedom men like MacIvor enjoyed before the clans were broken and English law extended to

[1] *Waverley*, ch. xviii.

Scotland; that 'the broods of grouse were yet too young' suggests that the time for armed rebellion had not yet come; and 'sportsman' defines MacIvor's attitude to the rebellion, gaily careless of life and death. Kingsley sees the detail, misses its point, and produces a muddle.

Kingsley's attitude to his villain remains curiously mixed. We never learn why Hawker really wants to marry Mary Thornton: whether for love or money. He has had plenty of the first, and stands to inherit enough of the second. We are not told how his coining is known to the police, how he escapes from prison, or why he chooses to become a bushranger in Australia among the very people who will recognize him. We do not even learn that he robs anybody; he merely haunts them. More than most Byronic heroes, Hawker is wrapped in mystery. But it is a mystery which Kingsley does not exploit imaginatively, because he is unaware of it. He is content to see Hawker as the opposite of a gentleman, a victim of his own excesses, of 'a new passion . . . which, like all his others, should only by its perversion end in his ruin'.[1] This is the Byronic hero become a stock devil; and it is in keeping with his appearance that Kingsley provides reasons for Hawker's actions. The elder Hawker, 'with a half-drunken satyr-like leer on his face'[2], hopes that his son dreams he is 'avenged on them all',[3] though we are not told what will be avenged by his marrying Mary Thornton. It sounds as if the old man is encouraging the younger to be able to repeat, with Manfred, 'I loved her, and destroy'd her'; but, unlike Manfred and the rest of the Byronic heroes, Hawker takes no pleasure in the crime. Hawker's Satanic descent is obvious in the remark of his cousin, whom he has seduced: 'He sold himself to the deuce . . . on condition of ruining a poor girl every year.' After unknowingly killing his son, he rides off 'laughing'. He is finally described as the 'arch-devil'. But there is no delight in it. Hawker is a motiveless enigma, a disturber of idylls, a bogey man to frighten children; very much indeed what Napoleon was to nineteenth-century Englishmen.

German independence was one reason for the Napoleonic and Crimean Wars, references to which open and close the novel; reference is maintained in the person of Doctor Mulhaus. He possesses the intelligence which the English characters

[1] *Hamlyn*, p. 141. [2] Ibid., p. 36. [3] Ibid., p. 37.

so lamentably lack. He is at ease with the strangeness of the new country, able to interpret it, 'like a man always reading a new and pleasant book'.[1] For him, knowledge is the path to wisdom. He is the only member of the Buckley society who does not try to make money out of Australia. He is curiously like Patrick White's Voss, who, 'knowing so much, would know everything',[2] of whom Laura Trevelyan says: 'He is not all money talk.'[3] Like Voss, he is also '*skeptisch*'. Interrupting the vision of Australia where Major Buckley proudly sees 'the Anglo-Saxon race', Mulhaus says: 'Don't forget the Irish, Jews, Germans, Chinese, and other barbarians.'[4] He also remarks: 'You English should never sneer at those two nations [the Dutch and Spanish]: they were before you everywhere.'[5]

Two reasons suggest themselves for the curious likeness, one of which F. H. Mares touches on when discussing Kingsley's other novel, *The Boy in Grey*, a political allegory, the climax of which, as Mares points out, 'is the trial in the desert'.[6] The comparison the novel contains: 'so lies Leichhardt' is also the origin of White's *Voss*. It might be that Kingsley, in creating Mulhaus, had Leichhardt in mind—or any one of the numerous Germans who contributed to an understanding of Australia while satisfying their *Wanderlust*. For us, however, it is more useful to observe that Henry Handel Richardson in *The Fortunes of Richard Mahony*[7] introduces Baron von Krause, a botanist, who similarly interprets Australia merely by knowing about it. These three *Gelehrten* are not the results of parallels or influences, but rather evidence that Australian literature has always shared with English a tradition that has not always been clear in English literature. From Schiller's *Die Räuber*, Goethe's *Götz von Berlichingen*, and Scott's translation of it, Coleridge's interest in Fichte and Kant, even Wordsworth's 1898–9 visit to Goslar, there has been a powerful but often underestimated connection between German and English literature. Its epitome is Goethe's *Faust*, in which Euphorion, the son of Faust and Helen, is based on Byron, as Goethe explained to Eckermann; while Byron, who dedicated both *Sardanapalus* and *Werner* to 'the illustrious Goethe', based *The Deformed Transformed* 'partly

[1] Ibid., p. 238.
[2] Op. cit., p. 27.
[3] Ibid., p. 28.
[4] *Hamlyn*, p. 410.
[5] Ibid., p. 379.
[6] *The Literature of Australia*, p. 249.
[7] London 1930.

on the "Faust" of the great Goethe.' The story of Faust, however, is only the measure of the connection between the two literatures, the summation of a shared Protestant faith, from Marlowe to Shaw. It is of course possible to see this connection in English literature constantly warring with that of France and Italy, much as the history of the English language itself shows the conflict between its Romance and Germanic origins. The struggle is summarized in the book by Henry Kingsley's brother Charles, called *The Roman and the Teuton*[1]; and, being a disciple of Carlyle, Charles leaves us in no doubt about the outcome: 'the welfare of the Teutonic race is the welfare of the world.'[2] In periods like the nineteenth century, when English history, philosophy, and philology were pro-German, there was added reason for the villains of literature to appear as Byronic, Italianate brigands rather than German *Räuber*; and for the 'heroes', as Kingsley uses the word, to be noble northern gentlemen.

The German cause has had its greatest appeal among Celts, or 'provincials'. Even Kingsley was marginally a Celt, at least a provincial from Devon. Coming from the outlying areas of Great Britain, such writers have seemingly felt themselves obliged to prove their characters more noble, like Scott's John Duke of Argyle or Kingsley's Sam Buckley, or more strikingly intelligent, like Shaw's many self-portraits, or more at ease with the world of God or nature, like Mulhaus, than any Englishman. Although Kingsley in creating Mulhaus and being consistently anti-French, is sharing an English tradition to which Prince Albert gave fresh impetus, he is also introducing into Australian literature an attitude peculiarly attractive to Australians who, while speaking English, live at the furthest point on the globe from the origins of the culture which that language was developed to express. If in Mulhaus there is a sceptical intelligence working on comparatively metropolitan English stuffiness, the opposite appears in *The Boy in Grey*. The boy arrives in Australia:

> All the male adult colonists were down on the shore; and every man had brought his grandmother, and every man had brought an egg, and was showing his grandmother how to suck it.

[1] Cambridge, London 1864.

[2] There is a more detailed discussion of this in my article 'The German Element in Australian Fiction', *Wascana Review*, vol. 5, no. 2.

'Come here,' they cried, as Gil and the Prince coasted along; 'come here, you two, and learn to suck eggs. We will teach you to suck all kinds of eggs, not merely those of the emu and the talegalla, but those of the blue-throated warbler. And we will teach you to suck eggs which we have never seen.'[1]

Kingsley is here writing of Australians; but an involved provincial similarity is apparent when Tom Troubridge says to Burnside, a Scot: 'A Frenchman is conceited enough, but, by George, he can't hold a candle to a Scotchman.' The fellow-feeling many Australians have for Scots and Irishmen is as great as that which Voss felt for the aborigines. Scots and Irish are felt also to be victims of English metropolitan government and all it entails, just as Voss felt, among so much else, that the aborigines were the victims of people like the Bonners and others in the vicinity of Government House, and all that that entails. The similarity helps explain why one corner of South Australia has more pipers than the whole of Scotland, most of them originally from the great clan Brown, or 'army' as Thomas Hughes calls them, whose members 'are scattered over the whole Empire, on which the sun never sets, and whose general diffusion I take to be the chief cause of that empire's stability'.[2]

Another result of considering Kingsley's novel not as an example of 'Colonial Fiction' but as a work of fiction in English is that supposedly distinctive Australian phenomena, such as 'mateship', are seen to have more general origins. Bill Lee, an ex-convict, has his mate Dick, who comes over to England with him, and who, in Australia, is heart-broken at the thought that Lee may imagine he has 'slipped away'. When Hamlyn does Lee a service, Dick is told by his mate to stay close to Hamlyn—for the rest of his days, it seems; and he does his mate's bidding. Lee is older than Dick, but apart from vague hints about common experience we are not told precisely why Dick and Lee have become mates. We do learn in passing, however, that convicts sentenced to the chain-gang were chained together to prevent their escaping: a powerful influence on the nature of mateship in early Australian society, although an example of mateship that Australian literature has surprisingly

[1] London 1894, p. 47.
[2] Thomas Hughes, *Tom Brown's Schooldays*, ch. i.

not yet explored. By the casualness with which he presents the origins of the bonds binding Dick and Bill Lee together, Kingsley seems to be suggesting there is nothing unusual about them. In other words he accepts such friendship without feeling obliged to lather it in romance as Lawson does, or even apologize for it, as post-Freudian writers feel they must. He accepts that men have mates or 'butties' in much the same way that, say, Sean O'Casey does in *Juno and the Paycock*, where the same word, 'butty', is used.

Kingsley feels free when mentioning 'mateship', because he sees that masculine friendship, though it does not in this novel at least cross the class barriers, is not peculiar to any one class. He accepts it as naturally, or as unnaturally, as Tennyson or the Pre-Raphaelite Brotherhood or Durham miners or a 'ship's Daddy'. In dealing with the friendships of gentlemen, however, Kingsley does suggest their origins in trials shared, in public school or the army. Early in the novel, referring to the death of Major Buckley's brother, John, at Trafalgar, Kingsley tells of the letter sent to the father: 'It was just three hasty lines from the great Collingwood himself. That brave heart, in the midst of the din of victory, had found time to scrawl a word to his old school-mate, and tell him that his boy had died like a hero, and that he regretted him like a son.'[1] Major Buckley established his friendship with Brentwood by saving his life at Waterloo. Charley Biddulph, alias 'Captain Saxon' the card-sharper who was once Buckley's friend, 'could not die without sending a tender love to his good old comrade . . . he remembered him and loved him to the very end.'[2] The existence of such love among 'brother-officers', as well as among other ranks,[3]

[1] *Hamlyn*, p. 8.

[2] Ibid., p. 152.

[3] Compare this stanza from the Victorian music-hall song called 'Comrades' by Felix McGlennon:

We from childhood play'd together,
  My dear comrade Jack and I,
We would fight each other's battles,
  To each other's aid we'd fly;
And in boyish scrapes and troubles,
  You would find us everywhere,
Where one went the other followed,
  Naught could part us, for we were
Comrades, comrades, ever since we were boys,

suggests why mateship could have 'its last fling with the A.I.F.'.[1] Extended in this way, mateship also helps explain why Australia's one constantly influential tradition is its military tradition. Paradoxically, in the context of Australia, 'that working man's paradise', as Kingsley calls it, the tradition is traceable at least to the English public schools of the nineteenth century: 'From the cradle to the grave, fighting, rightly understood, is the business, the real highest, honestest, business of every son of man';[2] and this in spite of the humility proposed by the Son of Man. Hughes is not referring to personal combat, nor, as he stresses, is Kingsley concerned with a hero. Kingsley is depicting the victory of the Buckley society, of a segment of civilization, in 'the natural growth of which', John Stuart Mill remarks, 'power passes from individuals to masses, and the weight and importance of an individual, as compared with the mass, sinks into greater and greater insignificance'.[3] The real opposition to a 'mass', or even a 'society', is not another mass or society, but the individual, who, if he will not sink quietly, must be held under. This is the 'levelling process', which 'in modern times, corresponds, in reflection, to fate in antiquity'.[4] Kierkegaard is speaking about a European historical process in which 'fighting, properly understood', means foreign war; for 'in a burst of momentary enthusiasm people might, in their despondency, even long for a misfortune in order to feel the powers of life'.[5] Thus, to feel threatened by a foreign power, as England was by France or Russia, is a response meant to indicate that a nation is still alive. Ghosts, of Bonaparte or anyone else, can only threaten the living.

In America and what used to be called the 'white dominions', Australia, New Zealand, and Canada, where smaller, less technically efficient native populations were quickly subdued, the

Sharing each other's sorrows,
Sharing each other's joys.
Comrades when manhood was dawning,
Faithful whate'er may betide,
When danger threatened, my darling old comrade was
there by my side.

[1] Douglas Pike, op cit., p. 229.

[2] *Tom Brown's Schooldays*, ch. v.

[3] 'Civilisation: Signs of the Times', *Westminster Review*, xxv, April 1836.

[4] Søren Kierkegaard, *The Present Age*, London (Collins) 1963, p. 57.

[5] Ibid., p. 56.

levelling process has been faster, for reasons such as the belief that hierarchy was responsible for those European social ills that settlers wished to get away from, or because the colony was distant from the home of hierarchy, or because of the wish to rearrange that hierarchy. In Australia, however, the process has been even more accelerated; and the reason lies in the nature of the country's foundation. Australia began as a place of correction, a place where non-conformists—individuals, in Kierkegaard's sense—would be made to conform. With the advent of free settlement, a wider dialectic was established: those who had been 'corrected', still bearing the marks of the experience, had to be assimilated or erased by time in the greater conformity their presence made necessary and strong. For Trollope, for Dickens in *David Copperfield*, *Great Expectations*, and *Nicholas Nickleby*, for George Eliot in *Adam Bede*, for Thackeray in *Pendennis*, for Charles Reade, for Lytton in *Paul Clifford*, for almost any novelist who mentions the place in the nineteenth century, Australia was a prison, to which one was sent.[1] Mr Micawber was sent to help administer it. One must assume it had this meaning for the readers of such novels. To overcome this impression, free settlers to Australia established a more rigorous conformity—called Victorianism elsewhere—than was necessary even in the home of Victorianism. Gentlemen, and ladies—who were considered equal and allowed to vote much earlier than in Britain—became the rule rather than the exception. Heroes—for there has never been an Australian heroine—were killed, or forgotten and allowed to die a natural death, or simply ignored.

To recognize this process is to understand why the Byronic hero has so frequently died and been so often resuscitated in Australian cultural history, from Kingsley's George Hawker to Sidney Nolan's Ned Kelly. For the trouble with Byron, as Hazlitt pointed out in *The Spirit of the Age*, is that he 'goes to the very edge of extreme and licentious speculation, and breaks his neck over it';[2] but in Australian fiction, the pieces have

[1] I am aware of another view, most recently expressed in Coral Lansbury's interesting book *Arcady in Australia* (Melbourne 1970); but the reason why Samuel Sidney, Caroline Chisholm and Dickens argued so strongly in *Household Words* that 'Arcady' was to be found in Australia was that so many people, including Dickens in his novels, suspected it wasn't, though the place might do for the poor, despite Edward Gibbon Wakefield's notions.

[2] William Hazlitt, *The Spirit of the Age*, London (World's Classics) 1966, p. 114.

been put together again and again, till in *The Fortunes of Richard Mahony* or *Voss* or *To the Islands*, one recognizes the reason: the development of the levelling process 'is in spite of everything, a progress because all the individuals who are saved will receive the specific weight of religion, its essence at first hand, from God himself'.[1] The foundations of the Christian existentialist position are discernible sooner in Australian fiction than in English partly because the country's history was so cruelly secular. Though theology is not taught even today in any of Australia's universities—while military studies is—that position can already be seen in Marcus Clarke's *For the Term of his Natural Life*.

[1] Kierkegaard, op. cit., p. 94.

6 Marcus Clarke, *For the Term of his Natural Life*

MARCUS CLARKE was seventeen when he arrived in Australia in 1863. Seven years later his serial, *His Natural Life*, began in *The Australian Journal*;[1] in 1874, under the same title but considerably altered, it was published in book form.[2] Under its 1885 title[3] it is this text, slightly revised, that L. H. Allen follows in his edition in the Oxford World's Classics series,[4] and the one by which Clarke's name is best known.

The novel begins in England and ends in Australia. Young Richard Devine, 'whose name is a bye-word for all that is profligate and base'[5], is physically threatened by his father, the elderly 'knight, shipbuilder, naval contractor, and millionaire . . . the son of a Harwich boat carpenter'.[6] He is saved from this assault by his mother's admission that he is not his father's son, but the love-child of her cousin, Lord Bellasis, 'a remarkable scamp and dandy'.[7] Richard, whose father's plebeian care for money he has already offended so that some of it is spent on a commission for his cousin Maurice Frere, is himself threatened with disinheritance and told to leave the house for ever. His cousin is to inherit all; while he, no matter how dire his condition, must never use the name Devine. If he disobeys, his mother's shame will be exposed.

Wandering over Hampstead Heath, he sees his father, who has left the house before him, hurrying back. A while later he finds the body of Lord Bellasis, and is caught still looking at it. Although a horseman has been seen in the area, and Lord Bellasis' pockets are as empty as Richard's, he is nevertheless condemned, under the name Rufus Dawes, to imprisonment in Tasmania.

[1] March 1870 to June 1872.

[2] Melbourne.

[3] *For the Term of his Natural Life*, London, Melbourne 1885.

[4] Ibid., London 1952; reprinted 1954, 1956, 1961 (hereafter referred to as *Term*).

[5] Ibid., p. 1.

[6] Ibid., p. 5.

[7] Ibid., p. 6.

The ship that takes him out also carries the new prison governor, Major Vickers, his wife and small daughter Sylvia and their maid Sarah Purfoy, as well as a detachment of soldiers, one of whom is Maurice Frere. Among the convicts is John Rex, forger and dandy, who in England was Sarah Purfoy's lover.

During the voyage, besides a mutiny led by Rex, for which Dawes is blamed, the monotony is interrupted by the appearance of a burning ship. It is the one which Richard had told his mother he was taking to India. The fire removes all apparent evidence of Richard Devine's existence and is also the occasion for the belligerent and officious Frere to recount how death not only cheated him of a fortune, but cheated his cousin, too: the elder Sir Richard Devine had been hurrying home across Hampstead Heath to await his lawyer, but had died before he could alter his will.

The remaining five-sixths of a long book are taken up mainly with Dawes's experiences as a convict and his love for Sylvia Vickers. She becomes Frere's wife after he has posed as the man who saved her when both of them, with her mother, were abandoned at Macquarie Harbour. The convict settlement there had been broken up and Major Vickers had gone to Port Arthur with the main body of convicts, leaving Frere to bring the rest as well as look after Mrs. Vickers and her small daughter. The boat they sail in is seized by the convicts—again led by John Rex—who puts them ashore at Hell's Gates. There they meet the escaped convict Dawes, and by his exertions they eventually reach safety. The credit, however, goes to Frere; for Mrs. Vickers never recovers from the experience, and Sylvia suffers from amnesia, despite Dawes's attempts during several escapes to revive her memory of the time when as a child she scratched on the sand 'Good Mr. Dawes'.[1] Only in the last chapter does she fully recover her memory. With the escaped and disguised Dawes, she is by then in the ship which was to bear her and the Rev. James North, who loves her, to the mainland. The ship is wrecked and crew and passengers drowned; but the moment of recognition has been experienced: 'entangled in the rigging were two corpses—a man and a woman. The arms of the man were clasped round the body of the woman, and her head lay on his breast. . . . The tempest was over.'[2]

[1] Ibid., p. 229. [2] Ibid., p. 603.

The theme of Dawes's repeated escape, re-capture and punishment is interwoven with that of John Rex and Sarah Purfoy. He is sent to Tasmania as a convict, while she travels as a free woman. She loves him and retains her freedom. She eventually becomes rich, having for a time been at least Frere's mistress, besides much else. She accomplishes Rex's escape, with the help of Blunt, the erring captain aboard the convict ship, whom she has fascinated as she does Frere. When Carr, her servant, dies, Rex takes his place and name and becomes her husband. He is soon as keen to escape from her as he was from the convict settlement. Despite the opportunity for blackmail which both the law and his breaking of it have given her, he obtains his freedom in order to use the secret of Dawes's identity. He returns to England and poses as Lady Devine's long-lost son, whom he closely resembles. He lives freely, spending his newly acquired wealth, putting off the day when he must decide to sell house and land in order to feel completely unencumbered by responsibility and suspicion. He becomes the crony of racing men and loose women, gets drunk and generally abuses Lady Devine's credulity. Sarah arrives from Australia to claim what she feels is her own, having recognized an Australian reproduction of a picture of 'Richard Devine', the noted English horseman. She insists on being recognised as his wife, but Lady Devine as rigidly insists on knowing from Rex the secret which she and her son shared—the cause of her son's leaving the house so many years ago. Rex does not know the answer. Sarah rescues him by taking advantage of Lady Devine's indisposition and hurries him off to a ship. Rex has a stroke and returns to Australia as Sarah's captive husband, an invalid for life.

The machinery is old: the disinherited love-child; his punishment for a crime he did not commit; the resemblance between the hero and the villain; and the use of coincidence to keep it moving. There is no use in tracing its possible sources, for they are embarrassingly many, as Clarke recognised when he said it was his purpose to write 'a sensation novel'. What is interesting is the way the book holds together despite its ragged string. It does so mainly because of the constancy of Clarke's anger that such a system of punishment should ever have existed; it does not matter—as it does not in Dickens's *Bleak House*—that the abuses should have already disappeared by the time he came to write about them. He seems not to have been impelled so much by a social conscience, as by a feeling of collective and inherited guilt. He recognized in his Preface that he was partly working within the nineteenth-century tradition of protest: 'Charles Reade has drawn the interior of a house of correction in England, and Victor Hugo has shown how a French convict fares after the fulfilment of his sentence. But no writer—so far as I am aware—has attempted to depict the dismal condition of a felon during his term of transportation.'[1] He also intended a warning for society in general:

It is true that the British Government have ceased to deport the criminals of England, but the method of punishment, of which that deportation was a part, is still in existence. Port Blair is a Port Arthur filled with Indian-men instead of Englishmen; and, within the last year, France has established, at New Caledonia, a penal settlement which will, in the natural course of things, repeat in its annals the history of Macquarie Harbour and of Norfolk Island.[2]

The important element in these remarks is that Clarke sees himself the possessor of history. Even had he read *Quintus Servinton*, that history would have lost none of its uniqueness. Savery was an English convict describing the conditions of his punishment. His experiences would go under the heading of 'News from foreign parts'. Clarke is writing as an Englishman whose exile became permanent, who had to live not only with the world described by Henry Kingsley—the descriptions of which he praised—but also with the history of the 'convict country', as Rowcroft called it. Clarke summarizes the second thus: 'All that the vilest and most bestial of human creatures could invent and practise, was in this unhappy country invented and practised without restraint and without shame.'[3] In other words, he is not only the first of many Australian historical novelists, but the first Englishman to attempt in print to come to terms with the harsh origins of the country of his adoption. The constancy of his anger is the result of the double shame he felt: as an Englishman whose countrymen had 'invented and practised' what 'Price Warung' was to call The System;[4] and as an Australian who, like his countrymen, had to live with the whole of his past.

[1] *Term.*, Preface, p. xxv.

[2] Ibid., Preface, pp. xxv–xxvi.

[3] Ibid., p. 116.

[4] 'Price Warung' (William Astley), *Convict Days*, Sydney 1960, a selection of stories collected under different titles much earlier. See Bibliography.

Just how difficult such a task is even for more recent Australians is suggested in Dr. Allen's Introduction to *For the Term of his Natural Life*. In answering the question, 'What led Clarke to choose this dismal theme?', he pertinently invokes the name of Byron, but applies it not to the book but to its author. Once started on psychoanalysis—as a reason for this 'dismal' rather than fascinating theme—Allen cannot leave it. Clarke, he says, was melancholic. The proof? First, Clarke's preface to Adam Lindsay Gordon's poems, which ends: 'The phantasmagoria of that wild dreamland termed the Bush interprets itself, and the Poet of our desolation begins to comprehend why free Esau loved his heritage of desert sand better than all the bountiful richness of Egypt.' What Allen wants to say is that Clarke should have admitted—which in fact he does—that at least some of Australia is not 'desert sand', no matter how small the fraction.

Again, Allen writes of Clarke: 'He is equally unsympathetic with the sea . . . he suppresses the transparent beauty of our Australian coastal waters, no less lovely than those described by Shelley in his "Stanzas written at Naples".' Although they would not be 'consonant with the mood to be induced', Allen would nevertheless like them to be at least mentioned, for Australia can compete—even in the quality of its sea-water—with the best in Europe.

In the third example, Allen comes near to critical objectivity, when he records Professor Tucker's criticism of the novel, that it is untypical of Australian conditions: 'Why did not Clarke give a . . . picture of convicts in happier conditions, and of well-to-do emancipists? There must have been many like Mary Reiby, a girl transported for a hoyden prank, who eventually made a happy marriage, conducted a thriving business, and became the grandmother of a Tasmanian Premier.' Lucky Mary Reiby; but the instance offers nothing except special pleading. Allen comes nearer the truth when he says: 'The sombre monotone had to be maintained', but he is still happy to hedge with Tucker and Desmond Byrne: 'Clarke never intended to give a picture of the whole class of convict. He deals only with the worst class of convict.'

These three examples from Allen, and that from Tucker, suggest how difficult it is for Australians, even today, to accept and live with both their history and geography. Or at least it is difficult when they are conscious of a European audience. Objectivity, critical values, all are so often put aside in favour of a defensive nationalism. It is one of Clarke's achievements that a humane anger and not a national sensitivity gives his book its unity.

Clarke, as well as appreciating what he called the 'grotesque' in Australia, was capable of doing justice to Australia's natural beauty, as the following passage shows:

> About a hundred and seventy miles to the south of this mill-race lies Van Diemen's Land, fertile, fair, and rich, rained upon by the genial showers from the clouds which, attracted by the Frenchman's Cap, Wyld's Crag, or the lofty peaks of the Wellington and Dromedary range, pour down upon the sheltered valleys their fertilizing streams. No parching hot wind—the scavenger, if the torment, of the continent—blows upon her crops and corn. The cool south breeze ripples gently the blue waters of the Derwent, and fans the curtains of the open windows of the city which nestles in the broad shadow of Mount Wellington. The hot wind, born amid the burning sand of the interior of the vast Australian continent, sweeps over the scorched and cracking plains, to lick up their streams and wither the herbage in its path, until it meets the waters of the great south bay; but in its passage across the straits it is reft of its fire, and sinks, exhausted with its journey, at the feet of the terraced slopes of Launceston.
>
> The climate of Van Diemen's Land is one of the loveliest in the world. Launceston is warm, sheltered, and moist; and Hobart Town, protected by Bruny Island and its archipelago of D'Entrecasteaux Channel and Storm Bay from the violence of the southern breakers, preserves the mean temperature of Smyrna; whilst the district between these two towns spreads in a succession of beautiful valleys, through which glide clear and sparkling streams.[1]

This is a handsome appreciation; it is, moreover, a description of Tasmania, an island which no earlier novelist had had the chance to sit back and appreciate. The element of 'sitting back' is important: the island, or the eastern half of it, had been settled since Rowcroft's time, and was by now in a condition to allow its inhabitants to rest as well as to receive guests; and Clarke is looking at it as a visitor might. Such details as he gives are the prominent ones a tourist with a map would remark upon. His audience is clearly European in origin and experience,

[1] *Term.*, pp. 107–8.

people who might have heard of Hobart but who would more readily know what it was to enjoy the 'mean temperature of Smyrna'.

This flatness of description, however, has its uses in the novel. It is at once the distant background to the story, and the immediate contrast to the foreground scenery, which Clarke paints thus:

> But on the western coast, from the steeple-rocks of Cape Grim to the scrub-encircled barrenness of Sandy Cape, and the frowning entrance to Macquarie Harbour, the nature of the country entirely changes. Along that iron-bound shore, from Pyramid Island and the forest-backed solitude of Rocky Point, to the great Ram Head, and the straggling harbour of Port Davey, all is bleak and cheerless. Upon that dreary beach the rollers of the southern sea complete their circuit of the globe, and the storm that has devastated the Cape, and united in its eastern course with the icy blasts which sweep northward from the unknown terrors of the southern pole, crashes unchecked upon the Huon pine forests, and lashes with rain the grim front of Mount Direction. Furious gales and sudden tempests affright the natives of the coast. Navigation is dangerous, and the entrance to the 'Hell's Gates' of Macquarie Harbour—at the time of which we are writing (1833), in the height of its ill-fame as a convict settlement—is only to be attempted in calm weather. The sea-line is marked with wrecks. The sunken rocks are dismally named after the vessels they have destroyed. The air is chill and moist, the soil prolific only in prickly undergrowth and noxious weeds, while fœtid exhalations from swamp and fen cling close to the humid, spongy ground. All around breathes desolation; on the face of nature is stamped a perpetual frown. The shipwrecked sailor, crawling painfully to the summit of basalt cliffs, or the ironed convict, dragging his tree-trunk to the edge of some beetling *plateau*, looks down upon a sea of fog, through which rise mountain-tops like islands; or sees through the biting sleet a desert of scrub and crag rolling to the feet of Mount Heemskirk and Mount Zeeharn—crouched like two sentinel lions keeping watch over the seaboard.[1]

This is a lumpier description, despite the occasional alliteration and heightened language. The man who wrote it walked on the spongy ground and got his feet wet. It also suggests the feeling of loneliness there is in the spot, the knowledge any man has who stands there, that it is, save for the Southern Pole, the end of the world. The terror has nothing to do with Clarke's melancholia.

[1] *Term.*, p. 108.

It is in the nature of the place, where even ships, let alone men, can disappear suddenly and without trace.

In the main body of the book Clarke explores the lumps with more care, uncovering the symbolism which both man and nature have created. Clarke writes that, according to Colonel Arthur, the spot which bore his name was a 'natural penitentiary',[1] an opinion which earlier in the book Mr. Pounce, of the 'Civil list', has expressed over soup: 'This island seems specially adapted by Providence for a convict settlement; for with an admirable climate, it carries little indigenous vegetation which will support human life.'[2] As is evident in the title, Clarke's overt theme is going to be 'Australia as a prison'; but as much to his point is the constant presence of the sea and the symbolic quality he extracts from it. Its encircling terror is real: in the convict ship that goes from England; for Dawes in punishment, chained, like the legendary St. Gregory, to a rock in the bay; for Frere, Mrs. Vickers, and Sylvia when they are abandoned by convicts on the coast where Dawes finds them; but that it is more than real is apparent in the last pages of the novel. Sylvia and Dawes 'escape' by doing as Conrad's Stein would have had them do, namely, 'in the destructive element immerse'. 'The tempest was over,'[3] Clarke writes. As the sea ensures a 'natural penitentiary', it is also the symbol of Dawes's restless and encircling love for Sylvia; 'the transparent beauty of our Australian coastal waters' would hardly have served the purpose. They are rather the equivalent of Mr. Pounce's soup.

To say that Clarke works with a sense of Australia's past and is willing to exploit the symbolism of both her history and geography is not to say that his attitude is free of ambiguity. Although he can pour scorn on the Rev. Meekin's 'London-learnt platitudes', he is not without admiration for the society which made them into laws. Meekin, however, is meant for contempt. He is a hypocrite, or at best has mistaken meekness for humility. His appearance in 'faultless tie, his airy coat, his natty boots, and his self-satisfied Christian smile' contrasts well with his description of himself as 'a poor labourer in the vineyard, toiling through the heat and burden of the day'.[4] He is also the friend of a bishop more temporal than spiritual. His literary

[1] Ibid., p. 393. [2] Ibid., p. 311. [3] Ibid., p. 603.
[4] Ibid., p. 239.

antecedents are in Fielding, Goldsmith, and Trollope. Clarke scorns him not merely because he is one of the Pharisees, but because he is in Australia a 'new-chum'. His summary of Hobart society as 'composed of very curious elements', as he writes to his patron in England, Clarke emphasizes with irony by placing him in it. He is effeminate compared to these curious elements. He is also less honest, not because he is a hypocrite, but because English society protects and even encourages falsity:

> The population that was abroad on that sunny December afternoon had certainly an incongruous appearance to a dapper clergyman lately arrived from London, and missing, for the first time in his sleek, easy-going life, those social screens which in London civilization decorously conceal the frailties and vices of human nature.[1]

More unforgivably, Meekin is writing back to his patron with the conviction of knowledge after he has been in Tasmania only 'seven days'. He continues throughout the novel to expose his ignorance of local conditions and to be as opinionated as ever. Here, at least, the irony suggests that Clarke see himself as an Australian—an old hand; though the tone is at odds with that used to describe Dawes's action in helping to support a social screen around his mother's secret.

The suggestion is strengthened by the portrayal of Meekin's 'opposite', the Rev. North, who is as rugged as his name. Not only does he dress badly, offend authority out of real concern for the prisoners' sufferings, and experience 'honest doubts' as well as the trials of alcoholism; he also loves Sylvia Vickers, Maurice Frere's wife. Instead of returning to England, however, which, Clarke suggests, would be no place for such an uncompromising character, he considers in his diary the only alternative: 'I have made up my mind to leave this place, to bury myself again in the bush, I suppose, and await extinction . . . I will write the reason plainly: "I covet my neighbour's wife."'[2] For him, an honest man, with an honest man's faults, the Australian bush is the only escape. It is also, of course, a prison; for him there is no escape from it. He must escape from himself: that is, await extinction. An analogy thus seems to be intended—or can be drawn—between North's passion and alcoholism and the bush where 'the hot wind, born amid the

[1] *Term.*, pp. 238–9. [2] Ibid., pp. 548–9.

burning sand of the interior of the vast Australian continent, sweeps over the scorched and cracking plains to lick up the streams'. North accepts more or less willingly his Australianness, and prepares to spend his life in purgatory.

What emphasizes Clarke's attitude as ambiguous is the Prologue to Book I of the novel. The style is not markedly different from that used in the rest of the book, but the attitude informing it, the attitude to that English society which Clarke later contemns, is different.

To clarify this ambiguity, the first consideration must be of Rufus Dawes's origins. His mother is a 'lady', while her husband is older, rich, self-made and a cuckold. Clarke, as a Victorian, neither allows himself nor encourages others to indulge in Chaucerian laughter. Instead he portrays the husband as a boor and a bully, whose wife could be forgiven for preferring her gay cousin, but at the same time insists that her peccadillo must remain a secret between her, the husband, and the blameless son, twenty years after the event. In the novel, the secret lasts another twenty years, and is the motivation behind the whole plot. Without this Victorian compromise, there would have been no novel, whose 'superiority to the serial', Dr. Allen says, 'is evident. Suffering for a mother's honour was much more calculated to appeal.' Thus easily is superiority equated with appeal, suggesting that the compromise did not end with Victoria.

In social terms, the Victorian compromise meant the acceptance by the middle class of aristocratic values, including that which says an aristrocracy is valuable. In literary terms, it meant an acceptance, however uneasy, of the Byronic hero. True to the ideal, Richard Devine is illegitimate but highly born: he has 'superior mental abilities', a 'haughty temper and powerful frame', black eyes, and white skin. He is disinherited by a rich member of the middle class, and protects the secret—and thus the honour—of an aristocratic mother. He is a gentleman as the elder Sir Richard was not—he was prepared to use his wife's shame to blackmail her into getting rid of her bastard son. Dawes is different from the other convicts, who use him, distrust him, and learn to fear him, until he becomes the leader of the Ring, proud, uncompromising, but sensitive. He can be moved to tears by kindness and can bear fearful punishment because a child calls him 'Mr.'. He becomes leader among the convicts because of his knowledge, the same knowledge which he displays when he finds Frere, Sylvia, and Mrs. Vickers abandoned by convicts on the desolate coast: 'Might was Right, and Maurice Frere's authority of gentility soon succumbed to Rufus Dawes's authority of knowledge.'[1] This is what the Frontier meant. Knowledge was a proof of adaptability; and adaptability, a proof of one's Australianness. Its use here is an example of Clarke's Australianness; but it is worth remembering that Dawes was more intelligent than other convicts, more than his captors, and especially more than his plebeian cousin, Maurice Frere, whose gentility, like his commission, was acquired, not to say bought. As Sir Richard Devine's favourite, he inherited his qualities instead of his wealth.

Devine is a late Byronic hero, whose virtues obscure his vices. Despite temptations, he does not steal; he does not strike a man but quells him with a look; he does not murder; he does not let another down; he is not a sodomite; he does not even commit suicide, though he tries and is sorry; he is lonely, silent, and apart. He breaks only one commandment: he covets his neighbour's wife. This is hardly the stuff of which sensation novels are made, the recipe for which Clarke outlined when he was twenty-three, in an essay called 'Sham Criminality':

> The standard of the present-day is the hero of the sensation novel—the cool, calm, impassable, gentlemanly scoundrel, and all young men want to be cool, calm, impassable, and gentlemanly scoundrels. A few years back Byronic heroes were in vogue, and everyone tried to write verses and break the seventh commandment. Now they confine themselves to the latter amusement, and mercifully let versification alone, except when a Swinburne or a Walt Whitman arises to sing the poetry of prurience. Oh dear! will nobody say anything really worth listening to in praise of poor, honest, ugly, neglected virtue.[2]

The explanation of the apparent contradiction is in the mixing of the two love themes, Dawes–Sylvia and Rex–Sarah. Although Dawes is the hero, it is John Rex who provides the sensation. He is the gentlemanly scoundrel, a forger, popular with both men and women, whom he does not scruple to betray; who is intelligent enough to delude Meekin, but not Frere, into

[1] *Term.*, p. 197.

[2] *The Peripatetic Philosopher by 'Q'*, Melbourne 1869, essay entitled 'Sham Criminality', p. 16.

thinking him pious; who is called the Dandy and has a certain gay courage when he leads the small party of convicts in seizing a boat and abandoning Frere, Mrs. Vickers, and Sylvia with Bates, the pilot:

> 'Come!' cried the Dandy, shaking off his momentary melancholy, 'look alive there! Lower away the jolly-boat. Mrs. Vickers, go down to your cabin and get anything you want. I am compelled to put you ashore, but I have no wish to leave you without clothes'. Bates listened, in a sort of dismal admiration, at this courtly convict. *He* could not have spoken like that had life depended on it. 'Now, my little lady,' continued Rex, 'run down with your mamma, and don't be frightened.'[1]

Despite the superficial qualities of a gentleman, however, Rex remains what he always was: a confidence man, whether as 'Mr. Lionel Crofton', a 'gentleman sportsman', or as 'Richard Devine', the long-lost son. That he is not completely to the manner born is emphasized by his assumed roles; he recognizes his deficiencies, Clarke is saying, and by trying to make up for them, adds to the suggestion in the novel that those qualities which Dawes actually possesses are admirable. His falsity is apparent when he is compared with the real thing. Lady Devine finds his conduct 'brutal', while her brother, who is a gentleman, calls it 'unnatural'.[2]

The punishment which Clarke metes out to him is significant. After his exposure, it is not the officers of the law who take him into their power, but the woman who loves him. Weary of her though he is, he does not break the seventh commandment. He begins and ends as the 'gentlemanly scoundrel', whose failure to be adulterous provides the essential difference between him and the Byronic hero.

Sarah Purfoy's first appearance is in the tradition of the *femme fatale*:

> The convict raised his eyes and saw a young girl of eighteen or nineteen years of age, tall, and well developed, who, dressed in a loose-sleeved robe of some white material, was standing in the doorway. She had black hair, coiled around a narrow and flat head, a small foot, white skin, well-shaped hands, and large dark eyes, and as she smiled at him, her scarlet lips showed her white even teeth.

[1] *Term*, pp. 167–18. [2] Ibid., p. 579.

He knew her at once. She was Sarah Purfoy, Mrs. Vickers's maid, but he never had been so close to her before; and it seemed to him that he was in the presence of some strange tropical flower, which exhaled a heavy and intoxicating perfume.[1]

Black hair, dark eyes, white teeth, white skin, red lips, an air of mystery and passion, Sarah has a long ancestry in European literature. True to her kind, she loves her man, whatever he is, prepared to sell her favours to anyone who will help him. That she may prove treacherous to others in order to serve her beloved is in the nature of the *femme fatale*: her treachery will be understood. There is, Clarke writes, 'a sort of love—if love it can be called—which thrives under ill-treatment'.[2] She is not entirely irresistible. Dawes, for instance, the convict in the above passage, resists her; as significantly, Maurice Frere cannot.

An explanation occurs years later in North's diary. Sarah Purfoy is now known as the widow of a rich squatter, Carr, in fact Rex, who has escaped from her:

She is a well-preserved creature, about thirty-four years of age, and a clever woman—not in a poetical sense, but in the widest worldly acceptation of the term. At the same time, I should be sorry to be her husband. Women have no business with a brain like hers—that is, if they wish to be women and not sexual monsters. Mrs. Carr is not a lady, though she might have been one. I don't think she is a good woman either. It is possible, indeed, that she has known the factory before now.[3]

The 'factory' was 'a prison for females' where 'the vilest abuses were committed'. Prostitution was common, despite the example of Mary Reiby, 'who conducted a thriving business and became the grand-mother of a Tasmanian Premier.' North is drawing attention, not to the woman's possible criminality, but to her sexual monstrosity. Most important, she is not a lady, 'though she might have been one'. It is inevitable, within these terms, that Rex, who was no gentleman but might have been one, should be her lover; and as inevitable that Dawes should not. As she tells Rex, 'I love you because you are a villain. A better man would be wearisome to such as I am.'[4]

[1] *Term.*, p. 22. [2] Ibid., p. 102. [3] Ibid., p. 469.
[4] Ibid., p. 481.

So far, Sarah is a late example of a European convention; but Clarke then uses specifically Australian social conditions to change the convention. He has already suggested them in the early pages, where Sarah emigrates as a free-woman on the same ship as her convict-lover. He takes them up again after Sarah has helped Rex to escape:

After he was landed in Sydney by the vessel which Sarah Purfoy had sent to save him, he found himself a slave to a bondage scarcely less galling than that from which he had escaped—the bondage of enforced companionship with an unloved woman. The opportune death of one of her assigned servants enabled Sarah Purfoy to instal the escaped convict in his room. In the strange state of society which prevailed of necessity in New South Wales at that period, it was not unusual for assigned servants to marry among the free settlers, and when it was heard that Mrs. Purfoy, the widow of a whaling captain, had married John Carr, her storekeeper, transported for embezzlement, and with two years of his sentence yet to run, no one expressed surprise . . . But John Rex had no notion of remaining longer than he could help, and ceaselessly sought means of escape from this second prison-house. For a long time his search was unsuccessful. Much as she loved the scoundrel, Sarah Purfoy did not scruple to tell him that she had bought him, and regarded him as her property. He knew that if he made any attempt to escape from his marriage-bonds, the woman who had risked so much to save him would not hesitate to deliver him over to the authorities, and state how the opportune death of John Carr had enabled her to give name and employment to John Rex, the absconder . . .

'I know you don't care for me now, John,' she said, with grim complacency; 'but your life is in my hands, and if you desert me I will bring you to the gallows' . . .

'I am home-sick,' John Carr retorted. 'Let us go to England, Sarah.'

She tapped her strong white fingers sharply on the table. 'Go to England? No, no. That is what you would like to do. You would be master there. You would take my money, and leave me to starve. I know you, Jack. We stop here, dear. Here, where I can hand you over to the first trooper as an escaped convict if you are not kind to me.'[1]

Rex's reply is to call her a 'she-devil'; but she is more. She is, up to the time Clarke wrote, the most complete naturalization in Australian literature of a stock European convention.

[1] Ibid., pp. 479–81.

Because the altered convention was firmly set in Australian conditions, she persisted in Australian literature long after her prototype, the *femme fatale*, had disappeared from the literature of Europe. For John Rex, all Australia is a prison. The law wanted to keep him there; and woman embodied the law.

After Rex's exposure in England, Sarah, in fulfilling her womanly role of captor, hears the explanation for his superficial gentlemanly qualities; an explanation for his close resemblance to Dawes is also incidentally afforded. Like Dawes, he is the illegitimate son of Lord Bellasis, and it was he who killed Bellasis.

In shifting the scene back to England, Clarke does more than merely tidy the story; he also enforces two constant themes. The first he summarizes thus:

> 'Gentleman seems to have had a stroke,' said a boatman.
>
> It was so. There was no fear that John Rex would escape again from the woman he had deceived. The infernal genius of Sarah Purfoy had saved her lover at last—but saved him only that she might nurse him till he died—died ignorant even of her tenderness, a mere animal, lacking the intellect he had in his selfish wickedness abused.[1]

In other words, the woman holds her man captive. The second is that, despite having the same father, Richard Devine and John Rex are as different as gentleman and scoundrel. Richard Devine's mother was a lady, John Rex's was not.

This insistence on a mother's all-powerful influence may be because Clarke himself was early deprived of his mother. There is also evidence of its importance in his story, 'A Mysterious Coincidence', where he writes: 'Thrice fortunate is he among us who can look back on a youth spent in the innocent enjoyment of the country, and who possesses a mind moulded in its adolescence by the cool fingers of well-mannered and pious women.'[2] More important, there is the evidence in *For The Term of his Natural Life*: Richard Devine 'became reckless and prodigal. The mother . . . tried to restrain him, but the headstrong boy, though owning for his mother that strong love which is often a part of such violent natures, proved intractable. . .'.[3] Her attentions are not without success, however, for

[1] *Term.*, p. 588. [2] Ibid., quoted L. H. Allen, Introduction, p. v.
[3] Ibid., p. 6.

he proves himself his mother's son when he does protect her secret and her honour, responding, not like a Byronic hero, but like a gentleman: 'Bound by the purest and holiest of ties,—the affection of a son to his mother—he had condemned himself to social death, rather than buy his liberty and life by a revelation which would shame the gentle creature whom he loved.'[1] The outline of legend is blurred when Clarke shows that Richard Devine did not murder his father: murder was beyond a gentleman. It needed a scoundrel like Rex to do that, even accidentally; and Rex's mother was a valet's wife, fond of her son and socially ambitious for him, but neither well-mannered nor pious.

By using for motivation the relationship between a mother who is a lady and her son who is a gentleman, Clarke shows himself an English Victorian novelist; and by using the Sarah Purfoy–John Rex relationship as an alternative he shows himself an involuntary Australian; but, though he links and condemns Swinburne and Whitman in his essay, as Byronic heroes as well as poets of prurience, he shows in his portrayal of his hero a knowledge of, and a willingness to use, a stock figure of European literature. This gives his work a wider relevance, and eventually increases the worth of the novel. The extensions of the figure can best be considered under three headings: the image of woman; the theme of mateship; and the story of Christ.

Sylvia Vickers first appears as a small child of five. She sees Maurice Frere strike Dawes, who has returned her ball; the memory stays with her only as a dislike for Frere. She next appears, as a gay, fair-haired, blue-eyed, precocious child of eleven, with her mother, Maurice Frere, and Bates, when they have been put ashore by mutinying convicts at the abandoned settlement of Macquarie Harbour. Here Dawes, who has escaped and is starving, finds them. Bates having died, and Mrs. Vickers being ill, Sylvia welcomes Dawes as an interesting alternative to Frere, whom she continues to dislike. And it is he, not Frere, who knows how they can best survive:

> Sylvia began to look upon Dawes as a second Bates. He was, moreover, all her own. She had an interest in him, for she had nursed and protected him. If it had not been for her, this prodigy would not have lived. He

[1] Ibid., p. 224–5.

felt for her an absorbing affection that was almost a passion. She was his good angel, his protectress, his glimpse of heaven. She had given him food when he was starving, and had believed in him when the world—the world of four—had looked coldly on him. He would have died for her, and, for love of her, hoped for the vessel which should take *her* back to freedom and give *him* again to bondage.[1]

Dawes's dilemma has the elements of a trial of courtly love; the difference is in the quality of the reality. There is nothing hypothetical about the problem: both the freedom and the bondage are real. The theme of the prison is thus strengthened. It is strengthened still further by the apparent choice Dawes has. If the awaited vessel does not come, he can either refuse to help in building some sort of boat, or he can build it and navigate it. It is, however, not the choice which is real, but the inevitability of Dawes's response to it. He is the one equipped not only with the right sort of knowledge, but the one most effectively imprisoned by his responses. Love is his response to kindness.

From this point, Clarke shifts his emphasis. Dawes's love for his mother is superseded by his love for a child. Five years after the rescue, 'The whole world was his foe: there was no honesty or truth in any living creature—save one . . . In the depth of his degradation, at the height of his despair, he cherished one pure and ennobling thought—the thought of the child whom he had saved, and who loved him.'[2] His original love for the child is as real as that of Mr. Jarndyce for Ada Clare in *Bleak House*, but the quality changes because of Clarke's emphasis on a girl of sixteen remaining a 'child'. He has moved away from the real world, which even sentimentality subsumes, to the borders of a world as unreal as Swinburne's. It is unnecessary to examine 'The Mind Reader's Curse' in Clarke's *Sensational Tales*[3] or his story of *The Man with the Oblong Box*,[4] both of which are concerned with such unreality; the evidence is in *For the Term of his Natural Life*.

Dawes has again escaped, been caught, and sent to the Coal Mines:

The day on which he started for this place he heard that Sylvia was dead, and his last hope went from him.

[1] *Term.*, p. 198. [2] Ibid., pp. 300–1.
[3] Marcus Clarke, *Sensational Tales*, Sydney 1886.
[4] Marcus Clarke, *The Man with the Oblong Box*, Melbourne 1878.

Then began with him a new religion. He worshipped the dead. For the living, he had but hatred and evil words; for the dead, he had love and tender thoughts. Instead of the phantoms of his vanished youth which were once wont to visit him, he saw now but one vision—the vision of the child who had loved him. Instead of conjuring up for himself pictures of that home circle in which he had once moved, and those creatures who in the past years had thought him worthy of esteem and affection, he placed before himself but one idea, one embodiment of happiness, one being who was without sin and without stain, among all the monsters of that pit into which he had fallen. Around the figure of the innocent child who had lain in his breast, and laughed at him with her red young mouth, he grouped every image of happiness and love. Having banished from his thoughts all hope of resuming his name and place, he pictured to himself some quiet nook at the world's end—a deep-gardened house in a German country town, or remote cottage by the English seashore, where he and his dream-child might have lived together, happier in a purer affection than the love of man for woman.[1]

We see here in European literary terms, a movement away from the lonely, fatal hero towards the hero who is sustained in life by a beautiful, dead, woman. Clarke has brought about what Swinburne could only hope for:

I would my love could kill thee; I am satiated
With seeing thee live, and fain would have thee dead.[2]

The beloved dead is here, however, a child: but in blurring the literary connection, Clarke has the hero and his dream-child live together 'happier in a purer affection than the love of man for woman'. Coming after the mention of the 'red young mouth', the phrase 'purer affection' has a false ring. Whatever else he was, Swinburne was never hypocritical in this way. The unorthodox vices of his heroes did not become orthodox virtues. If they had, they would have lost their connection with Satanism which it was Swinburne's purpose to proclaim. What makes the passage significant in the Australian literary tradition is that the purest kind of love is that which is unfruitful, an insistence which Clarke enforces when, in his pursuit of poetic injustice, he makes Sarah the matrimonial captor of the crippled Rex.

[1] *Term*, p. 303.

[2] *The Complete Works of Algernon Charles Swinburne*, ed. Sir Edmund Gosse and Thomas James Wise, 20 vols., London, New York 1925; reissued 1968, vol. 1, 'Anactoria'.

Sylvia is not dead, however; instead, Frere is engaged to marry her; and it is to him that Sarah Purfoy, his former mistress, describes the kind of woman Sylvia is: 'She is good—and virtuous—and cold.'[1] She is Sarah's traditionally golden-haired opposite; and Frere marries her.

Their marriage is at first successful—'Yet there were times when her lips were cold to his kisses, and her eyes looked disdainfully upon his coarser passion.'[2] The sentence is ambiguous, for it can be read either as a comment on Frere's generally coarse nature or as a comment on sexual love. That it is the second is made clear later: 'we will not presume to set forth in bare English the story of this marriage of the Minotaur. Let it suffice to say that Sylvia liked her husband least when he loved her most.'[3] It is possible so far to accept Sylvia's plight as real, but doubts crowd in when Clarke continues:

> In this repulsion lay her power over him. When the animal and spiritual natures cross each other, the nobler triumphs in fact if not in appearance. Maurice Frere, though his wife obeyed him, knew that he was inferior to her, and was afraid of the statue he had created. She was ice, but it was the artificial ice that chemists make in the midst of a furnace. Her coldness was at once her strength and her weakness. When she chilled him, she commanded him.

Before Sylvia's marriage Sarah has described her as cold; Dawes loves her because she is a child, without sexuality; her frigidity, equated with spirituality, is finally offered as the ideal in woman.

The ideal is supported by the thoughts which North confides to his diary. North is forty-seven, Sylvia twenty-five, when he writes, 'Charming little Sylvia, with your quaint wit and weird beauty, [Frere] is not good enough for you. . . .'[4] Her 'littleness' is curiously emphasized when North applies Christ's words to a twenty-five-year-old woman:

> I am a coward not to throw off the saintly mask, and appear as a Free-thinker. . . . The scandal of a priest turned infidel [however] would do more harm than the reign of reason would do good. Imagine this trustful woman for instance—she would suffer anguish at the thoughts of such a sin, though another were the sinner. 'If any one offend one of these little ones it were better for him that a millstone be hanged about his neck and that he be cast into the sea.'[5]

[1] *Term.*, p. 264. [2] Ibid., p. 381. [3] Ibid., p. 519.
[4] Ibid., p. 470. [5] Ibid., p. 471.

Her 'littleness' reappears in the next entry, and with it an explanation of her 'weird beauty', which supports the contention that it was not merely Sylvia's childishness Dawes was recalling when he imagined 'her red young mouth':

> Mrs. Frere is about five-and-twenty. She is rather beneath the middle height, with a slight, girlish figure. This girlish appearance is enhanced by the fact that she has bright fair hair and blue eyes. . . . Her cheeks are thin . . . [which] makes the eyes appear larger and the brow broader than they really are. Her hands are white and painfully thin. . . . Her lips are red with perpetual fever.[1]

This is still the world of Swinburne and not of Baudelaire—sickness used to titillate desire, not to clarify, or even to enlarge, experience. Mental masturbation is again suggested when North writes: 'At night I become a satyr. While in this torment I at once hate and fear myself. One fair face is ever before me, gleaming through my hot dreams like a flying moon in the sultry midnight of a tropic storm.'[2] Frere is a Minotaur, North a satyr, and the object of their desires a frigid, fevered, girl-child. Clarke seems to condemn the bestialism of both, but his real values appear in the way he does it; for he allows Dawes, the hero, to applaud the same qualities the other two have observed in Sylvia. Dawes, however, recognizes them as signs of 'spirituality' and welcomes their implicit sterility.

Clarke also allows North to be the mouthpiece of condemnation in the following passage where North is talking to Maurice Frere:

> I broached my theory, that strong intellect in women went far to destroy their womanly nature.
>
> 'Desire in man,' said I, 'should be Volition in women: Reason, Intuition; Reverence, Devotion; Passion, Love. The woman should strike a lower keynote, but a sharper sound. Man has vigour of reason, woman quickness of feeling. The woman who possesses masculine force of intellect is abnormal.' He did not half comprehend me, I could see, but he agreed with the broad view of the case. 'I only knew one woman who was really "strong-minded," as they call it,' he said, 'and she was a regular bad one.'
>
> 'It does not follow that she should be *bad*,' said I.
>
> 'This one was, though—stock, lock, and barrel. But as sharp as a needle, sir, and as immovable as a rock. A fine woman, too.'[3]

[1] Ibid., p. 473. [2] Ibid., p. 530. [3] Ibid., p. 475.

Frere's reference, which North recognizes, is to Sarah Purfoy, whom North has already condemned. The ideal, which North expresses as a 'theory', is much the same as Frere's and Dawes's. The condemnation lacks conviction when we remember the care with which North and Dawes have imagined the concomitants of this ideal woman: the little child with feverish red lips, who is sick mentally as well as physically. The conclusion that this was Clarke's ideal is unavoidable when Sylvia herself comments to Frere: 'Well, you see, that is the reason why I am angry with myself for not loving you as I ought. I want you to like the things I like, and to love the books and the music and the pictures and the—the World *I* love; and I forget that you are a man, you know, and I am only a girl. . . .'[1] In European literature, the sterility of this ideal led to Swinburne's Lesbia Brandon and in the nineties to the more directly logical ideal of masculine homosexuality. Clarke, with his concern to 'appeal', was also careful not to offend, though the reality of the conditions in which he chose to set his novel offered more than sadism to a writer who purported to give the truth. The account Clarke does give of the experience of Kirkland, a new young pious convict, is indicative. The youth is put in the 'yard' for a night as punishment and 'In the morning, Rufus Dawes . . . was struck by the altered appearance of Kirkland. His face was of a greenish tint, and wore an expression of bewildered horror'.[2] Later we learn that the cell in which six men spend their period of solitary confinement, 'a mere name', is called the 'nunnery', which was also the name of the women's prison.[3] While it is unnecessary to speculate how much 'le vice anglais' had to do with the details Clarke feels obliged to give of the beatings common in the settlement, what does bear speculation is why his public could accept such details, though unprepared for an account of the Freres' sex life. More significant is the way Clarke's ideal of woman is supported by the theme of mateship.

It has become part of Australian mythology to say, in explanation of the phenomenon, that mateship had convictism as one of its sources. Though there is nothing in 'Price Warung' to support this belief, there is some evidence in Clarke, but it is ambiguous and at times contradictory.

Clarke early makes clear the convicts' feelings of being set

[1] *Term.*, p. 291. [2] Ibid., p. 350. [3] Ibid., pp. 500–1.

apart from society, which 'was the common foe, and magistrates, jailers, and parsons, were the natural prey of all noteworthy mankind. Only fools were honest, only cowards kissed the rod, and failed to meditate revenge on that world of respectability which had wronged them.'[1] The tone of disapproval is shared by Dawes when he is on the convict-ship going to Australia, but he is forced into admitting something like a feeling of solidarity: 'Though he conversed but little with his companions, these men were his berth mates, and he could not but know how *they* would proceed to wreak their vengeance on their jailers.'[2] That the solidarity is more apparent than real is shown when Dawes tries to warn the authorities that a mutiny is afoot, and is blamed by the other convicts for starting it. This is explicable in terms of the Byronic hero being distrusted by all; but Frere, in echoing a sentiment expressed in Charles Rowcroft's *Tales of the Colonies*, accounts for it in another, more obvious way to the Rev. Meekin: 'Why, my dear sir, if the prisoners were as faithful to each other as we are, we couldn't hold the island a week. It's just because no man can trust his neighbour that every mutiny falls to the ground.'[3] Frere works on this principle, and is successful; and it is part of Dawes's function, after he has suffered the brutality that makes him one of the outcast group, to oppose Frere's 'realism' by his keener understanding of its origins as well as its purpose. When Frere offers to make him a constable, Dawes answers: 'And betray my mates? I'm not one of that sort.'[4] This is not so much a reference to mateship as a reminder that Dawes is still a gentleman; though sometimes the two are difficult to separate, as D. H. Lawrence remarks of Australians like Jack and 'the quiet well-bred . . . upper-class young Englishmen, who have the same yearning for intimate comradeship, combined with a sensitive delicacy really finer than a woman's'.[5] But by using the word 'mates' Clarke is implying that Dawes recognizes his new community of interest, and loses nothing by such recognition.

Mateship, in Lawson, however, meant more than a community of interest. It meant the relationship existing between two men, a relationship that was perhaps the result of the working conditions of the goldfields where men needed to

[1] Ibid., p. 46. [2] Ibid., p. 68. [3] Ibid., p. 321.
[4] Ibid., p. 527. [5] *Kangaroo*, p. 119.

work at least in pairs. Shepherding had early provided similar conditions, one man looking after the sheep while the other slept, and acted as hut-keeper. Clarke shows that the same social necessity existed in at least some convict activities, in the chain-gang for instance, where men were chained in pairs; but here the sterility of such a relationship is manifest in the uses which were made of it:

> Not many months before, one of the companions of the chain, suffering under Burgess's tender mercies, had killed his mate when at work with him, and, carrying the body on his back to the nearest gang, had surrendered himself—going to his death thanking God he had at last found a way of escape from his miseries, which no one would envy him—save his comrades.[1]

This man had a mate. Clarke's ironic use of inverted commas to describe John Rex, at one time Dawes's companion of the chain, as Dawes's 'mate'[2] means that he accepts the convention of mateship and recognizes the code which Rex abuses. Death was literally its end, while Rex cheats by preferring life. Clarke's use of mateship can thus be seen as widening the theme of the prison as well as supporting the ideal of sterile love.

Dawes also has a mate, as well as a 'mate', though Clarke calls him a 'friend'—Blind Mooney. The explanation for their friendship is significant, very different from those feelings of group solidarity generally attributed to the convicts:

> Perhaps this oddly assorted friendship was brought about by two causes—one, that Mooney was the only man on the island who knew more of the horrors of convictism than the leader of the Ring; the other, that Mooney was blind, and, to a moody, sullen man, subject to violent fits of passion and a constant suspicion of all his fellow-creatures, a blind companion was more congenial than a sharp-eyed one.[3]

The ultimate purpose to which this friendship is put involves a third member. They draw lots to decide who is to be killed, who to kill, and who to be the witness, thus ensuring that at least two men will 'escape'. It is Mooney and the third who go to 'Heaven', while Dawes remains the witness in 'Hell'. Of Mooney, Clarke has already said that 'His wife was long since dead, and he stated, without contradiction, that his master,

[1] *Term.*, p. 383. [2] Ibid., p. 345. [3] Ibid., p. 524.

having taken a fancy to her, had despatched the uncomplaisant husband to imprisonment. Such cases were not uncommon.' We should not be surprised that a convict might prefer a mate; or that Australian fiction should so often celebrate a Robin Hood, but never a Maid Marion.

Clarke's ambiguous attitude to mateship among convicts is apparent in the following, where Frere is discussing with Warder Troke the case of Gabbett, who has returned after bolting: ' "How many mates had he?" asked Maurice, watching the champing jaws as one looks at a strange animal, and asking the question as though a "mate" was something a convict was born with—like a mole, for instance.'[1] Clarke disapproves of Frere's cynicism, but he draws attention to Gabbett's champing jaws, for Gabbett has eaten his 'mates'. The temptations of cannibalism, or John Rex's readiness to betray his mates to ensure his own safety, would seem to suggest that there were disadvantages in being a mate; and that in literature the theme should not so readily be applauded as a reflection, both accurate and admirable, of what happened in convict society. In Clarke, the theme at the social level proves to be as sterile as his literary ideal of love between man and woman. Its 'spirituality' has death as its logical, even necessary conclusion.

It appears fruitful when Clarke extends it to mean not so much the brotherhood of man, as 'I am my brother's keeper', because it seems not to be in conflict with the normal sexuality existing between man and woman; and in literary terms the extension supports the symbolism of the book. Clarke's achievement in using symbolism has gone unremarked because of the care with which he set the story in the history and geography of Australia.

Reference has already been made to his use of the sea, which is the title he gives to Book I. It has also been shown how he continues to employ its encircling quality to provide in the last chapter, called 'The Cyclone', the culmination of Dawes's imprisoned love. In Book II, he begins to use the details of allegory on which to base his symbolism; and he did not need to invent his allegorical world. As Port Arthur was 'a natural penitentiary', so nature also provided at Macquarie Harbour 'a rocky point, which runs abruptly northward'[2] and 'almost touches, on its eastern side, a projecting arm of land which

[1] *Term.*, p. 128. [2] Ibid., p. 109.

guards the entrance to King's River'. This is the formation known as Hell's Gates, the entrance to that hell in which Dawes is imprisoned. In the chapter called 'The Power of the Wilderness', Dawes escapes only to wander lost in this wilderness, and, Clarke writes, 'He never *could* escape'.[1] This is what hell means.

It is in this hell that Dawes finds Mrs. Vickers, Sylvia, and Frere; it is where he is sorely tempted to save himself in the boat that he alone has made, and to desert the others:

> He was within three feet of the boat, when he suddenly checked himself, and stood motionless, staring at the sand with as much horror as though he saw there the Writing which foretold the doom of Belshazzar. He had come upon the sentence traced by Sylvia the evening before, and glittering in the low light of the red sun suddenly risen from out the sea, it seemed to him that the letters had shaped themselves at his very feet.
>
> GOOD MR. DAWES[2]

The reference is in fact not to Belshazzar but to Christ's temptation at Gethsemane. That Dawes acts in a Christlike way, Clarke makes clear by concluding the chapter: 'The sacrifice was complete.' Which is to say that Richard Devine justifies his birth name. His pseudonym Dawes is merely the imprisoning opposite of Frere's name.

Should this seem a too facile interpretation, even though some of the chapter headings 'The Writing on the Sand', 'A Labourer in the Vineyard', and 'The Valley of the Shadow of Death'—where Gabbett once again eats his mates—seem to confirm it, there is further support in the theme of the Old Testament God, which Meekin encourages Dawes to worship in the chapter called 'The Consolations of Religion', and the theme of New Testament salvation which ends with the chapter called 'The Redemption'.

Meekin's character has already been sufficiently indicated. It is now only necessary to quote from the ironically titled chapter, 'The Consolations of Religion', where Dawes, expecting North, has been sent the new parson, Meekin, who leaves him a Bible, with 'some twenty marked texts':

> Good Meekin, in the fullness of his stupidity, had selected the fiercest denunciations of bard and priest. The most notable of the

[1] *Term.*, p. 156. [2] Ibid., p. 229.

Psalmist's curses upon his enemies, the most furious of Isaiah's ravings anent the forgetfulness of the national worship, the most terrible thunderings of apostle and evangelist against idolatry and unbelief, were grouped together and presented to Dawes to soothe him. . . . Before his eyes was held no image of a tender Saviour (with hands soft to soothe, and eyes brimming with ineffable pity) dying crucified that he and other malefactors might have hope, by thinking on such marvellous humanity. The worthy Pharisee who was sent to him to teach him how mankind is to be redeemed with Love, preached only that harsh Law whose barbarous power died with the gentle Nazarene on Calvary.[1]

North, the man whom he expected, came into his life after Dawes was ordered to flog Kirkland, the young Methodist. Up to this time, Dawes had been sustained by the 'memory of his [own] sacrifice and love'. As it is dissipated by the conditions of the hell in which he lives, Dawes accepts the order to flog Kirkland, an event which North has said he will not allow to happen. As he does not arrive, Dawes begins to flog: 'But he had miscalculated his own capacity for evil. As he flogged he blushed; and when he flung down the cat and stripped his own back for punishment, he felt a fierce joy in the thought that his baseness would be atoned for in his own blood.'[2] It is, then, Dawes whose actions admit that he is after all, his brother's keeper. His Christlike quality is greater than that of North, the minister of God, because North fails to keep his appointment. He finds Dawes later, recovering from his own flogging, and explains why he had not arrived in time:

'I wanted to save him, God knows! But I have a vice; I am a drunkard, I yielded to my temptation, and—I was too late. I come to you as one sinful man to another, to ask you to forgive me.' And North suddenly flung himself down beside the convict, and catching his blood-bespotted hands in his own, cried, 'Forgive me, brother!'

Rufus Dawes, too much astonished to speak, bent his black eyes upon the man who crouched at his feet, and a ray of divine pity penetrated his gloomy soul. He seemed to catch a glimpse of misery more profound than his own, and his stubborn heart felt human sympathy with his erring brother. 'Then in this hell there is yet a man,' said he; and a hand-grasp passed between these two unhappy beings. North arose, and, with averted face, passed quickly from the cell.

[1] Ibid., pp. 387–8. [2] Ibid., p. 382.

Rufus Dawes looked at the hand which his strange visitor had taken, and something glittered there. It was a tear. He broke down at the sight of it, and when the guard came to fetch the tameless convict, they found him on his knees in a corner, sobbing like a child.[1]

At this admission, Dawes accepts North's qualities as genuine. Clarke explains that 'he who would touch the hearts of men must have had his own heart seared', and thus enforces, by his appeal to shared travail, the connection between mateship and brotherhood in Christ. The 'hand-grasp' signifies the first, the tears signify the second. The power of the experience is summed up after Meekin's visit: 'And filled with a strange wild pity for himself, and yearning love towards the man who befriended him, he fell to nursing the hand on which North's tears had fallen. . . .'[2] The theme is pursued to the end. Dawes, sentenced to death, is North's only 'brother', for the minister has incurred Frere's displeasure. His attempt to help the convicts results only in their being punished further. For Dawes, this holds little terror, and he continues to receive North's visits. 'It seemed to the fancy of the priest—a fancy distempered, perhaps, by excess, or superhumanly exalted by mental agony—that this convict, over whom he had wept, was given to him as a hostage for his own salvation. "I must save him or perish," he said. "I must save him, though I redeem him with my own blood." '[3] Despite the increasing severity of Frere's punishments, 'Dawes clung to North as the saviour of his agonized soul'.[4]

Thus far, Clarke's use of the Christian story has enriched the novel by increasing the possibilities his symbolism can carry; but, by allowing two of his main characters Christlike qualities, he presents himself with a dilemma. To some extent he has already prepared a solution by differentiating the kinds of love North and Dawes have for Sylvia. The one is 'spiritual', the other 'physical'; and from what has gone before in the novel, it is certain that the 'spiritual' will triumph. But the contest will still be between the two Christs. It is the nature of the triumph, however, which weakens the work.

North, true to his character, appeals in his diary to Christ's humanity, not to his divinity, rejecting the Old Testament God

[1] *Term.*, p. 370. [2] Ibid., pp. 388–9. [3] Ibid., p. 558.
[4] Ibid., p. 560.

whose law, he feels, should make him forswear Sylvia's company and suffer because of it: 'Art thou not sated with blood and tears, O God of vengeance, of wrath, and of despair? Kind Christ, pity me. *Thou* wilt—for thou wast human! Blessed Saviour, at whose feet knelt the Magdalen!'[1] For a time, he does not see her and endures his agonies. Eventually, he succumbs to his temptation and tells Dawes that he has resigned his position, and will leave on the same boat as Sylvia, who is returning to the mainland. He also admits it was a lie that Sylvia had forgiven Dawes the shocks his escapes had caused her when he tried to revive in her the memory of his part in saving her. The lie, and the fact that they are leaving together, give Dawes the clue to their love. His response is the culmination of the character Clarke has created out of the Byronic hero and the Christian legend:

'No, madman, I will not let you go, to do this great wrong, to kill this innocent young soul, who—God help her—loves you! . . . I say you shall *not* go! You shall not destroy your own soul and hers! You love her! So do I! and my love is mightier than yours, for it shall save her!'

'In God's name—' cried the unhappy priest, striving to stop his ears.

'Ay, in God's name! In the name of that God whom in my torments I had forgotten. In the name of that God whom you taught me to remember! That God who sent you to save me from despair, gives me strength to save you in my turn! Oh, Mr. North—my teacher—my friend—my brother—by the sweet hope of mercy which you preached to me, be merciful to this erring woman!'

North lifted agonized eyes. 'But I love her! Love her, do you hear? What do you know of love?'

'Love!' cried Rufus Dawes, his pale face radiant. 'Love! Oh, it is you who do not know it. Love is the sacrifice of self, the death of all desire that is not for another's good. Love is Godlike! *You* love?—no, no, your love is selfishness, and will end in shame! Listen, I will tell you the history of such a love as yours . . . I will tell you the secret of my life, the reason why I am here . . .'[2]

Dawes thus expresses the moral in the story of his life: 'The punishment of sin falls not upon the sinner only'; which is a variation on the Old Testament law that the sins of the fathers shall be visited on their children. He is here uniting in his person the characters of Jehovah and Christ.

[1] Ibid., p. 551. [2] Ibid., pp. 577–8.

Despite the melodrama, the scene is not without its effect, but the effect is spoiled when Dawes's argument is examined. His love is mightier than North's, because, he says, it will save Sylvia; at the same time, 'Love is a sacrifice of self', 'the death of all desire that is not for another's good'. It is unnecessary to dwell on the presumption in this kind of thinking; but that his love will 'save' Sylvia is difficult to comprehend or perhaps to sympathize with. He evidently intends to keep her as a child, in his 'German garden' or 'by the English sea-shore'; at least he intends to deny her recognition of that sexuality which a woman of twenty-five can normally be assumed to have, for only thus will his decision to impersonate North and take his place on the boat be justified. For he too 'covets his neighbour's wife'.

What Clarke is asking the reader to do is either to accept this special pleading, or to accept his constant implication that love is most perfect when sterile; or to anticipate the deaths of both hero and heroine, and so make the conclusion of the book superfluous. He seems to have realized, when he presents Dawes's worship of the child as occurring in dreams about a person he has heard is dead, that this picture of sterility had to be preserved from any contact with reality. It could exist only in the conditions he gives it; that is, he uses it as a literary convention. By his emphasis on the brutality of convict life. however, and by the constancy of his anger, he forces the reader to concern himself with reality.

The same difficulty attends his use of the gentleman who becomes a Byronic hero as a result of brutal experience and at the same time a Christlike man intent on saving a pretty little girl from herself. We can follow the reality from honour to proud loneliness and blighted love; but how can this kind of love suddenly become sustaining? The change from Byronic hero to Christlike man is not in doubt, if by a Christlike man we mean a man who can see, and act upon the knowledge, that 'the sharp scythe of the leveller makes it possible for every one individually to leap over the blade—and behold, it is God who waits.'[1] But such a man, whom Kierkegaard calls an 'unrecognisable', an individual, 'neither can nor dares help man, not even his most faithful disciple, his mother, or the girl for whom

[1] Kierkegaard, *The Present Age*, p. 94.

he would gladly give his life: they must make the leap themselves, for God's love is not a second-hand gift'. Yet Dawes and Sylvia leap together, responding not as Christians leaping 'into the arms of God', but as a lady and gentleman who are found in each others'.

What finally prevents his success is the realism of his setting and the conviction of his anger: for they conflict with the ideals embodied in his main characters. Scene and anger give unity to his novel, but he fails to preserve the tension that comes from a constant opposition of morality and psychology. Where morality, with allegorical and stock figures, condemns and applauds, psychology, through sybolism, precludes both condemnation and applause, offering instead a bewildered pity. Clarke reverses the functions, trying to extract pity from morality, and applause for his psychology. His intention was to write a 'sensation novel', and he ended by offering his public a novel of protest. It is as much his intentions as his achievement that are in doubt.

7 'Rolf Boldrewood', *Robbery under Arms*

WHEN Thomas Alexander Browne chose in 1881 to write *Robbery under Arms*[1] under his pen-name 'Rolf Boldrewood', he was completing what his earlier sketches[2] had been intended to do but could not, because of their form, fulfil: to show in Australian terms his admiration for and indebtedness to Scott. His reliance on Scott was as great and as conscious as Thomas McCombie's had been nearly forty years earlier. Boldrewood records[3] that he had 'always been a devoted admirer of Walter Scott', and took the pen-name Boldrewood from the first canto of *Marmion*, merely adding the Norse or Saxon forename. The aristocratic pretensions which the name 'Boldrewood' held were thoroughly, and repellently, explored in his *My Run Home*;[4] but in 1881 it was the literary connection that he was most anxious to establish.

The serial was successful in Australia; and its London publication as a book confirmed its success. Its present appearance as one of the World's Classics many times reprinted, implies that it has continued as it began. The main reason for Boldrewood's initial success was that he chose a bushranging theme one year after Australia's most notable and flamboyant bushranger, Ned Kelly, was executed. The theme was thus topical and finally reassuring. It was also traditional, the bushranger being part of the stock-in-trade of the Australian novelist, whom English reading habits and expectations compelled to include danger in any tale of a new land, and whom the novel's traditions compelled to give to danger a local habitation and a

1 *Robbery under Arms: A Story of Life and Adventure in the Bush and in the Goldfields of Australia*, 3 vols., London 1888. It was first serialized in the *Sydney Mail* in 1881.

2 *In Bad Company and Other Stories*, London 1901: includes 'A Kangaroo Shoot' and 'Shearing in Riverina', written 1865.

3 Quoted by Thomas Wood in Introduction to *Robbery under Arms*, O.U.P., World's Classics, London 1949, reprinted 1951, 1955, 1957 (twice), 1961 (hereafter referred to as *Robbery*), p. vii.

4 London 1897.

name. The novelists used the bushranger because Australia's 'blacks are the stupidest, laziest beggars in the whole world';[1] and flood, fire, and drought, being acts of God, left so little room for the interest of human conflict. Boldrewood gave the theme a new turn. Instead of being an escaped or freed convict, Boldrewood's bushranger hero—like Kelly himself—was a free-born native 'cornstalk'. Transportation had ended. Australia had begun to produce her own felons. The country had, as it were, come of age.

With topicality and literary tradition, Boldrewood also uses the history of his country. Marcus Clarke, seven years earlier, had recognized the value of Australian history to the novelist who felt himself to be a part of that history. Boldrewood, in the year after the Melbourne International Exhibition and the laying of the Sydney–San Francisco cable, was less concerned with Australia's macabre origins. Their uniqueness seemed not to impress him. He uses instead the whole historical process, only touching on the country's origins through old Ben Marston, the narrator's father, a freed convict. The process continues through George Storefield, his free-born neighbour, who, from a small farmer, prospers to become a magistrate, the equal in generosity, if not in wealth, of Mr. Falkland, the pastoralist. The process ends ten years after the enriching and disturbing discovery of gold in 1850, which hastened the spread of towns and consolidated the existence of cities, despite the misgivings, complaints, even denials of small farmers and pastoralists then and since. *Robbery under Arms*, written a generation after Kingsley's *Geoffry Hamlyn*, offers a more certain picture of the process that Kingsley used and admired. In Boldrewood's novel, where one bush character happily takes a city job, the process is complete.

Boldrewood's large use of Australian history, exemplified in character and experience, is matched by his use of Australian geography. The gang of bushrangers canter and occasionally gallop freely across the south-western quarter of the continent, relying—as Kelly did— on a network of friends and relatives to 'give them the office', and on their own ability to accept this land as theirs, reading its signs and moods as others would a diary. Their area of operation is Queensland and its ports,

[1] *Robbery*, p. 297.

Sydney, Melbourne, and the land behind; at the same time they are aware of the Islands, New Zealand, America, and of course England. The days when convicts, unconsciously denying their isolation, thought that Australia was a continuation of the Malayan peninsula are long past. The limits of the land are known, the interior is being explored; knowledgeable men can cross both with a fair degree of safety and certainty—this is the suggestion behind the novel. The important point is that the story's conclusion belies this. Australia still constrains, still imprisons.

Such a conclusion, which by 1881 could be called traditionally Australian, is anticipated, and in some way prepared for, by the third element in the novel's success: its use of what by 1881 were already types and conventions in Australian literature—the bushranger; his companion in crime, the aborigine; the convict. Mates and women are similarly typed. The mere names 'bushranger', 'convict', 'aborigine' are Australian by origin or historical association; so that when an Englishman reads *Robbery under Arms*, without reference to previous Australian literature, he feels he recognizes much that the word 'Australian' means. The novel is like a variation on the theme of '*Waltzing Matilda*', itself a late but, to Australians, an often embarrassingly better-known summary.

The reader, English or Australian, is also encouraged to accept the novel's types and conventions as authentically Australian by Boldrewood's own conviction, that they are real. His confidence in presenting them provides this ambience of reality, a confidence that comes from doing something done many times before because it was once a reflection of Australian society. That Boldrewood's society had changed, despite Ned Kelly, mattered no more than that present-day Australian society seems to have no relation to Sidney Nolan's paintings of Kelly, or that his mural of the Eureka Stockade would seem oddly housed in Melbourne's Reserve Bank of Australia. Boldrewood, like Nolan, is using a tradition large enough to embrace rather spurious types and conventions. Though these are severed by time and habit from the society which produced them and gave them meaning, they have renewed their meaning in reflecting the concerns which artist or writer, who is, however unwillingly, a member of society, sees as his own. Boldrewood's types also benefit from the exactness with which he transposes history and geography into time and place. His stylizations are thus able to act out their obvious ends amidst the concreteness of things observed and the accuracy of work performed, sharing their solidity and action.

Boldrewood wrote more than a dozen other novels. They are, however, for the most part unread, not to say unreadable. Each deals with one aspect of Australian life already found in *Robbery under Arms*; and treated singly, even the richest theme, for instance that of gold in *The Miner's Right*,[1] is meagre in comparison. They are further marred by Boldrewood's increasing complacency, which, as an old man, he mistook for wisdom. Conflict disappeared from his novels as from his life. Australia becomes merely a better-off England, as for example in *The Ghost Camp*,[2] where material wealth is always the criterion of success, the opportunities for leisure the criterion of civilization. In *A Colonial Reformer*,[3] 'the leaders of a democracy' are compared, without anger, pity, or regret, to cattle, 'doomed to blind progression'.[4] In *The Crooked Stick*, the tendency, evident in *Robbery under Arms*, to see Australia as a better-off England, provides an early example of that historical fudging which was prevalent in Australian literature, creative and critical, for the next fifty years. Pollie, an Australian heroine, is speaking to a recent immigrant:

> 'But what always entertains me about you recent importations is, the mild air of surprise with which you regard the smallest evidence that the men that preceded, and built up these great cities, this wonderful country, were of much the same birth, breeding and social status as ourselves.'
>
> 'But many were not, surely? That must be admitted.'
>
> 'The majority were; the leaders, certainly, in every branch of civilization: how else would the miraculous progress have been effected? The rank and file were much like other people—good, bad, indifferent.'[5]

The free-born Boldrewood doth protest too much; but the reason is clear and accounts for more than his protestations.

1 *The Miner's Right: A tale of the Australian Goldfields*, 3 vols., London 1890.

2 *The Ghost Camp, or the Avengers*, London 1902.

3 3 vols., London 1890.

4 *A Colonial Reformer*, 1 vol., London 1890, p. 225.

5 *The Crooked Stick, or Pollie's Probation*, London 1895, p. 231.

Nationalism relies for its success among other, often conflicting, nationalisms on being at least as respectable as they. Australia got off to a 'bad' start and has been over-compensating ever since, except in those times like the thirties when 'bad', under the influence of a mild Marxism, was reinterpreted to mean 'good'. The search for respectability of course remained constant, despite the change in terminology. Scott, being a Scottish lawyer wishing to compete with older-established English gentlemen, felt himself similarly compromised. His heroines are more virginal, his heroes more manly, than was either necessary in literature or true in history. His influence on Australian writers, because his predicament was similar, was reinforced and lasted longer than it did in England. When influence waned, affinities either disguised the fact or did duty for it. This can be most clearly seen in *Robbery under Arms*.

Like *Geoffry Hamlyn*, the novel has a narrator, Dick Marston, who, unlike Hamlyn, is a 'Sydney-side native'. Like Henry Savery's main character, Quintus Servinton, Dick Marston is, significantly, in prison, condemned to death, writing with pride and blame of the exploits of the gang of bushrangers to which he once belonged. Boldrewood's picaresque treatment—gone from European literature, which deals with compact societies, but common in Australian literature from McCombie's *Arabin* to Randolph Stow's *To the Islands*[1]—allows him the freedom that made it popular in eighteenth-century English literature, and the freedom that Scott exploited in, say, *Rob Roy*. It allows him to open up the unknown land, as it were; and by making Dick, his brother Jim, their father Ben, and the Englishman Captain Starlight, bushrangers, Boldrewood is the better able to display with proprietary pride the wonders of this treasure-box. His box is larger than Joseph Furphy's, but the lid opens in the same way, and the patter and accompanying gestures are the same: Such is Australian life, each is saying. Only bushrangers enjoyed even more freedom of movement than Furphy's Deputy-Assistant-Sub-Inspectors; and, unlike highwaymen, they were not confined to the established trade-routes. They were interested in all sources of other people's wealth: outback stations, banks, gold-fields, cattle, and horses. They were obliged to escape over unmapped country,

[1] London 1958.

hunted by mounted police, black-trackers, and by anyone who fancied his chance of earning a reward. Their movements, even when recounted by a prisoner, had to be wary, wide, and rapid.

The gang's headquarters is a secret rendezvous, known as the Terrible Hollow, near the Marstons' small and rundown farm. To this they escape when hard pressed; but they are not immediately averse to lying low on the gold-fields as honest miners, on outback stations as fencers and shearers, or even as tourists and occasionally in cities as manual workers. Their activities progress from simple pastoral pursuits like cattle-stealing to station hold-ups, and finally to robbing the gold escort. The process mirrors Australia's own advance from small-time farming by free men or freed convicts, to the pastoralism of squatters and wealthy men keen to ensure their families of what Rowcroft calls a 'competency', and to gold-mining. The last was as far-reaching and permanent in its effects on the bush-ranger as it was on Australian history. Gold opened up the land, brought more women and police, both in search of quick promotion and at one in their desire for a peaceful life. Both share in the breakup of Starlight's gang.

The Marstons have a sister, Aileen, who like her mother is brought up a Catholic. (This is Boldrewood's only gesture to Anglo-Irish relations, which, Ned Kelly said in his Jerilderie Letter, were one of the main causes of his taking to the road.) Mrs. Marston and Aileen are the believing good, constantly at pains to reform what they cannot understand. Starlight falls in love with Aileen, dying with her name on his lips before he can fulfil what he has so ardently promised. Aileen, like Flora in *Waverley* though in different circumstances, becomes a nun. Her mother is dead, her brother Jim has been shot during the gang's last stand, Dick is in prison awaiting death and then serving the long sentence that replaces it. Her father, Ben Marston, dies with his dog Crib in the secrecy of the Terrible Hollow, a place which is only discovered when the fever for gold takes prospectors there. Gold thus completes what indirectly it began.

There are two further groups of characters—grouped by function rather than fortune or family. While Dick and Jim are in Melbourne, after the gang has auctioned a thousand head of stolen cattle in Adelaide, they meet two girls, Jeanie and Kate Morrison, recently arrived in Australia. Jeanie, fair and good, loves and marries Jim. Kate, dark and treacherous, loves and loses Dick, and eventually betrays him.

The second group is represented by Mr. Falkland, the rich and noble-born pastoralist, for whom the neighbouring Marston boys occasionally work; and his daughter, whom Jim has once saved from being killed on a bolting horse. With them can be included George Storefield, whose name indicates his nature, and his sister Gracey, whom, when she was a child, Dick had saved from drowning. She waits for and marries Dick after his sentence is complete. George, who is everything the Marstons could have been had they wished and worked as hard as he—for Boldrewood is ever intent on pointing a moral even in a tale most adorned—supports Mr. Falkland's petition to save Dick, as Jim had once saved Miss Falkland. In the unanimity of interest and responsible citizenship which George's rise to fortune has ensured, the appeal is successful. As Dick tells George on the eve of their becoming brothers-in-law: 'What's left of Dick Marston's life belongs to [Gracey] and you.'[1]

As usual in Australian fiction—a 'frontier' fiction about what often appears a fictional frontier—Boldrewood's emphasis is on doing, rather than on the psychological necessity for it; but for the question which any modern reader asks, 'Why, in such a land of plenty, do so many fine but ill-assorted men become bushrangers?', Boldrewood is careful to provide an answer, several answers. To examine them one must examine the assorted bushrangers.

Boldrewood's novel contains two gangs, Starlight's and Dan Moran's, which combine on great occasions, such as the robbing of the gold escort. Though led by Starlight—who, like many places and events in the novel, is no doubt a judicious blending of fact and fiction—they are brought together and, in the main, held together by Ben Marston, the former convict. His original crime was poaching, which Dick Marston likens to a gentle form of duffing:

But as for father, he'd been a poacher in England, a Lincolnshire man he was, and got sent out for it. He wasn't much more than a boy, he said, and it was only for a hare or two, which didn't seem much. But

[1] *Robbery*, p. 657.

I begin to think, being able to see the right of things a bit now, and having no bad grog inside of me to turn a fellow's head upside down, as poaching must be something like cattle and horse duffing—not the worst thing in the world itself, but mighty likely to lead to it.[1]

He is the original Lincolnshire Poacher, it would seem, caught and shipped out to Australia. His continuing presence there, after the expiration of his sentence, is explained by the law that sent him there: expirees were not allowed back into England. Despite the greater returns on gold, Ben prefers his first love, and, in his fashion, remains true to it. He refuses to turn from wickedness completely because, Starlight says, he 'had a long account to square with society, and he has a right to settle it his own way'.[2] He is an uneducated man, socially a plebeian, but one who had had his hopes. When Aileen is reading him an account of Trafalgar, he tells her that as a boy he had twice tried to run away to sea and been prevented, once being 'fetched back and flogged, and pretty nigh starved. I never did no good afterwards. But it's came acrost me many and many a time that I'd been a different sort o' chap if I'd had my will then.'[3] His choice of the navy, rather than the army, would seem to have been sound. As Sir Walter Elliot ruefully complains, in Jane Austen's *Persuasion*, the navy was 'the means of bringing persons of obscure birth into undue distinction, and raising men to honours which their fathers and grandfathers never dreamt of'.[4]

Dan Moran and his 'mates' are Ben Marston's friends, socially his equals, as Boldrewood shows in their similar passion for revenge, which involves their killing four disarmed men, an act that sickens the two Marston sons. On another occasion, the revenge motive appears to be introduced as typical of 'working chaps'. Moran disagrees with Starlight's suggested leniency towards the pastoralist Knightley, his family, and friends, who, during a raid by the combined gangs, have fired back and killed one of Moran's men:

'I suppose you think you and Starlight's going to boss the lot of us, because you've been doing it fine at the Turon races along with a lot of blasted swells as 'ud scrag us if they had the chance, and we're

[1] Ibid. pp. 7–8. [2] Ibid., p. 66. [3] Ibid., p. 470.
[4] Ch. iii.

to take so much a head for our dashed lives, because we're only working chaps. Not if Dan Moran knows it. What we want is satisfaction—blood for blood—and we're a-goin' to have it, eh, mates?'[1]

The vocabulary—'boss', 'swells', 'scrag'—also suggests that Boldrewood is keen to attribute the difference to class. He is careful not to be too obvious by providing another explanation, one that Henry Kingsley would have approved, though Walter Scott might not. Dick Marston says of Moran:

A sulky, black-hearted, revengeful brute he always was—I don't think he'd any manly feeling about him. He was a half-bred gipsy, they told us that knew where he was reared, and Starlight said gipsy blood was a queer cross, for devilry and hardness it couldn't be beat; he didn't wonder a bit at Moran's being the scoundrel he was.[2]

It is hard not to guess at the other half of Moran's ancestry. His name is as Irish as those of his friends Daly and Bourke. This suggests that Boldrewood, despite his kind words about Mrs. Marston's Irishness, is taking a swipe at Irish 'working chaps', of whom Ned Kelly was the most famous. Mrs. Marston's being a woman is enough, in Boldrewood's sentimental logic, to prevent her belonging to the idle poor. Like Kate Lawless in his *Nevermore*,[3] the sister of the notorious Edward Lawless, as fond of him as Kate Kelly was of Ned, Mrs. Marston merely cohabits with and is made unhappy by Australia's Irish problem. The class antagonism, however, is sufficient reason for Moran and his gang's bushranging, clumsy, greedy, and bloody though their efforts necessarily are.

Boldrewood gives quite different reasons from these for Dick and Jim becoming bushrangers. Dick says:

I say again, if it weren't for the horse-flesh part of it, the fun and hard-riding and tracking, and all the rest of it, there wouldn't be anything like the cross-work that there is in Australia. It lies partly between that and the dry weather. There's the long spells of drought when nothing can be done by young or old . . . Then the youngsters, havin' so much idle time on their hands, take to gaffin' and flash talk; and money must be got to sport and pay up if they lose . . .[4]

Small farmers though the Marstons are, there is no suggestion here of economic hardship driving them to crime. 'The ground

[1] *Robbery*, p. 554. [2] Ibid., p. 429. [3] 3 vols., London 1892.
[4] *Robbery*, p. 69.

like iron and the sky like brass', as Dick says, quoting the prison chaplain, are not starving but boring them. There is simply nothing to do. They are not, like Dan Moran, what is magisterially called 'naturally vicious'. They are somehow of a better class than mere 'working chaps', as Dan Moran suspects; but, being young, they have jumped the traces. This feature helps Boldrewood to overcome, as in *Moll Flanders* Defoe overcame, the novel's moral problem: whether crime, purveyed as exciting literature, ceases to be criminal. This device relies for success on the assumption that the reader will accept class as part of a social hierarchy which, for Boldrewood, corresponds to a hierarchy of moral worth. This view of Boldrewood's permeates the whole novel and is supported by the fates meted out to the characters. It thus gives the novel a moral unity and offsets the weakness inherent in the picaresque technique: a tendency for the book to disintegrate into a series of events connected only because they happen to the same characters.

Occasionally Boldrewood suggests that fate has played a part in making the Marston boys what they are. Aileen, whom Dick admiringly describes as 'fit to teach in a school or sell laces and gloves', puts the middle-class point of view. She is defending George Storefield, who is the principal champion of that middle-class view:

'Oughtn't a steady worker to rise in life, and isn't it sad to see cleverer men and better workers—if they liked—kept down by their own fault?'

'Why wasn't your roan mare born black or chestnut?' says Jim, laughing, and pretending to touch her up. 'Come along, and let's see if she can trot as well as she used to do?'

'Poor Lowan,' says she . . . 'she was born pretty and good. How little trouble her life gives her. It's a pity we can't all say as much, or have as little on our minds.'

'Whose fault's that?' says Jim. 'The dingo must live as well as the collie or the sheep either. One's been made just the same as the other. . . .'[1]

It is an argument that Dick has already anticipated:

Some people can work away day after day, and year after year, like a bullock in a team or a horse in a chaff-cutting machine . . . But

[1] Ibid, pp. 157–8.

there's other men that can't do that sort of thing, and it's no use talking. They must have life and liberty and a free range. . . .

Besides, sometimes there's a good-looking girl even at a bush public, the daughter or the barmaid, and it's odd, now, what a difference that makes. There's a few glasses of grog going, a little noisy, rattling talk, a few smiles and a saucy answer or two from the girl, a look at the last newspaper, or a bit of the town news from the landlord. . . . Well, it doesn't amount to much, but it's life—the only taste of it that chaps like us are likely to get.[1]

In each instance it can be seen that the influence of fate is blurred, even superseded, by that of boredom—boredom with the unrewarding grind which was existence for the small farmer in Australia; and, coming between the agricultural labourer and the pastoralist, he *was* the middle-class until the discovery of gold. Despite the real history of this class, carefully documented by Russel Ward, Boldrewood allows the type and the dream to succeed. George Storefield prospers, while Dick Marston, the gang's lone survivor, by marrying Gracey Storefield rejoins the class from which youthful boredom had divorced him. A lack of 'life', Boldrewood is saying, hurts only the hectic young; economically, the small farmer is a sound creation and a credit to his maker. The argument throughout is self-consistent; historically, it was false, as Boldrewood knew better than most. Having himself been financially broken twice, he wisely took refuge in law and literature.

Boldrewood's way of making his argument plausible is interesting and instructive, for in literature it involves an affinity with Scott, in politics with Disraeli. The most outspoken protagonist of his views is Mr. Falkland, who as a poor but well-born youth, emigrated to Australia and made his fortune on the land:

'This was the best country in the whole world,' he used to say, 'for a gentleman who was poor or a working man.' The first sort could always make an independence if they were moderately strong, liked work, and did not drink. There were very few countries where idle, unsteady people got rich. 'As for the poor man, he was the real rich man in Australia; high wages, cheap food, lodging, clothing, travelling. What more did he want? He could save money, live happily, and die rich, if he wasn't a fool or a rogue. . . .'[2]

[1] *Robbery*, pp. 88–9. [2] Ibid., p. 81.

What more did he want indeed? Perhaps Miss Falkland, whom Dick compares to the Virgin Mary. Nor does Dick, speaking to Falkland, balk at what her father becomes:

> 'Every one of you gentlemen wants to be a small God Almighty. . . . You'd like to break us all in and put us in yokes and bows, like a lot of working bullocks.'
>
> 'You mistake me, my boy, and all the rest of us who are worth calling men, let alone gentlemen. We are your best friends, and would help you in every way. . . . But your class might, I think, always rely upon there being enough kindness and wisdom in ours to prevent that state of things [of keeping all the good things to ourselves]. Unfortunately neither side trusts the other enough. . . .'[1]

Falkland's argument does not conflict with Dick's, though it goes some way to explain the former paradox that the poor man is the rich man in Australia. What is meant here by poor man is the working man, or 'chap'. No matter how much money he has, he will remain of a different class, the working class, for it is as a shearer that Dick is employed by Falkland; and if the lower had trust in the higher, all would be well. This is an Australian 'peasant and pastoralist' version of Disraeli's successful 'labourer and lord' formula for social stability. In *A Sydney-Side Saxon*,[2] Boldrewood is even more forthright: 'Newly-come people don't understand this. Generally they think that money does everything, and that there are no ranks or differences in colonial society. There they're quite wrong. . . .' If this seems to conflict with what Storefield represents—the striving, ultimately prospering middle class—it is because there is the other, aristocratic side of the Victorian compromise. The landed aristocracy encourages the aspirations of the middle class, allies with its wealthier members, remains intact and becomes richer, and at the same time denies the need and the chance of any radical change in the class structure. The middle class, or those members of it so selected for advancement, have their aspirations justified and their hopes actually or vicariously confirmed and so are concerned to preserve the structure. These were the reasons Marx gave for not expecting revolution to emanate from the middle class; and in Australia at least, despite the Eureka Stockade, as Boldrewood illustrated in *The*

[1] Ibid., pp. 82–3. [2] London 1891, p. 204.

Miner's Right, they afforded a more correct reading of history there than in other countries. These same reasons led Kierkegaard to write, in almost the same year as Marx: 'In the present age a rebellion is, of all things, the most unthinkable. Such an expression of strength would seem ridiculous to the calculating intelligence of our times.'[1]

The real clash occurs between the lower and the middle classes. Storefield, the epitome of rectitude and effort, is convinced that he will 'always be able to get a few pounds to go on with, however the season goes'. Such a conviction will keep a man honest. Dick, who does not share it, puts the other view: he, and those like him, should take some of the big pastoralists' land and stock; for, as he says with splendid succinctness, 'I don't think it pays to be too honest in a dry country'. This is one expression of that 'presumptive dishonesty', as Russel Ward calls it, practised by determined bushworkers like James Tyson and the later knight, Sidney Kidman. Australian geography and climate, supported by land laws meant to satisfy England's demand for wool rather than a prospective small farmer's hunger for land, ensured that such 'presumptive dishonesty' should be practised only by those who wanted as final a security on the land as, for instance, their American counterparts enjoyed. Revolutionary views like Dick's failed; for success would have meant only the replacement of one big pastoralist by another: the size of the holding, in a dry country, would have had to remain the same, which was one reason why the various Free Selection Acts failed in their purpose. Falkland remained, the extent of his acres reinforcing his aristocratic claims, while the laws of nature and man protected his patrimony. Boldrewood is thus correct in seeing Falkland's kind and class at the head of Australian society. Whether that class is represented by a Falkland, an ennobled working chap or a bank does not matter. They all share the same values, a fact that permits such social movement as there is. The distinctions between them are quantitative and reduceable to terms of horsepower, one or two, twenty or thirty.

Dick, in talking about 'unlocking the land', is accused of talking 'like Frowser, that's always spouting at the Shearers' Arms'. He is, Boldrewood suggests through Storefield, again

[1] Kierkegaard, *The Present Age*, p. 36.

guilty of voicing the 'working chap's' point of view, which in a small farmer is incongruous, not to say treacherous. Dick's ambiguous class sympathies here reveal his plight throughout but the personal qualities that underlie the conflict also point to the ambiguity in the portrait of the Australian 'frontiersman'. The opening paragraph is a self-portrait:

> My name's Dick Marston, Sydney-side native. I'm twenty-nine years old, six feet in my stocking soles, and thirteen stone weight. Pretty strong and active with it, so they say . . . I can ride anything —anything that ever was lapped in horsehide—swim like a musk-duck, and track like a Myall blackfellow. Most things that a man can do I'm up to, and that's all about it. As I lift myself now I can feel the muscle swell on my arm like a cricket ball, in spite of the—well, in spite of everything.

One recalls Deerslayer, Fenimore Cooper's archetypal frontiersman:

> In stature, he stood about six feet in his moccasins, but his frame was comparatively light and slender, showing muscles, however, that promised unusual agility, if not unusual strength. His face would have had little to recommend it except youth, were it not for an expression that seldom failed to win upon those who had leisure to examine it, and to yield to the feeling of confidence it created.[1]

The differences in the descriptions demonstrate the differences in the national types. Deerslayer has an honest youthful face; whereas Dick is describing himself from a police cell, which he thinks he fully deserves. The American frontiersman remained an innocent possessed of all the skills necessary to his life in the wilderness. The Australian, equally adept, remained something of a rogue, more engaging than his convict predecessors perhaps, but in Furphy and Lawson and his other celebrants still with a touch of the rogue if not actually a criminal. The conditions of geography, climate, and land-legislation would oblige him to be so, if he wished to stay on the frontier. One can also see the frontiersman to be as closely related to the convict past as Dick is to his father. In other words, inherited history is also helping to form him.

There is a second difference. Deerslayer is wearing the moccasins that match the physical prowess and skills originally

[1] Fenimore Cooper, *The Deerslayer*, ch. i.

distinctive of the North American Indian from whom he has acquired them; but Dick is measured in his socks, having presumably taken his boots off and his mention of the aborigine implies only equality, not indebtedness. A clearer sign of civilization is in the description of his arm muscles, which swell 'like a cricket ball'. The socks and the simile, together with his being the son of a small farmer, suggest a difference between the Australian and the American frontier. The two certain characteristics of the American frontier were that it was constantly moving, as constantly as the frontiersman could find new land to take; and that it moved from east to west. In Australia supplies of new land were soon exhausted, so that the frontiersman soon settled to become a small farmer or more usually a bushworker on the large dry holdings that defined the Australian frontier, but still within cooee of socks and cricket; while settlement moved quickly and briefly inland from those areas now marked by the Australian State capitals. Russel Ward, basing his remarks on the ill-defined belief that settlement in Australia 'As in the United States . . . proceeded inland from the eastern coastal plain',[1] is able to generalize that 'the typical noble frontiersman should be an uncultivated workman'.[2] This is not true of the frontiersman in Australian literature. Not only did he have the white man's socks and lust for organized sport, he was also able to read and write. Although woman primarily represented in fiction as in fact the civilizing influence, being always in Boldrewood's phrase 'well-taught', the frontiersman, whose rough skills she also practised, was able even in prison to take advantage of available books. It is a characteristic which Furphy's frontiersmen, handing on copies of *The Australasian* or their 'swapping book', proudly share. The ability to read was perhaps one reason why the Australian frontiersman accepted political organization more readily than did the American. Which is perhaps finally to say that he was more bushman than frontiersman, working-class in his background, middle-class in his aspirations and at least some of his attainments. Disraeli would have appreciated the situation; as evidently did Sir Robert Menzies.

Boldrewood's second way of making his argument plausible—involving an affinity with Scott—is of more immediate concern:

[1] Russel Ward, *The Australian Legend*, p. 225. [2] Op. cit., p. 231.

his practice of taking an aspect of reality and grafting it on a literary stock to get an effect both colourful and real. He is helped by the suggestions of feudalism, or at least paternalism, which Falkland's argument contains, though mainly he works through the interplay of gentleman and Byronic hero. And so one comes back to Captain Starlight and his reasons for taking to the road:

'Mr. Starlight is an edicated man,' said father . . . 'and many a man has looked at his own beast, with the ears altered and the brand faked, and never dreamed he ever owned it. He's a great card is Starlight. It's a pity he ever took to this kind of life.'

Father said this with a kind of real sorrow that made me look at him to see if the grog had got into his head; just as if his life, mine, and Jim's didn't matter a straw compared to this man's, whoever he was, that had so many better chances than we had and had chucked 'em all away.

But it's a strange thing that I don't think there's any place in the world where men feel a more out-and-out respect for a gentleman than in Australia. Everybody's supposed to be free and equal now; of course, they couldn't in the convict days. But somehow a man that's born and bred a gentleman will always be different from other men to the end of the world. What's the most surprising part of it is that men like father, who have hated the breed and suffered by them, too, can't help having a curious liking and admiration for them. They'll follow them like dogs, fight for them, shed their blood, and die for them; must be some sort of a natural feeling. Whatever it is, it's there safe enough, and nothing can knock it out of nine-tenths of all the men and women you meet.[1]

Dick's opinions before he has met Starlight seem to coincide with Moran's, who considers Starlight 'a half-bred swell'; but the last paragraph, the result of years in Starlight's company, corrects the balance. The feudal concept of 'natural feeling' is triumphant, even in nineteenth-century Australia, over such new-fangled notions as freedom and equality. There is conclusive evidence in the old lag's reference to '*Mr*. Starlight'. As Boldrewood wrote in *A Sydney-Side Saxon*: 'It's a curious thing . . . how one man is made much of, and spoken everywhere as Mr. So-and-so, while another never gets beyond Jack or Bill—or Smith or Jones—as the case may be.'[2] Henry Savery's Quintus Servinton and Marcus Clarke's Rufus Dawes

[1] *Robbery*, p. 59. [2] p. 204.

both made the same point, and Joseph Furphy's Tom Collins accepts the distinction without comment.

Boldrewood, however, had more cause to make it than they; and his cause—maintaining the established order—was very much Scott's, and certainly that of Scott's readers. A great part of Scott's appeal, during what still seemed a revolutionary era, was to those conservative elements in English life which tolerated *liberté et égalité* within limits, but did not wish to let them upset the established, or natural, order; for the natural order was by definition an expression of *fraternité*. History that was garish and safely dead—such as the Stuart defeat and the Hanoverian victory—obviously had a ready readership. Nothing was changed much apart from religion and dress, a change that brought a small diminution of local colour.

Boldrewood was writing during a similar era in Australian history. Transportation was over and gold had been found by at least some working chaps who, like Arizona Bill in *Robbery under Arms*, did not give a damn about the natural order. As Boldrewood points out, Arizona Bill was wrong, as were those other predominantly foreign hotheads in *The Miner's Right* who thought they could succeed at the Eureka Stockade in substituting a new and unnatural order. Now, whatever the success or defeat the Eureka rising in reality was on Sunday 3 December 1854, its symbolism had hardened thirty years later. It had become for many Australians the national equivalent of the storming of the Bastille. Boldrewood's work, like Scott's, was a call to good men and true to hold fast. Similarly it was a reassurance that history need not be a tempest, but could instead be seen as a system of canalization: that alteration, not change is the one great absolute; and, in Australia, it was not Heraklitus but Rolf Boldrewood who was right.

Ben Marston calls Starlight an 'edicated' man, but for Ben it is the altering of a brand that is the sure sign of education. He appreciates in Starlight those qualities which he himself possesses, as any traditional peasant does those of his traditional prince. And he respects Starlight's English gentlemanly qualities. These are clearly indicated for all to see, and it is their general acceptance that allows Starlight to play his many confidence tricks. He has only to wear an eye-glass, produce a Sandhurst 'r', and talk of shooting in England and hunting in India to be known as an equal by both ladies and gentlemen. When he plays cards with Mr. Knightley, it is not euchre or poker, which his Australian rabble prefer, but piquet and hazard. Mr. Knightley anticipates his preference with the same certainty of approval with which he offers cigars and claret. Starlight is gallant to women, tactful and amusing. He can sing well, talk well, ride well, and has a proper disregard for his safety and an understandable concern for his comfort. He is very much a very old literary type. Castiglione described him.

At the same time, Boldrewood specifically says, Starlight is the descendant of Claude Duval and Dick Turpin, a brevet colonel as it were in the Sherwood Foresters, a rank held by Australian bushrangers as early as Charles Rowcroft's. Like them he is something more than an outlaw. Moreover, he was born free, though his origins are uncertain:

> Nobody knew who he'd been, or almost where he had come from—next to nothing about him had ever come out. He was an Englishman—that was certain—but he must have come young to the colony. No one could look at him for a moment and see his pale, proud face, his dark eyes—half-scornful, half-gloomy, except when he was set up a bit (and then you didn't like to look at them at all)—without seeing that he was a gentleman to the tips of his delicate-looking fingers, no matter what he'd done, or where he'd been.
>
> He was rather over the middle-size; because he was slight made, he always looked rather tall than not. He was tremendous strong, too, though he didn't look that, and as active as a cat, though he moved as if walking was too much trouble altogether, and running not to be thought of.[1]

Small wonder that Aileen felt that she 'had never seen a man before'; for this is no ordinary man, or even, as Dick thinks, just a gentleman, like Mr. Falkland and Mr. Knightley. This is the Fatal Man, the Byronic hero, of the delicate fingers, dark gloomy eyes, and proud face. He has the soft voice, 'which no woman could fight against long'. He speaks only more distinctly when roused, and 'His eyes were worse than his voice at such times. There weren't many men that liked to look back at him, much less say anything.'[2] Starlight is the most complete of Australian Byronic heroes, even to his reasons for becoming a bushranger: 'I have my own reasons for leading the life I do,'

[1] *Robbery*, pp. 478–9. [2] Ibid., p. 206.

he said, 'and must run my own course, of which I foresee the end as plainly as if it was written in a book before me.'[1] This is far more fateful than anything Dick or Jim Marston might try to present as a reason for their behaviour. Boldrewood, concerned to make him plausible, offers one or two additional reasons for Starlight's activities, though the first again reflects literary convention, being the type's typical reason. Dick, a fellow prisoner, questions Starlight about his unrepressed spirits: 'Why don't I feel it? My good fellow, I have felt it all before. But if you sear your flesh or your horse's with a red-hot iron you'll find the flesh hard and callous ever after. My heart was seared once—ay, twice—and deeply, too. I have no heart now, or if I ever feel at all it's for a horse. . . .'[2] It is a reason that Byron himself provided:

> In self-inflicted penance of a breast
> Which tenderness might once have wrung from rest;
> In vigilance of grief that would compel
> The soul to hate for having loved too well.[3]

The second reason is more interesting in that it is similar to the one given by the socially very different Ben Marston. Starlight says: '. . . If my people had let me go into the army, as I begged and prayed of them to do, it might have been all the other way. I recollect that day and hour when my old governor refused my boyish petition, laughed at me—sneered at me. I took the wrong road then. . . .'[4] This is an example of the same kind of parental delinquency that Swinburne experienced. Starlight did not, however, share Swinburne's passion for the sea, on which, Boldrewood suggests, Starlight's father obliged him to sail for a living. The service was no doubt galling to one who wanted 'the paltry vanity of leadership, and being in front of [his] fellow-men'.[5] As E. S. Turner records, the 1840 Royal Commission into Navy and Military Promotion found that all forty admirals were over sixty-five years of age, one of them over ninety. There was no rear-admiral under fifty, and the senior lieutenant had been appointed to the rank in 1778.[6] The same source provides a nice irony: had Starlight got his own

[1] *Robbery*, p. 66.
[2] Ibid., p. 208.
[3] Lord Byron, *Lara*, Canto I, xvii.
[4] *Robbery*, pp. 404–5.
[5] Ibid., p. 404.
[6] *Gallant Gentlemen*, London 1956, p. 256.

way as a youth, he might still have ended as an English highwayman, for cadets at Sandhurst, which was known to nearby Wellington College as 'Hell-over-the-Hill', held up a stagecoach in the 1850s.[1]

Turner's information provides more evidence for what has already been observed in the work of Rowcroft and Kingsley: the lack of professional employment for commissioned soldiers and sailors between the Napoleonic and Crimean Wars. In Rowcroft and Kingsley, they emigrate to find a competency and something which their training fits them to tell others to do. Starlight, on the other side of the law but displaying the same qualities, emigrates for the same reasons. Although a bushranger, he does not cease to be both Byronic hero and a gentleman of the half-pay-officer kind.

Boldrewood pursues the relationship between bushranger and soldier in a way that makes clear the growing divergence between what Australian writers thought about England and the truth. Starlight says:

> 'By Jove, boys, it's a pity we didn't belong to a troop of irregular horse instead of this rotten colonial Dick Turpin business, that one can't help being ashamed of. They would have been delighted to have recruited the three of us, as we ride, and our horses are worth best part of ten thousand rupees. What a tent-pegger Rainbow would have made, eh, old boy?' he said, patting the horse's neck. 'But Fate won't have it, and it's no use whining.'[2]

England has become in Boldrewood the legendary lost land that it showed evidence of becoming in Kingsley. It is suggested that Australian colonists will one day help, joyously, to fight England's wars, naturally in India. Although Starlight's view of war, like many a contemporary's, appears limited to polo,[3] his prognostication was true: 'they' were delighted to recruit such men.[4] In the first World War, the Australian people refused conscription, choosing to rely instead on volunteer armies,

[1] Ibid., p. 205.

[2] *Robbery*, pp. 279–80.

[3] The view lasted at least to the end of the century. Cf. Lord Kitchener's remark on arriving in South Africa during the Boer War: 'People here do not seem to look upon the war sufficiently seriously; they consider it too much like a game of polo with intervals for afternoon tea.' Quoted E. S. Turner, *Gallant Gentlemen*, p. 265.

[4] 'A New South Wales contingent went to Britain's aid in the Sudan even before the Imperial Bushmen's Corps of Cavalry went to South Africa.' Douglas Pike, *Australia: The Quiet Continent*, p. 142.

whose military record was impressive as well as brutal.[1] That the reality of war did not match the ideal—it was set in Europe and not on an Imperial Frontier—affected many besides a writer like Leonard Mann; yet disillusionment mattered less in the evolution of Australia than did the creation of a tradition by which to announce, to explain, even to excuse her maturity. The tradition—the strongest, perhaps the only, tradition Australia has, which all classes helped form and still assiduously foster through the Returned Servicemen's League—was a military tradition.

Such a tradition is the second most rigorous conformity possible, the first being imprisonment. It announces its conformity with uniforms, badges, marches, and public demonstrations of strident masculinity. It continues to exist not only because frequent wars keep up a demand for recruits, but also because it is the simplest expression of that conformity to which international urban civilization is directed. Many Australians do not belong to the Returned Servicemen's League; but it is an influential political instrument because it embodies a powerful ideal. This is the reason why Lawrence in *Kangaroo* was so attracted to it, though he misunderstood it, not because he was an Englishman, but because he had not lived long enough. He thought it could be used to help 'blow a cleavage through the old system'.[2] He did not realize how tied to the old system such organizations were, or, to express it in the terms of a more distant history, how close was the interdependence of convicts and soldiers, each justifying, defining, the other's existence. Not until Patrick White's *Riders in the Chariot* do we find international historical experience used as the basis for the questioning of such an organization, and the military tradition which it most immediately embodies. 'The pressures of conformity, which in itself becomes an ideal, and which eventually destroys "Zanadu" as the same ideal destroys Durilgai in *The Tree of Man*, are exactly those that turn the Rosetrees' lives into a tragedy, as comparable but more highly organized pressures turned recent German history into a tragedy.'[3] This evolution—from 'outcast scum of all the world' to bushrangers to military heroes,

[1] Cf. Robert Graves: 'The troops with the worst reputation for acts of violence against prisoners were the Canadians (and later the Australians).' *Goodbye to All That*, London 1929; 1957, p. 164.

[2] p. 178.

[3] Barry Argyle, *Patrick White*, Edinburgh, London 1967, p. 57.

guardians of what *all* must cherish—is very like that whereby Noel Byron, the lame and lovely boy, became the hero of Missolonghi. By acting on behalf of a community, or an association of people, Byron was forgiven those characteristics which had made him heroic and distrusted. He was like one of those early convicts who, because of 'good behaviour'—i.e. socially acceptable behaviour—became a gaoler. But the ideal which association embodies is conformity, what Kierkegaard calls the 'levelling process': 'Association is the scepticism, which is necessary in order that the development of individuality may proceed uniformly, so that the individual will either be lost or, disciplined by such abstractions, will find himself religiously.'[1] This last reward is the fate of Mordecai Himmelfarb, and to a lesser extent of Richard Mahony. As far as one knows, Byron did not share it; which is why, when Byron's body returned to London from Missolonghi, 'rigid moralists could not refrain from weeping for one so young, so illustrious, so unhappy, gifted with such rare gifts, and tried by such strong temptations'.[2] They wept for joy, that the Byronic hero was dead: *dulce et decorum est pro patria mori.*

Boldrewood is more explicit than historical parallels, however fanciful, permit. Starlight may say that Fate will not allow his going for a soldier, but he expresses himself Byronically. Among his bushranging kit, he carries 'a good many books, poetry, and all kind of things'.[3] Like Byron, who professed to value nephews more than sons, Starlight is able to say: 'I can bear my fate, because my blood does not run in the veins of a living soul in Australia. If it were otherwise I could not bear my reflections.'[4] The picture is completed by his having a retainer, Warrigal, an aborigine. His function links the novel as much to the Sade tradition in English literature, represented by Swinburne, as to the earlier Crusoe–Friday tradition. There is the same master-and-servant relationship between white and coloured, which Max Weber has rightly made much of, but the vocabulary suggests Rowcroft's master-and-dog rather than Defoe's father-and-child:[5]

[1] *The Present Age* p. 90. [2] Macaulay, *Edinburgh Review*, liii, June 1831.

[3] *Robbery*, p. 477. [4] Ibid., p. 478.

[5] Cf. Charles Rowcroft's *The Bushranger of Van Diemen's Land*, vol. 3, p. 3, where the aboriginal girl Oinoo, the last of her tribe, becomes the heroine's 'companion' and is described as showing 'by her manner that she commiserated

Warrigal . . . throws himself down at his feet, bursting out crying like a child. He was just like a dog that had found his master again. He kept looking up at Starlight just like a dog does, and smiling and going on just as if he never expected to see such a good thing again as long as he lived.

'Well, Warrigal', says Starlight, very careless like, 'so you've brought me a horse, I see. You've been a very good boy. Take Rainbow round the long way into the Hollow. Look after him, whatever you do, or I'll murder you'[1].

The threat is that of the prefect to his fag, who happens to be black and whose name means 'native dog'; but sustaining each other, the British Empire and the public school also sustained *le vice anglais*. The connection is further suggested when Dick Marston says: 'As for Warrigal, Starlight used to knock him down like a log if he didn't please him, but he never offered to turn upon him. He seemed to like it, and looked regular put out once when Starlight hurt his knuckles against his hard skull.'[2] Although Warrigal is said to like it, Marston makes clear that this is only if Starlight does it. It is, in every sense of the word, a special relationship.

With this minor example of sadism—whose significance must be seen in the whole context of Australian history, including its convict origins, its ignoble savages, and military tradition—there is the suggestion of Satanism. Warrigal is referred to as the 'devil's limb' who was never intended for anything better than a tragic end, whose 'sleepy eyes . . . were like a half-roused snake's'. Taken with Starlight's reference to himself as an outlaw from birth, plus his gratuitous description of French executions—'performances' he has seen 'more than once'—and his quoting 'some German fellow' on the nature of the devil's steeds, the fashionable European Satanic colouring of the time becomes stronger. The brief appearance of a Dr. Schiller—the German scientific type who is also in Kingsley—

their distress, much in the same way as an attached dog looks up into the face of its master, and wags its tail and shows an inclination to sympathize with his affliction if he could only understand what the matter was, and how he could assist him'. Compare Crusoe's Friday: 'Never man had a more faithful, loving, sincere servant, than Friday was to me; without passions, sullenness, or designs, perfectly oblig'd and engag'd; his very affections were ty'd to me, like those of a child to a father . . .' (Daniel Defoe, *Robinson Crusoe*, London 1960, (Everyman), p. 152).

[1] *Robbery*, pp. 238–9.

[2] Ibid., p. 105.

offers the name of the author of *Die Räuber* as a possible influence on the novel,[1] and certainly, as Mario Praz has argued, as a source for the tradition within which such novels work. Or the German scientific figure can be traced back to the Faust tradition; or the novel can be seen as generally Goethean in origin, combining a little of *Faust* and more of *Götz von Berlichingen*; but Boldrewood provides his own evidence. One of Starlight's gentlemanly digger friends says to him: 'You're like the fellow in Scott's novel (*Anne of Geierstein*) that I was reading over again yesterday—the mysterious stranger that's called for at midnight by the Avenger of Blood, departs with him and is never seen more.'[2] The German references can thus be accounted for. Scott, having translated *Götz von Berlichingen*, later used it as a source for *Anne of Geierstein*. With Byron, who said he had read many times everything Scott had written, Scott helped make *Robbery under Arms* a successful Australian novel.

One important aspect of Byronism—omnivorous love—seems to be lacking in Boldrewood, though there are traces of it in *Robbery under Arms*. Starlight, like Rowcroft's Mark Brandon, is a 'carneying devil' with women, and has had his heart seared twice; but without Byron's usual insistence on 'high bloodedness', he chooses the simple devout farm-girl Aileen Marston. Boldrewood uses her presence to display his Australian patriotism, by putting into the mouth of her refined but broken English schoolteacher: 'I defy any village in Britain to turn out such girls—plenty of rosy-cheeked gigglers—but the natural refinement and intelligence of these little damsels astonishes me.'[3] What is important to a consideration of the Australian literary tradition is that, unlike Scott's simple devout farm-girls, Aileen Marston, her friend, Gracey Storefield, and Jim Marston's wife, Jeanie Morrison, continue to be presented throughout the book, despite the passing of years and beauty, as 'little damsels'. Their differences are only perfunctorily indicated. They resemble rather a Gilbertian trio whose patter is interchangeable. Of Gracey Storefield, Dick Marston says: 'She

[1] The raid on the household of Mr. Knightley is said to have been based on an actual raid on the house of a Mr. Keighley (see Clive Hamer's article in *Southerly*, no. 4, 1966) at which a German guest was present. But his name was not Schiller.

[2] *Robbery*, p. 393.

[3] Ibid., p. 17.

looked into my face with that pleased look that put me in mind of her when she was a little child and used to come toddling up to me, staring and smiling all over her face the moment she saw me.'[1] When Jeanie enters the church to marry Jim Marston, the picture she presents is much the same: 'As she came in with her slight figure and modest sweet face that turned up to Jim's like a child's, there was a sort of hum in the church . . .'[2] This is not so much man and wife as brother and sister; and on this subject Dick Marston fully commits himself:

There's a great deal said about different kinds of love in this world, but I can't help thinking that the love between brothers and sisters that have been brought up together and have had very few other people to care about is a higher, better sort than any other in the world. There's less selfishness about it—no thought but for the other's good.[3]

Goethe, Wordsworth, Byron, Shelley, Poe, would not have disagreed.[4]

But if the Romantic poets anticipated Boldrewood's theme of genteel incest, the Australian *frisson* he gives it might have surprised them. Jeanie Morrison, whose affection matches Jeanie Deans's, is the means of delaying Jim and thus of causing his destruction. Kate, her wayward sister, in the small role of *femme fatale*, betrays Dick to the police out of pique and natural disposition, her face that 'of an evil spirit more than of a woman'. Gracey waits for her Dick to finish his long prison sentence; yet there must seem to any reader not aware of Australian literary tradition something macabre in her reward:

A man with a set kind of face, neither one thing nor the other, as if he couldn't be glad or sorry, with a fixed staring look about the eyes, a half-yellowish skin, with a lot of wrinkles in it, particularly about

[1] *Robbery*, p. 162. [2] Ibid., p. 346. [3] Ibid., pp. 36–7.

[4] There is a passage in William Empson's *Some Versions of Pastoral* (London 1935; Harmondsworth 1966) that brings together in an enviably brief way some of the issues dealt with here, though his concern is not with Australian literature: 'Byronism is almost consciously the poet as Macheath. Its peculiar mixture of aristocracy and democracy is just that mixture of outcasts from heroic and pastoral: the relations of Manfred with the Swiss shepherd on the mountain are those of two demigods above the falsity of civilization. The importance of incest, so baffling to poor Augusta, was that the hero's family as well as himself must be too great to keep the common rules of humanity, and unable to find a fit mate elsewhere; an appeal to the Pharaohs rather than the Borgias.' p. 168. Boldrewood changes the tradition a little: peasant and poet are there, but 'incest' protects goodness rather than greatness.

the eyes, and gray hair. Big streaks of gray in the hair of the head, and as for my beard it was white—white. I looked like an old man, and walked like one. What was the use of my going out at all?[1]

The answer is that it will make Gracey happy. The Law has been appeased; and the Law is female and English, set up by women and enforced by Englishmen. The dying Starlight, speaking to Sir Ferdinand Morringer, the Police Commissioner who has hunted him down, says:

'. . . I say, Morringer, do you remember the last pigeon match you and I shot in, at Hurlingham?'

'Why, good God!' says Sir Ferdinand, bending down, and looking into his face. 'It can't be; yes, by Jove, it is—'

He spoke some name I couldn't catch, but Starlight put his finger on his lips, and whispers—

'You won't tell, will you? Say you won't?'

The other nodded.[1]

Starlight dies, at peace with himself, his class, his nation, and the Law; although the Hurlingham Pigeon Shooting Club was founded only in 1867.

It is not the first time that he and Aileen and her brothers have known such quiet righteousness. Mention has been made of Terrible Hollow, so called because of its past, of which rags, a lock of hair, gold, and legend remain. In presenting the Hollow, Boldrewood uses the machinery which Kingsley, like Cooper and Hawthorne, had from Scott. It is marked by Nulla Mountain, variously described as 'the old needle rock', 'a big black lump, without sign of tree or rock', 'dark and overhanging all the valley'. This is how the gang and the reader recognize the Hollow, for there is no other way of knowing of its existence. Its implications, however, are wider. The Hollow

grew stunning fine grass . . . there was beautiful clear fresh water in all the creeks that ran through it . . . [there were] wild raspberries . . .

The gully widened out bit by bit, till at last we came to a little round green flat, right under the rock walls which rose up a couple of thousand feet above it on two sides. On the flat was an old hut—very old it seemed to be . . .

Outside had been a garden; a few rose trees were standing yet, ragged and stunted. The wallabies had trimmed them pretty well, but we knew what they were. Been a corn-patch too—the marks where it had been hoed up were there, same as they used to do in old

[1] *Robbery*, p. 653. [2] Ibid., p. 621.

times when there were more hoes than ploughs and more convicts than horses and working bullocks in the country.[1]

Boldrewood must have been one of the first Australian writers to apply the phrase 'old times' to Australia; but he is conscious of his adopted country's history, brief as it was in the 1850s, the period of the novel. It is possible to accept the whole passage as nothing more than a reference to a newly acquired history, and to appreciate it for that alone.

Jim Marston provides a further interpretation, however, when he refers to the man who lived there 'in old times' as 'this Robinson Crusoe cove'. Ben Marston, a product of those times, grows fretful in the Hollow, unable to 'content himself with this sort of Robinson Crusoe life'; while Aileen interprets even Defoe's original: 'How strange all this is', she said one day; 'I feel as if I were living on an island. It's quite like playing at "Robinson Crusoe," only there's no sea. We don't seem to be able to get out all the same. It's a happy, peaceful life, too. Why can't we keep on for ever like this, and shut out the wicked, sorrowful world altogether.'[2] She sees the Hollow as a kind of Eden, where all is good and peaceful, where people are as innocent as children, and as lacking in sexuality: 'Oh! if we could have come here when we were little how we should have enjoyed it! It would have seemed fairyland to us.'[3] It is an opinion which Dick shares, although he is supposed to be in love with the absent Gracey: 'Those were out and out the pleasantest days we ever spent in the Hollow—the best time almost Jim and I had had since we were boys.'[4] Starlight pertinently summarizes the experience by calling it 'an Australian Decameron without the naughty stories'.

When the description of this Eden is analysed, however, it is apparent to an English reader that what the Hollow holds is a good deal less than exotic—green grass, streams, wild raspberries, and roses. This may be Happy Valley, but it is very like rural England seen from amidst the alien corn. Dick is more definite in his description:

It was a beautiful warm evening, though summer was over, and we were getting into the cold nights and sharp mornings again, just before the regular winter weather. There was going to be a change, and

[1] *Robbery*, pp. 260–1. [2] Ibid., pp. 475–6. [3] Ibid., pp. 472–3.
[4] Ibid., p. 475.

there were a few clouds coming up from the north-west; but for all that it had been quite like a spring day. The turf on all the flats in the Hollow was splendid and sound.... We had two or three little creeks to cross, and they were pretty full, except at the crossing places, and rippled over the stones and sparkled in the sun like the brooks we'd heard tell of in the old country.[1]

An Australian autumn has become an English spring. By divesting themselves of their adulthood and putting on childhood's innocence, the later inhabitants of the Hollow fancy they are in England: the roses are still recognizable despite the nibbling of Australian wallabies. Certainly they are safe from the Law; but as Aileen says, there is no way out. They are prisoners, safe but unfree. Freedom is somewhere else, beyond Australia's coasts; but 'we had that feeling we didn't like to clear away altogether out of the old country; there was mother and Aileen still in it, and every man, woman, and child that we'd known ever since we were born.'[2] Although Australia has now become 'the old country', Gracey is still absent from these natural regrets, as she is from later half-made plans to flee to Honolulu, San Francisco, the Islands. Kate too is absent, understandably, as it is as much her as her allies the police they are anxious to escape; but, as she proves, indirectly assuring Gracey of ultimate satisfaction, these two women are at one in their purposes. Though the convict era is past—thankfully, Boldrewood suggests—woman is still the gaoler, Australia the prison, imprisoning and incapacitating man as effectively as Ned Kelly's home-made armour.

Of the theme of mateship, there is little in *Robbery under Arms*. In choosing to centre the novel on one man, the Byronic hero— 'a man proud, moody, cynical, with defiance on his brow, and misery in his heart, a scorner of his kind', as Macaulay defined him—Boldrewood eliminates the possibility at least from the experience of his main character. Such a hero is, curiously, in the same position as Patrick White's Mordecai Himmelfarb, the mystical Jew in *Riders in the Chariot*: each, according to his lights, has taken Providence for a mate.[3] As in *The Miner's Right* and *Nevermore*, the goldfields in *Robbery under Arms* provide opportunity for mates to show themselves. Even

[1] Ibid., p. 471. [2] Ibid., p. 137.
[3] Patrick White, *Riders in the Chariot*, Harmondsworth 1964, p. 308.

Starlight, preferring to emphasize his gentlemanly qualities, puts aside his lonely splendour to dig with his two English noble-born mates, becoming one of the team known as the Three Honourables. Dan Moran has his mates. This is mateship of a general professional kind. The closer personal kind exists between Dick and Jim, epitomized in the silent handshake: 'I didn't say anything, but I took hold of Jim's hand and shook it. We looked in each other's eyes for a minute; there was no call to say anything. We always understood one another, Jim and I.'[1] David and Jonathan could not say very much more. But the novel is not about Dick and Jim. They are merely part of Saul's local colour.

No one has argued that *Robbery under Arms* is a great novel or even, like *For the Term of his Natural Life*, a good one. Boldrewood called it a 'pot-boiler', but it is something more. The proof is that it is probably the only Australian novel widely known. Not only is it an integral part of Australian fiction, even when it appears most English; it is also a conscious attempt, as conscious as Furphy's later attempt, to convey reality by means of literary technique which, though old, was sophisticated in comparison with the reality to be communicated. By using phrases that promise truth, such as 'most of the books say so', and then allowing the unlettered narrator afterwards to explain that he found time to read in gaol, Boldrewood gives the novel an authenticity additional to the exact descriptions of cattle-branding, herding, duffing and selling, gold-digging, and the rest.

The most successful technique is the book's imagery, which holds together its wandering elements. The simplest example is perhaps Dick's laconic comment on his persuasive lawyer's efforts to save him during his final trial. The lawyer says: 'It was therefore incumbent on the jury to bring in a verdict for his client of "not guilty". But that cock wouldn't fight.'[2] The attitude behind the image—of pricking high-flown oratory with a humble pin—is one that has been highly praised in Furphy as somehow distinctive of Australians.[3] Boldrewood also possesses the quality.

[1] *Robbery*, pp. 259–60. [2] Ibid., p. 627.

[3] Though Canadians like William Toye also consider 'ironic humour a [national] speciality', to say nothing of the beliefs of 'hard-headed Yorkshiremen' and 'canny

A more extended use of this occurs in Dick's musings on 'man', particularly when man is ill:

> One day he'll be smiling and sensible, looking so honest all the time. Next day a knock on the head or a little vein goes crack in the brain (as the doctor told me); then the rails are down, and everything comes out with a rush into the light of day—right and wrong, foul and fair, station brands and clear-skins, it don't make no difference.[1]

Or the description of Bella Barnes's wedding:

> . . . as we went up the church all together, all in a heap, with the Barneses and the bride, they thought we must be related to 'em; and the church being choke-full they shunted us on to the place inside the rails, where we found ourselves drafted into the small yard with the bridegroom, the bride, the parson, and all that mob.[2]

Such imagery, echoing the main theme, gives the novel its predominantly Australian tang, encouraging such descriptions of it as 'Australian as the gums'. In explaining the origins of the bushranger's cry, 'Bail up', rather than the highwayman's 'Stand', as stemming from Australia's being at the time a mainly farming country, Dick comments: 'The same talk for cows and Christians.' The comment explains the book's unity and at least some of its appeal.

Scots'. It is perhaps an aspect of all colonial, not to say provincial literature, which defines itself by refusing, rejecting, or merely declining the unsubstantiated claims of what Mark Twain called 'smooth talkers'. For further information on this point, see A. Hausrath, *Corpus Fabularum Aesopicarum*, 1940.

[1] *Robbery*, p. 466. [2] Ibid., p. 521.

8 Joseph Furphy, *Such is Life*

THE story of Joseph Furphy's novel—or 'chronicle', as the narrator insists—*Such is Life*[1] is told by Tom Collins, a recently sacked Assistant Deputy Sub-Inspector of the Ninth Grade in the New South Wales Civil Service, 'Tom Collins' being the traditional name given to an Australian teller of tall tales. He professes himself a 'philosopher', by which he means he is beyond surprise; instead, there is the shrug of the shoulders and the laconic remark, said to have been Ned Kelly's last: 'Such is life.' Such an attitude to life might imply a freedom from all tension and an insensibility to most feelings; and might lead the reader to expect that a 'chronicle' based upon it would be inevitably banal. The chronicler, we learn, has 'three distinct attributes: an intuition which reads men like sign-boards; a limpid veracity; and a memory which habitually stereotypes all impressions except those relating to personal injury'.[2] The last unphilosophical attribute belongs rather to Joseph Furphy, and it is he that acknowledges the tensions of which Collins remains unaware. The novel is thus not as dull as Collins almost succeeds in making it.

The setting is the Riverina, an area for which the unemployed Deputy Assistant Sub-Inspector was formerly in some small, vague way responsible:

> Riverina Proper, consists of a wide promontory of open and level plain, coming in from the south-west; broken, of course, by many pine-ridges, clumps of red box, patches of scrub or timber, and the inevitable red gum flats which fringe the rivers. Eastward, the plain runs out irregularly into open forests of white box, pine, and other timber. Northward—something over a couple of hundred miles from the Murray—the tortuous frontier of boundless scrub meets the plain with the abruptness of a wall.[3]

'Northward—something over a couple of hundred miles' suggests that feeling of space which has since come to seem

[1] 'Tom Collins' (Joseph Furphy), *Such is Life*, Sydney 1903.
[2] *Such is Life*, Sydney 1962, (hereafter referred to as *Life*), p. 2.
[3] Ibid., p. 330.

distinctive of Australian novels; but if the description is analysed, it will be seen to present not the varied grandeur of Australia, which so attracted Kingsley and Boldrewood, or the terrifying vastness of its dry heart, which White and Stow record, but a relatively fertile fragment, or locality. The boundless is not Furphy's concern.

Published by the Bulletin Co., publishers of the Sydney *Bulletin*, that paper printed and for the most part written in Sydney for bushmen, Furphy is even more antagonistic to 'the spurious and blue-moulded civilization of the littoral', the advent of which both Kingsley and Boldrewood sometimes celebrated almost as joyously as they did the bush. Furphy writes:

> It is not in our cities or townships, it is not in our agricultural or mining areas, that the Australian attains full consciousness of his own nationality; it is in places like this, and as clearly here as at the centre of the continent. To me the monotonous variety of this interminable scrub has a charm of its own; so grave, subdued, self-centred; so alien to the genial appeal of more winsome landscape, or the assertive grandeur of mountain and gorge. To me this wayward diversity of spontaneous plant life bespeaks an unconfined, ungauged potentiality of resource. . . . Faithfully and lovingly interpreted, what is the latent meaning of it all?[1]

Furphy's ostensible reason, then, for choosing to limit his scene to one comparatively small region is that it is as representative of the whole as is the centre, and more representative than the settled areas; while in it, 'the Australian attains full consciousness of his own nationality'. That he can do this most easily when away from the general concourse of men may seem to be a variation on Wordsworthian anthropomorphism of the kind Henry Kendal and Charles Harpur had been attempting in more winsome landscapes; but if this is not a settled area, there would seem to be few Australians vouchsafed a national consciousness.

There were, however, more Australian nationalists here than Collins's philosophizing might suggest. The Riverina, in *Such is Life*, contained two interdependent communities: the squatters who held the land, and the bullock-drivers who supplied the goods they needed and carried away their produce. Despite the miles, there were homesteads for which one link

[1] *Life*, p. 81.

was the bullock teams, which, usually in the care of two men, went from one to the other. Another of their tenuous links was the Assistant Deputy Sub-Inspector, who camped on the track with the bullock-drivers, and at the homestead ate in the *narangies'* hut at the invitation of the squatter. Socially, he was, at least while employed, between the squatter and the bullock-driver.

There is a further reason for Furphy's limiting his scene. When *Such is Life* is read for the first time, it immediately impresses as a sprawling novel, linked only by the narrator's constant presence, accounted for by his assertion that he is writing no romance, with plot and denouement, but a chronicle of extracts taken with more or less arbitrariness from his 'twenty-two consecutive editions of Letts Pocket Diaries'. Its sprawl, like its arbitrariness, is more apparent than real. It first appears to be a picaresque novel, a series of loosely-connected anecdotes of the sort which talkative, semi-literate men might tell round a camp-fire. It is this picaresque quality plus a carefully-fostered suggestion of literary wilfulness that has led to the novel being compared with *Tristram Shandy*. There is also of course the 'philosophical' temper of its narrator, and even the presence of an equally 'philosophical' pipe, which seems to have been inherited from Uncle Toby. More important, there is a comparable prurience and furtive vulgarity.

But so much appearance and protestation mask a carefully constructed plot, to which the circumscribed locality offers a clue. Nearly everyone in the novel knows, has known, or is invited to know, everyone else. That bullock teams, and Collins, go from station to station across the Riverina, camping and yarning, provides the restless quality of a picaresque novel, but they never go where they are unknown. The success of the novel, like the success of their business, depends upon the treading of worn tracks. Beneath the literary wilfulness lies the story-teller's well-trodden but well-constructed path.

The novel opens with Collins taking the reader into his confidence, discussing the philosophical implications of his recent dismissal, an event which provides him with the time and the excuse for his writing, and immediately introduces a verisimilitude which the philosophizing heightens by contrast. Referring to the first of his diaries, he introduces his bullockies camping on, or not far off, the track—a piece of allegory which finds its explanation in the title to the novel. One of them, Cooper, tells that he had a sister, Molly, who, courted by a lad and kicked by a horse, was scarred and then jilted. Cooper believes she committed suicide, when she heard that the lad, Alf Jones, had married a shanty queen. Much later the reader learns, though Collins does not, that she did not commit suicide. She dressed as a man and became a boundary-rider calling herself Alf Morris, but known from her disfigurement as Nosey Alf. Like everyone else, Collins knows her only as a taciturn but unusually tidy and musically-gifted man. Her lover, Alf Jones—the lad whose Welsh name she almost assumes—finds his wife an adulterous slut, leaves her, and becomes a taciturn bullock-driver known as Warrigal Alf, who mourns his love while tending his guilt. Helped when sick by Collins, and at the same time providing the reader with the clues to his love, he afterwards leaves for Queensland in the employment of Stewart, a Scottish and Christian squatter. Some weeks after Collins has 'philosophically' offered this news to Nosey Alf, she—or he—also goes to Queensland.

Accompanying this love theme is the unromantic affection which the several-times widowed Madame Beaudesart, *née* Buckley, bears Tom Collins. She is the pretentious harridan Madame 'Bodysark', in every way Molly's opposite. Collins is her elusive prey, saved from capture only because he persuades friends to blacken his character in her hearing. As her maiden name is meant to indicate, she is a satire on Kingsley's heroines. She is the daughter of 'Hungry' Buckley, who is Furphy's idea of what Sam Buckley became, who 'went to beggary; and, being too plump of body and exalted of soul for barrow-work, and too comprehensively witless for anything else . . . was shifted by the angels to a better world—a world where the Christian gentleman is duly recognised, and where Socialistic carpenters, vulgar fishermen, and all manner of undesirable people, do the washing-up'.[1] Madame Beaudesart is a dependent of the Montgomerys, living with them at the romantically named Runnymede station. She is at the end of the track which Collins is travelling, an end to be avoided as long as possible. Like that of Nosey Alf and Warrigal Alf, this too is a barren track.

[1] *Life*, p. 205.

By the reappearance throughout the novel of the same characters riding its boundaries or driving along, or not far off, its main tracks, Furphy creates an air of casual, or fortuitous unity. The incident where old Sollicker, an oafish English boundary-rider, impounds Warrigal Alf's straying bullocks is such an instance. Collins meets him on the track, leisurely tailing the bullocks that Alf is too sick to look after, and slowly flatters him into releasing them. Sollicker is a butt of Furphy's satire on men who believe that 'orders is orders' and yet possess what Furphy sees as the typical English weakness of 'gentlemanly' pretensions, and at the same time he is a variant on the love theme. Inviting Collins to his hut, he explains that he has married, at his boss M'Intyre's request, a bullock-driver's Australian daughter who, while working at the homestead, has inexplicably quarrelled with Mrs. M'Intyre. The incident anticipates the quarrel between the servant girl Ida (whose name acknowledges her ugliness) and Madame Beaudesart at Runnymede station. Collins presents Sollicker's marriage as affectionate, unaware that the small son's Scottish appearance is because Sollicker was made to marry a woman already pregnant by another. The boy's name, Roderick, is also 'Hungry' M'Intyre's, a fact which widens the satire to include both sycophancy and marriage.

The situation recalls the earlier one concerning Collins's Irish Catholic new-chum friend, Rory O'Halloran, also a boundary-rider, married and with one child, Mary. Unlike Mrs. Sollicker, Mrs. O'Halloran angrily answers Collins's same waggish question about the child's age with a Protestant Irish concern for truth's simplicity. Even to the obtuse Collins, Rory and his wife appear unhappily wed. Mary, her father's single love, is the only reason for the marriage, Mrs. O'Halloran having been formerly something of a shanty queen whom marriage appears merely to have embittered. Her nature and her past are sufficient to indicate that she was Warrigal Alf's adulterous wife.

The reader learns of this incident, like so many, as the result of men yarning while they camp, for Collins assiduously notes it all in his diaries to use when he 'goes into print'. The talkative, camping bullock-drivers, besides linking the main contrasted themes of Warrigal Alf and Nosey Alf, and Collins and

Madame Beaudesart—which, as has been suggested, leads into an avowed literary critique—also epitomize, and voice, what many consider, with Furphy's encouragement, to be his main purpose in writing: to express his 'democratic bias'. Squatters and bullock-drivers were two interdependent communities. Without the one, the other could not have existed. Bullocks, however, had to feed, but the well-used tracks they travelled between homesteads were usually eaten out and waterless. To overcome this, teams camped off the track, in the squatters' paddocks; and this, as Folkstone, one of Furphy's typical English aristocrats, points out, is trespass. Thomson, a bullock-driver, early presents the problem and makes clearer what Furphy sees as implicit in this continuous struggle between the two classes:

'If you want a problem to work out, just consider that God constructed cattle for living on grass, and the grass for them to live on, and that, last night, and to-night, and to-morrow night, and mostly every night, we've a choice between two dirty transactions—one is, to let the bullocks starve, and the other is to steal grass for them. For my own part, I'm sick and tired of studying why some people should be in a position where they have to go out of their way to do wrong, and other people are cornered to that extent that they can't live without doing wrong, and can't suicide without jumping out of the frying-pan into the fire. Wonder if any allowance is made for bullock-drivers?—or are they supposed to be able to make enough money to retire into some decent life before they die?. . .'[1]

Remembering what Furphy says about such a region being the one where Australians gain a consciousness of their own nationality, we realize that he is here isolating what he and many others in the nineties saw as the political struggle, the struggle between 'them', who locked up the land even against bullock-drivers, and 'us'. Collins, who deals with 'them' and camps with 'us', is the striving middle-class whose concern is promotion to a higher grade and whose fear is the sack. As the Sydney official in the bush, he also represents the settled—or inclined-to-settle—city man that Furphy discounts. His easy meaningless job is to distribute lettered forms to squatters; his function in the novel is to observe and record the actions of others, actions which, though without the impetus of

[1] *Life*, p. 16.

encouragement or the distraction of fear, are more intelligible than his own. By making him, at the time of writing, one of the unemployed, however, Furphy blurs what objectivity—to give it a kind name—such a man might in such circumstances be thought to possess. Presented in this way, the class war assumes a simplicity more touching than earlier writers had thought possible. Its simplicity is in every sense pastoral, and even today is not without its devotees. Furphy encourages them thus: 'between the self-valuation of the latter-day squatter and that of his contemporary wage slave, there is very little to choose. . . . Either the anachronistic tradition must make suicidal concessions, or the better-class people must drown all plebeian Australian males in infancy, and fill the vacancy with Asiatics.'[1] In other words, the choice is between social revolution and mass coloured immigration. What happened was much more prosaic: the petrol engine was developed and two-thirds of Australia's population chose to live in the cities and townships. Joseph Furphy, the bullock-driver who like Holy Dan lost his team through drought and pleuro-pneumonia, was among the first to go. The land in Australia, as in Scotland, remained locked up in large holdings because it was better economics for everyone that it should be that way. And Australia remained as aggressively 'white' as Furphy could have desired. As a social prognostication, *Such is Life* was already out of date when it was written.

But the contemporaneity or political importance of Furphy's book is of secondary importance; as too are those extracts, omitted from the published version, which later appeared under the titles of *Rigby's Romance*[2] and *The Buln-buln and the Brolga*.[3] What does concern us is the way in which *Such is Life*—fabricated in 'near-isolation', as one critic once asserted—links with the by then established Australian literary tradition, and the way that tradition continued to show, even to depend on, its European origins. Indications of this link are apparent in the extracts already quoted. The first is in the emphasis Thomson, the bullock-driver, gives to the inevitable criminality there is

[1] *Life*, p. 256.

[2] 'Tom Collins' (Joseph Furphy), *Rigby's Romance: A 'Made in Australia' Novel*, Melbourne 1921. Another edition containing matter previously omitted was published by Angus and Robertson, Sydney 1946.

[3] 'Tom Collins' (Joseph Furphy), *The Buln-buln and the Brolga*, Sydney 1948.

in his job, a fact of life which parallels the literary convention embodied in the Byronic hero, and which Furphy exploits. The second is in the reference to Asian immigration and Furphy's fear of it, which had its original social parallel in those convict opinions most notably shared by Governor Macquarie and acknowledged in Rowcroft's *Tales of the Colonies*. Australia was the 'convict country', a prison; and one of the functions of prison walls is to keep people out. Both find support in Furphy's elaborated concern for the 'real' gentleman, and for those walks of life in which the gentleman has traditionally interested, and perhaps defined, himself. This concern is evident on the novel's opening page:

Unemployed at last!

. . . .

Scientifically, such a contingency can never have befallen of itself. According to one *theory of the Universe*, the momentum of Original Impress has been tending toward this far-off, divine event ever since a scrap of fire-mist flew from the solar centre to form our planet. Not this event alone, of course; but every occurrence, past and present, from *the fall of captured Troy* to the fall of a captured insect. According to another theory, I hold an *independent diploma* as one of the architects of our Social System, with a *commission* to use my own judgement, and take my own risks, like any other unit of humanity. This theory, unlike the first, entails frequent hitches and cross-purposes; and to some malign operation of these I should owe my present holiday.

Orthodoxly, we are reduced to one assumption: namely, that my *indomitable old Adversary* has suddenly called to mind *Dr. Watts's friendly hint* respecting the easy *enlistment* of idle hands.

Good. If either of the two first hypotheses be correct, my enforced *furlough* tacitly conveys the responsibility of extending a ray of *information*, however narrow and feeble, across the *path* of such *fellow-pilgrims* as have led lives more sedentary than my own—particularly as I have enough money, to *frank myself in a frugal way* for some weeks, as well as to purchase the few requisites of authorship.

If, on the other hand, my supposed safeguard of drudgery has been cut off at the meter by that *amusingly short-sighted old Conspirator*, it will be only fair to notify him that his age and experience, even his captivating habits and well-known hospitality, will be treated with scorn, rather than respect, in the paragraphs which he virtually forces me to write; and he is hereby invited to view his own *feather on the fatal dart*.[1]

[1] *Life*, p. 1.

Many have remarked on the tone of this first page, claiming it as an example of Furphy's celebrated irony. 'Debunking' more accurately describes the tone, irony perhaps defining the intention. It is the kind of deflationary exercise which C. J. Dennis was to perform in verse some years later.[1] What has gone unnoticed are the objects of Furphy's scorn. Most obvious in those words and phrases italicized above, they are: Learning, Christianity, Army and Empire, History, Literature, and the rhetoric which all employ; and this is an attack which Furphy carries on throughout the book. Furphy, however, was no anarchist. As H. J. Oliver has pointed out, his general theme is perhaps 'responsibility'. Having chosen his audience of fellow pilgrims whose lives were more sedentary than his own—in other words, the city-man—he states in the book's last paragraph what the object of that responsibility is: 'Such is life, my fellow-mummers—just like a poor player, that bluffs and feints his hour upon the stage, and then cheapens down to mere nonentity. But let me not hear any small witticism to the further effect that its story is a tale told by a vulgarian, full of slang and blanky, signifying—nothing.'[2] What he is attacking is the orthodoxy of the cultured, represented by the phrase 'cheapens down to mere nonentity', which recalls Sir Thomas Browne's 'The greater part must be content to be as though they had not been, to be found in the Register of God, not in the record of man.' What he is proclaiming is the unorthodoxy of the uncultured, whose representative, for Furphy, is always Shakespeare, who had little Latin and less Greek. Thus the battle is a simplified extension of the simplified political battle. To wage the same war on two fronts is the book's purpose. It turns out to be another phoney war as soon as the terms of the conflict are examined; for what Furphy is saying is that the vulgarian is as good as the cultured man, and he is good in the same ways. He is learned though untaught; he is a Christian though no church-goer; he will flatten an enemy though he is no soldier; he is a nationalist though no imperialist; history is what will be made in the future, not what has been done in the past; literature is a chronicle with a love interest, not a love story with a feature interest; while, to persuade and convince, Furphy

[1] *The Songs of a Sentimental Bloke*, Sydney 1915.
[2] *Life*, p. 371.

employs, even in the puns and alliteration on the first page, the devices of rhetoric—ironically, it is true; but irony is defensive, half in love with what it half condemns. Furphy thus upholds the same orthodoxy among different believers. But then, in what way are they different? This is the question facing all fundamentalists who refuse to be radicals. Their concern is with differences of degree, not of kind. Socially, they are the self-perpetuating middle-class, which, as more than one commentator has pointed out, is what Australian society predominantly is. As Douglas Pike has suggested with his usual exhilarating sharpness, this has come to mean complacent mediocrity, which is also one possible description of Furphy's novel.

The way in which such orthodoxy is established can be seen in his attitude to the bullock-drivers, whose presence throughout the book is constant enough, and who are so well wrapped in Furphy's sympathy that they can be called its heroes; and it can be seen in his attitude to women. With the exception of Mosey Price, an anarchical individualist with whom neither his comrades nor Furphy have much sympathy, all the bullock-drivers are big men. Thomson 'was tall and lazy, as bullock drivers ought to be'. Cooper 'was three inches taller, three stone heavier, and thirty degrees lazier, than Thomson'. Dixon 'was a magnificent specimen of crude humanity; strong, lithe, graceful, and not too big—just such a man as your novelist would picture as the nurse-swapped offspring of some rotund or rickety aristocrat'.[1] What virtue there is in this largeness, Furphy does not ask. He is content to assert that his plebeian heroes are at least as big as any novelist's aristocrats.

They are equals in other ways. Thomson 'was scarcely a typical bullock driver, since fifteen years of that occupation had not brutalised his temper, nor ensanguined his vocabulary, nor frayed the terminal "g" from his participles.' The typical bullock-driver's character resembles even more nearly that of the nineteenth-century aristocrat, at least as he appears in fiction. Like Thackeray's Lord Steyne, the bullock-driver is bad tempered, swears, and says, when occasion fits, huntin', shootin', and fishin'. Furphy later draws attention to the resemblance when he says; 'There are *bonâ fide* German names which no man of refinement cares about repeating except in a shearers'

[1] Ibid., pp. 3–4.

hut or a gentlemen's smoking-room'—shearers being here the social equals of bullock-drivers.

While establishing the heroic proportions of his heroes, Furphy hints at their roguishness:

> To avoid the vulgarity of ushering this company into the presence of the punctilious reader without even the ceremony of a Bedouin introduction—(This is my friend, N or M; if he steals anything, I will be responsible for it): a form of introduction, by the way, too sweeping in its suretyship for prudent men to use in Riverina—I shall describe the group . . .[1]

The tone is again obviously ironic, and consequently defensive. It lacks the combative quality, and the certainty, of satire. Furphy is arguing that bushmen are rascals, but likeable rascals—likeable because of their rascality. They have none of Lord Steyne's viciousness; they are harmless knaves in the way that Falstaff is often supposed to be. Presented thus, there can be no danger in their devilry, as Patrick White's Mordecai Himmelfarb is told, in *Riders in the Chariot*, when he is taken down from the tree to which jokers have strung him. At heart, they are sound chaps, even respectable chaps in an off-hand sort of way. What Thomas McCombie said, in *Arabin*, of the squatters who resembled the sons of landed gentry in *Rob Roy*, applies to Furphy's bullock-drivers: 'In their manners they were boisterous and abrupt; they assimilated pretty closely to the young squires of Osbaldistone—Messrs. Thorncliffe, Richard, John, and Wilfred Osbaldistone'. Equally to the point is McCombie's qualification: 'The eye wandered in vain for a Die Vernon to brighten the picture.'[2]

A clearer instance of cosy sentimental prevarication occurs when Furphy is describing Jack the Shellback, a boundary-rider, who, as his nickname denotes, was formerly a sailor. Furphy introduces him as a gusty old sinner whose language burns the air. He then qualifies the description, and directs the reader's sympathies, by saying:

> beyond this rollicking old blackguard there stood a second Jack, a soft-hearted, self-sacrificing other-phase, chivalrous to quixotism, yet provokingly reticent touching any act or sentiment which reflected real credit on himself. . . . Jack, for one thing, was eminently

[1] *Life*, p. 3. [2] p. 111.

religious—as indeed were those greater geniuses and equally hard cases, Dick Steele and Henry Fielding.[1]

Equally, of course, Dick Steele and Henry Fielding were gentlemen, though they did not share Jack's 'childlike simplicity'.

As the book's last paragraph makes clear, Furphy's intention is to show that ordinary men are worth writing about, a fact which Dickens, for instance, had assumed was self-evident. Collins's 'philosophical' pipe earlier argues the reasons, and explains the difficulties:

the man who spends his life in actual hardship seldom causes a trumpet to be blown before him. He is generally, by heredity or by the dispensation of Providence, an ornament to the lower walks of life; therefore his plea, genuine if ungrammatical, is heard only at second-hand, in a fragmentary and garbled form. Little wonder, then, that such a plea is received with felicitous self-gratulation, or passed with pharisaical disregard, by the silly old world that has still so many lessons to learn—so many lessons which none but that unresisting butt of slender-witted jokers can fitly teach, and which he, the experienced one, is usually precluded from teaching by his inability to spell any word of two syllables. Yet he has thoughts that glow, and words that burn, albeit with such sulphurous fumes that, when uttered in a public place, they frequently render him liable to fourteen days without the option.[2]

Although 'glow', 'burn', 'sulphurous fumes', and 'fourteen days without the option' introduce what might be called the 'Satan-convict' idea, the main point is that it is difficult for the common man either to write a book or to be made the hero of a book. These are the tasks Furphy sets himself. To overcome the problem of reproducing the common man's burning language, he adopts the literary convention of replacing such words as 'hell' and 'bloody' with euphemisms, but by making the substitutes rather more esoteric than, for instance, Boldrewood's 'by Jove', and by extending the convention to include such possible indelicacies as 'bed' and 'trousers', he pokes fun at it. By poking fun at it, however, the power of the convention is acknowledged; irony is not the weapon with which conventions are destroyed; and by choosing irony, Furphy suggests that he was not keen to see it go. To write the kind of realistic novel

[1] Ibid., p. 341. [2] Ibid., p. 106.

in which a spade is called a spade, he would have had to forego many of his knowing laughs; and, to those who admire the novel, such laughs are a great part of its attraction. As much in literary method as in political theory, Furphy was a conservative. Like Boldrewood, he favoured modification, not change. To fire literary squibs was his way of dealing with the hotheads.

Lest any reader, however, should imagine, by not sufficiently distinguishing between 'romances' and 'chronicles', that lowly men are illiterate, Furphy is quick to disillusion them. Thomson, the bullock-driver, has at one time heard of tangents, cube roots, and the square of the hypotenuse, as well as the retreat from Moscow. He has muddled them, but this does not matter. In speaking to Collins, he introduces them into his conversation as metaphors that denote a man of parts, for such he assumes Collins to be and he is anxious not to appear at a disadvantage. That he uses them wrongly shows Furphy being playfully ironic at Thomson's expense. That he uses them at all shows that he thinks the habit of using metaphors valuable; and if they are faintly learned, then their value is enhanced.

Thomson is not necessarily being ironical at Collins's expense: first because the line between pedantry and learnedness is never clear; secondly because there are so many direct and sympathetic references to the intellectual equipment which the common man possesses. Several of the characters, apart from Collins, have their 'swapping books'—Shakespeare, Zola, Ouida—and can say 'a Roland for your Oliver' with the best of them, including the farmers and squatters. Rory O'Halloran is even writing a thesis, whose 'style was directly antithetical to that curt, blunt, and simple pronouncement aimed at by innocents who deceive no-one by denouncing Socialism, Trades-Unionism, etc., over the signature of "A Working Man" '. Flowers of speech, which Collins also cultivates, are lovely things, even when the soil in which, for instance, Rory O'Halloran plants them, is, according to Collins, parched and barren.

The parallels between the attainments of gentlemen and plebeians having been drawn, it must be emphasized that their existence in reality is not in doubt. Furphy existed perhaps only to prove it. What is curious is the need he and others felt to assert the parallels; for there is no immediately evident virtue either in reading or in the ability to cap and quote, or in knowing mathematics and history, or being, like Jack the Shellback, religiously inclined. Furphy assumes there is. He assumes it, like Captain Starlight and Dick Marston, because such attributes and interests are gentlemanly.

The only time Furphy clearly allows learnedness to become so excessive as to be embarrassing, and therefore pedantic, is when characters like Willoughby, a broken English aristocrat, make a literary reference or a pun. Willoughby is one of Furphy's butts; we are thus encouraged to condemn the man who in conversation induces constraint among his audience. His action is unseemly. Anybody else is free to indulge in as many verbal tricks as he likes; for such men, silent or garrulous, are seemly men. Thus Furphy uses the gentlemanly code with which to measure every pretension, especially the pretensions of gentlemen.

The 'gentleman' or gentleman is a subject on which Furphy is most insistent, using inverted commas to indicate his contempt for what he considers false gods. In attacking the 'gentleman', he warns:

> Remember, however, that our present subject is not the 'gentleman' of actual life. *He* is an unknown and elusive quantity, merging insensibly into saint or scoundrel, sage or fool, man or blackleg. He runs in all shapes, and in all degrees of definiteness. Our subject is that insult to common sense, that childish slap in the face of honest manhood, the 'gentleman' of fiction, and of Australian fiction pre-eminently. . . . And it is surely time to notice the three-penny braggadocio of caste which makes the languid Captain Vernon de Vere (or words to that effect) an overmatch for half-a-dozen hard-muscled white savages, any one of whom would take his lordship by the ankles, and wipe the battlefield with his patrician visage . . .; which makes the rosy-cheeked darling of the English rectory show the saddle-hardened specialists of the back country how to ride a buck-jumper; which makes a party of resourceful bushmen stand helpless in the presence of flood or fire, till marshalled by some hero of the croquet lawn; above all, which makes the isocratic and irreverent Australian fawn on the 'gentleman', for no imaginable reason except that the latter says 'deuced' instead of 'sanguinary', and 'by Jove' instead of 'by sheol'. . . . The "gentleman" is not necessarily gentle; but he is necessarily genteel. Etymology is not at fault here; gentility, and gentility alone, is the qualification of the 'gentleman'.[1]

[1] *Life*, pp. 40–1.

Three points emerge from this apparently straightforward condemnation of the 'gentleman' of fiction. The first is that the democratic tone becomes confused with that of nationalism; and, while this was perhaps inevitable at the time, the condemnation is thus equivocal. Secondly, where he introduces a character such as Stewart of Kooltopa—who is 'the younger son of a Scottish laird'; who is as noted for his 'chivalry' and 'quixotism' as Jack the Shellback; who caps quotations with Collins; and who is rich because he knows his job as a pastoralist—Furphy then insists he is not a gentleman, but a Christian. The term has less to do with a belief in Christ than Furphy says it has to do with a belief in 'gentlemen'. The intention, however, is the same as Cardinal Newman's when he defined a gentleman:

> it is almost a definition of a gentleman to say he is one who never inflicts pain. . . . He is mainly occupied in merely removing the obstacles which hinder the free and unembarrassed action of those about him; and he concurs with their movements rather than takes the initiative himself. . . . The true gentleman . . . carefully avoids whatever may cause a jar or a jolt in the minds of those with whom he is cast; . . . his great concern being to make everyone at their ease and at home. He has his eyes on all his company; he is tender towards the bashful, gentle towards the distant, and merciful towards the absurd; . . . he guards against unseasonable allusions, or topics which may irritate; he is seldom prominent in conversation, and never wearisome. He makes light of favours while he does them. . . . He never speaks of himself except when compelled; . . . has no ear for slander or gossip. . . .[1]

In other words, the ideal though not the name is the same. Furphy is on the side of Newman in behaviour as in faith, orthodox in a way that Charles Kingsley, to whom his brother Henry dedicated *Geoffry Hamlyn*, perhaps misrepresented also out of a too Protestant concern for truth's simplicity.

The third point is the distinction Furphy says he is making between literature and life. He, as 'chronicler', deals only with reality. He is writing a novel not only in which a spade is to be called a spade, but in which it is essential for a spade to appear; yet, in its euphemisms this reality consists of an approximation to the reality of behaviour, or action, and in Stewart of Kooltopa as well as in more common men like Jack the Shellback, an

[1] J. H. Newman, *The Idea of a University*, London 1873, pp. 208–9.

approximation to the reality of intention, or idealism. Such a reality does not of course differ from that pursued by earlier Australian novelists, but Furphy insists that it does; and because he is so insistent, it is necessary to accept his terms in discussing the novel. For instance: Australians fawning on the likes of Captain Vernon de Vere (a name in the allegorical tradition which Furphy, like Herman Melville in *Billy Budd*, also follows) may be an attack on Boldrewood's remark, in the words of Dick Marston, that 'it's a strange thing that I don't think there's any place in the world where men feel a more out-and-out respect for a gentleman than in Australia'; but by making Stewart of Kooltopa the younger son of a Scottish laird, Furphy reproduces Boldrewood's gentleman hero, Mr. Falkland, to whom Dick Marston is specifically referring. Their qualities, like their origins, are the same, even to their 'genteel' habit of calling their employees and acquaintances by their surname, while getting 'Mr.' in reply. Quintus Servinton, like Rufus Dawes, had noticed the practice.

Furphy's remark, that men favour the memory of their fathers to the exclusion of their mothers, is perhaps intended as a repudiation of Marcus Clarke's assigning the opposite as the motive for his hero's behaviour; and Henry Kingsley is an object of Furphy's considerable scorn. Nameless Australian women novelists are also lambasted, because, it seems, they lack the courage to be convicted of naturalism. It is necessary, however, to emphasize the connection between political sympathy and literary technique. Romance—by which Furphy seems to mean the use of a plot—is old-fashioned or unreal; but *Such is Life* has a plot. That it is well disguised does not make the novel a radical exercise in literary technique; and so it cannot be usefully compared with either *Tom Jones* or *Tristram Shandy*, both of which were.

Politically, the same conservative attitude is evident. In *A Sydney-Side Saxon*, Boldrewood speaks of the existence in Australia of the class system: 'Newly-come people don't understand this. Generally they think that money does everything, and that there are no ranks or differences in colonial society. There they're quite wrong . . .'[1] Furphy says the same: 'Social status, apart from all consideration of mind, manners, or even

[1] p. 204.

money, is more accurately weighed on a right-thinking Australian station than anywhere else in the world.'[1] Thus the reality that both Boldrewood and Furphy are describing is the same. Neither is suggesting that this class structure is likely to give way to egalitarianism, or even that Australian society would be better if it did. Furphy is saying that it ought to be inverted, not for any faintly Marxist reason, but because it is the 'lower orders' who now possess those qualities which formerly were supposed to distinguish the gentleman. Furphy's 'gentleman', in losing them and relying instead only on 'gentility', has betrayed his trust. The qualities themselves are none the less desirable. Only Mosey Price, the 'anarchist', discounts them, and is therefore in turn discounted.

Neither Furphy's literary nor his political conservatism is surprising. Both imply a wish for a respectability comparable with that traditionally said to be possessed by the originator of the colony's literature and political system, namely Britain, so that Australian nationalism can begin to compete with Britain's imperialism. If the colony altered the terms under which she would compete, there could be no competition. Furphy goes to great lengths to ensure that they are the same. His heroes drink less and wash more often than any Englishman, he says, evidently believing, like Samuel Smiles, that cleanliness is next to godliness, and drunkenness an abomination. It is a remarkable claim, when almost every previous writer had noted there was more alcohol than water in the land. Furphy's heroes are thus having their virtues exaggerated at the same time as the viciousness is withdrawn from their vices. They are heroes not of the sixteenth or eighteenth century, but of the nineteenth.

In 1906, three years after he had been responsible for the publication of *Such is Life*, A. G. Stephens recommended John Murray's edition of Byron:

> Byron is one of those authors—like Shelley, Browning, Shakespeare, Spenser, Chaucer, and their high kindred—who by most of us must be read before twenty if they are to be read right through . . . it is in middle life that one wants knowledge of the classics to be sure and stimulating. Therefore, ye golden youth! vow to read and meditate your Byron while there is time: this new edition may confirm your vow.[2]

[1] *Life*, p. 255. [2] *The Bulletin*, Red Page, 15th February 1906.

Mad—even bad—Lord Byron thus takes his place alongside the Swan of Avon and the Ineffectual Angel 'and their high kindred', silencing those doubts Thomas McCombie had voiced in his novel *Arabin*, fifty years before, when young ladies like Martha Waller said: 'Alas! I regret that Byron was a licentious man; the beauty and power which break through everywhere fascinate the mind'; when young men became 'melancholy enthusiasts' from their 'solitary habits and the Byronian style of literature'; when authors 'observed in the world too great an anxiety to ape the misanthropy in which the Byron school of poets have so completely enveloped their heroes'. Byron had long since made his peace with Scott, but A. G. Stephens was reminding his readers of the fact. Furphy was one such reader, as he was also Byron's, and Scott's.

Along with references to Shakespeare, Sir Thomas Browne, Dr. Johnson, Dick Steele, and Henry Fielding, 'and their high kindred', Furphy quotes, as a man 'in middle life' should, from *Marmion*, *Rokeby*, and *Rob Roy*, whose hero was perhaps the first cattle-duffer in fiction. He establishes himself in the reader's mind as an untaught but well-read man, at the same time presenting Collins as something of a pedant who yet, in referring to himself in a ludicrous rather than dangerous situation as 'Alpine's son', is prepared to exploit or excuse his failing by being ironical. Used in the same way, there are quotations from Byron's *Hebrew Melodies* and a mention of 'Eve's curse on Cain, in Byron's fine drama'. More important, however, are asides such as 'in the Riverina of that period, it was considered much more disgraceful to be had by a scoundrel than to commit a felony yourself'; and the more sustained description of the bullock-driver, the inevitable criminality of whose work has been noted:

> The up-country man is decidedly open-handed: he will submit to crushing losses with cheerfulness, tempered, of course, by humility in those cases where he recognizes the operation of an overhanging curse; he will subscribe to any good or bad cause with a liberality excelled only by the digger; he will pay gambling debts with the easy, careless grace which makes every P. of W. so popular in English sporting circles—in a word, the smallest of his many sins is parsimony. But the penal suggestiveness of trespass-penalty touches the sullen dignity of his nature . . .[1]

[1] *Life*, p. 37.

Furphy is discussing 'up-country' men in general. They are always generous—as Henry Kingsley had been one of the first to remark; they are possessed of a 'sullen dignity', and sometimes marked with a heavy curse.

When he speaks of his two heroes, Warrigal Alf and Nosey Alf, Furphy's characterization becomes more exact and recognizable, and the irony in 'sullen dignity' disappears in order that the reader's sympathies shall be unequivocally committed. Warrigal Alf—whose nickname (the same as that of Captain Starlight's aboriginal companion, 'the devil's limb') means wild-dog—sells his saw-mill after his wife has deceived him, 'reserving to himself enough to start him in a line of life that he could follow without the annoyance of being associated with anyone'. Bullocking along, Warrigal Alf is beyond 'mateship'. His only company is the Riverina landscape, 'so grave, subdued, self-centred', Furphy matching its mood to that of his hero. Alf's wife 'humbly consented to his conditions,' he says, 'evidently looking forward to forgiveness and reconciliation, somewhere in time or eternity. But, by God! she mistook her mark!' Don Juan's couplet to describe such a situation was:

> Now hatred is by far the longest pleasure;
> Men love in haste, but they detest at leisure.[1]

Molly, his former sweetheart, was 'The only living thing he could not hate';[2] he believed that she, like Gulnare, was dead. He lived

> In vigilance of grief that would compel
> The soul to hate for having loved too well.[3]

Recounting his story to Collins, as though it were someone else's, Warrigal Alf says: 'The very curse that was on him seemed to protect him from the mishaps that befell other men in his line of work; and he found life worth living for the sake of hating and despising the whole human race, including himself. There's no pleasure like the pleasure of being a devil, when you feel yourself master of the situation. . . .'[4] The Satanic ancestry of the Byronic hero is apparent a little later when Mr. Smythe, a squatter, is recorded as having once fined Alf for

[1] Lord Byron, *Don Juan*, Canto XII, vii.
[2] Lord Byron, *The Corsair*, Canto III, xxi.
[3] Lord Byron, *Lara*, Canto I, xvii.
[4] *Life*, p. 187

trespass: 'It had caused [Alf] to speak a word in private to Mr. Smythe; and, from that time forward, the squatter hated the bullock driver considerably more than he hated sin, and feared him more than he feared his reputed Maker.'[1]

This 'unconscious outlaw', as Furphy calls him—meaning that Furphy wished the reader to be aware that Alf was very much a conscious outlaw—also possesses most of the physical attributes of the Byronic hero. The irony is directed at those who imagine that transference to the infernal regions of Australia diminishes the type:

Without being aggressively handsome . . . Alf, in his normal state, was a decidedly noble-looking man, of the so-called Anglo-Saxon type, modified by sixty or eighty years of Australian deterioration. . . . Physically, the Suffolk Punch had degenerated into the steeple chaser; psychologically, the chasm between the stolid English peasant and the saturnine, sensitive Australian had been spanned with that facilis which marks the descensus Averni.[2]

Though his eyes are not black but blue, they are 'stern, defiant'; he wears a 'habitual frown'; he has a 'fine forehead'. Speaking to Stewart of Kooltopa, Collins says of Alf: 'Now, I think that that temperament, though, perhaps, tending to the volcanic, must have been a sensitive and an amiable one; however it may have soured and hardened into misanthropy and avarice.' Stewart, with none of Collins's scientific mumbo-jumbo, neatly differentiates between Furphy's idea of the gentleman, or Christian as he says, and his typical hero: 'Capable fellow, too; fine combination of a cultivated man and an experienced rough-and-ready bushman. Strictly honest, also, I think—only for his d—nable disposition.'[3] Stewart eventually helps him by employing him in 'a warmer clime', in Queensland; for

With all that chilling mystery of mien,
And seeming gladness to remain unseen,
He had (if 'twere not nature's boon) an art
Of fixing memory on another's heart . . .
His presence haunted still; and from the breast
He forced an unwilling interest;
Vain was the struggle in that mental net,
His spirit seem'd to dare you to forget.[4]

[1] Ibid., p. 192. [2] Ibid., pp. 201–2. [3] Ibid., p. 213.
[4] *Lara*, Canto I, xix.

To the extent that she is a hero and not a heroine, Nosey Alf is presented in the same Byronic terms. Because of her accident, she is without a nose. Addressing the reader, Collins says: 'Your nose, in all probability, is your dram of eale—your club foot—your Mordecai sitting at the king's gate—but you would look very queer without it.'[1] As she is musically gifted, Collins assures her that 'if [a person is] an artist, as you are, what might otherwise be a disfigurement becomes the highest claim to respect and sympathy'. This may be another example of Collins talking rubbish for the sake of Furphy's irony, but Furphy is also using the injury to help hold the reader's 'respect and sympathy'. Thus he is employing the convention which equated the artist with the Byronic hero. Artist, she certainly is. Besides her playing, which 'was both a mystery and a revelation', she has a voice 'rich, soft, transcendent, yet suggesting ungauged resources of enchantment unconsciously held in reserve', while the 'tendency of her songs was toward love, and love alone'. Collins—or Furphy—then adds, 'chaste, sensuous, but purely human love'. The deformity is Byron's, but the love is Scott's. And we are to believe that 'such is life'!

This denial of woman's sexuality reads oddly when we know that Furphy allows her the youthfulness which is evident in at least one 'splendid, soft and luminous' eye, as well as in her 'thick, strong, coal-black hair'. It is even odder when we recall that Furphy uses the device of James Tucker, in *Ralph Rashleigh*, of dressing his heroine as a man; and like the rest of Furphy's 'Australiennes', she has a moustache. Her masculinity even when she was a girl had not escaped her brother, the bullock-driver Cooper. He says: 'The other girls was weeds aside of her; she stood inches higher nor any o' them, an' she was a picter' to look at. Strong as whalebone, she was . . .'[2] In reality of course there was a reason for masculinity. A woman had to work as hard as, often harder than, her man. Henry Lawson, though he stressed the claims and joys of 'mateship', was, with Barbara Baynton,[3] one of the few Australian writers to acknowledge that 'the settlement of the empty spaces of Australia has largely been made possible by [woman's] self-sacrifice'.[4] What she

[1] *Life*, p. 304. [2] Ibid., p. 26.
[3] *Bush Studies*, London 1902; Sydney 1965.
[4] Charles P. Mountford, *Brown Men and Red Sand*, London 1950, p. 9.

sacrifices is her womanliness. Her refusal, or inability, to do so may be the reason for some of Furphy's anti-feminism, as when he says of the hopelessly unlucky bullock-driver, Priestley: 'It is scarcely necessary to add that he had a wife and about thirteen small children, mostly girls.'[1] Neither the wife nor the children would immediately be able to do much work. Unless they become as men, they are useless. There is nevertheless a good deal of anti-feminine bias which is either gratuitously offensive, or must be accounted for in another way.

Collins says: 'I always make a point of believing the best where women are concerned', but his tone, as well as his behaviour, converts the remark into yet another of Furphy's ironies. Apart from Warrigal Alf's jilting one girl, and leaving another, there are the three stories he tells in which women are tragically unfaithful in the way that the convict origins of Australia had encouraged them to be. None of these three women was married to a convict—for Furphy ignores the convict era—but the habits of that era seem to have persisted. Old Sollicker's wife was one whose loyalties were early mixed, or mixed for her. Rory O'Halloran's wife—whose title of 'Mrs.' is conspicuously frequent and therefore suspect—is a shrew who, though 'married' to a darling of a man, has yet 'explored the profound depths of masculine worthlessness'. Cooper's half-admiring complaint has a different source. He has found that women 'can't suffer to be idle, nor to see anybody else idle'. He realizes that woman's 'settlement of the empty spaces of Australia' involves not only a willing self-sacrifice, but also a willingness to sacrifice the 'up-country' man's dream of himself. Settlement would also change those empty spaces, 'so grave, subdued, self-centred', as much as it would change the matching mood of man. The only men in *Such is Life* who find women desirable are Sunday-School teachers and Willoughby, the Englishman, all of whom are objects of Furphy's contempt. Willoughby 'was detected —ha-ha! *Sua cuique voluptas*—in a liaison with a young person who resided with [his] uncle's wife'. The reader is evidently intended to shudder; and the reader might very well oblige, if he were given less ambiguous encouragement of this kind:

There is nothing dainty or picturesque in the presentment of a naked character washing himself; yet how few of our later novels or notes

[1] *Life*, p. 268.

of travel are without that bit of description. . . . It would be much more becoming to wash our dirty skins, as well as our dirty calico, in private.

We might advantageously copy women-writers here. Woman, in the nature of things, must accumulate dirt, as we do; and she must now and then wash that dirt off, or it would be there still. (Like St. Paul, I speak as a man). But the scribess never parades her ablutions on the printed page. . . . Woman must be more than figuratively a poem if she can promenade a dusty show-yard for a long, hot afternoon without increasing in weight by exogenous accretion; but her soulfulness, however powerless to disallow dirt, silently asserts itself when that dirt comes to be shifted.[1]

There is prudery in all this, and only a writer obtuse in the manner of Saint Paul could liken dirty skins to any kind of dirty calico. In attacking writers like Kingsley—who allowed his characters a 'tubbing' almost as frequently as Furphy allows Collins a bathe in a stagnant water-hole, where he always seems to 'lose his virility' in what can only be a lonely orgasm among the duckweed—Furphy switches to attack those women-writers who coyly leave their characters clean but unwashed. He thus introduces a prurience in the service of what he takes to be a sort of 'no nonsense' realism, the sort that calls a spade a bloody shovel. 'Exogenous accretion' may be an ironic euphemism; but what about Furphy's own coyness in depriving his characters of their sexuality? Most civilizations have considered a bed more important than a bath; and it might be thought that in Australia, where people are as scarce as water, it would be more realistic to increase the one while conserving the other.

Furphy's hearty but limited, and therefore unhelpful, vulgarity—if that is what it is—is apparent in the frequency with which he has his characters untrousered. Rory O'Halloran is the first to appear thus, out of forgetfulness; Collins is the next, out of carelessness. And Ida, Madame Beaudesart's good but ugly allegorical maid, who 'had a straggly goatee of dirty white, with woolly side-boards of the same colour', says with some truth to Collins: 'I picked up this little buckle aside o' your b–d; it's come off the back of your tr—rs. I'll sew it on for you any time, for I notice you're bothered with them slippin' down.' What is one to make of so many naked men and bearded trousered women?

[1] *Life*, pp. 258–9.

This seaside-postcard stuff has been described as 'comic variation'; yet its comedy is slight, and its variation none. Collins, in a chapter of such naked fun, sets light to a haystack in order to distract the owner's attention while he steals a pair of trousers from the washing-line. Accused of incendiarism, he makes play with the word 'sansculotte'. As punning is his pastime, he encourages the reader to discover a *double entendre*. The encouragement is evident in Chapter Three, where Collins says: 'I incur a certain risk in thus unbosoming myself, as will become apparent to the perfidious reader who hungrily shadows me through this compromising story.' It yet remains remarkable that a man 'unbosoms' himself whenever he takes his pants off.

Thus 'unbosomed', Collins accosts various pairs of lovers driving home from the Sunday-School outing. One lover is 'a large fair young man, fashionably dressed':

> 'What do you want?' he gasped.
>
> 'I want your—', I replied sternly. 'I'm getting full up of the admiration of the gods; I want *the admiration of my fellow-men*. In other words, I'm replete with the leading trait of *Adamic innocence*. . . . Come! off with them!' and with that I snapped the laces of his balmorals; for *he had sunk to the ground*, and *was lying on his back*. '. . . I'll just take the complete outer ply while *my hand's in*. . . . Let me impress upon you that *I don't attempt to defend this action on strictly moral grounds* . . . I think we may regard the transaction as a pertinent illustration of Pandulph's aphorism—to wit, that "*He who stands upon a slippery place, makes nice of no vile hold to stay him up*". When the hurly-burly's done, I must get you to *favour me with your address*, so that'—Here my antagonist suddenly *gave tongue*.
>
> During an eventful life, I have frequently had occasion to observe that when a woman finds herself in a *tight place*, her first impulse is to set the wild echoes flying; whereas, man *resists* or *submits* in silence, except, perhaps, for *a few bad words* ground out between his teeth . . .
>
> Within the next few minutes, several people on horseback came up to the scene of the late attempted *outrage* . . . I would *solicit* this impracticable generation no longer.[1]

The italics are not Furphy's, but the words, phrases, and comparisons are. At least one perfidious reader is surprised that the Australian censors, who have banned so many better books,

[1] Ibid., pp. 135–6.

have not sought to ban *Such is Life*. By their chaste criteria, it seems to be a book most likely to pervert its readers to 'acts of buggery' and 'sodomitic orgies'.

When Collins at last happily meets the trousered, moustached Jim, and discovers she is a woman, 'the revulsion of feeling was one of the quickest and fullest [he] ever experienced'. He forgives her for being what she not very obviously is, content that, if not a man, she is at least called Jim Quarterman. As he says when discounting heroes rescuing heroines: 'I repudiate shifts.' Even his stallion is called Cleopatra.

Should this reading of *Such is Life* be thought to rely too heavily on omissions and italics, it must be said again—as so many have said before—that the book has, in the words of H. J. Oliver, 'a most subtle and original plan'. Similarly, its verbal intricacies have long provided cause for comment. 'Irony' has been the word most on scholars' lips; it could equally well have been 'vulgarity'. There is, for instance, the water tank known as Faugh-a-ballogh, which is pronounced by one bullock-driver as 'Fog-a-bolla'—an approximation to what in Australian speech (lately called 'Strine') would be 'Fuck a bullock'. Under the influence of the same accent, the name of the noxious English aristocrat, Folkstone, would become 'Fuckson'; while the obsequious English peasant, 'old Sollicker', who believes that 'orders is orders', would be 'arse-'ole licker'. These are isolated examples. There may well be others.

Englishmen are, on the whole, the most hated among Furphy's hates. For him, they epitomize that orthodoxy which he attacks on the first page. They are victims of his satire, not of Collins's irony. They are foolish and pretentious, unloved and unloveable. The Chinese, whom Collins always addresses in the Australian variant of 'black-feller talk', are the most despised. They are 'our lowest types', 'the Turanian horde', 'partners with opium and leprosy', 'joss devotees', whose greatest fault is to be considered 'cheap and reliable' by employers. The Irish have a 'noxious innocence and all-round ineptitude'. Germans, appearing in their traditional literary role of scientists, are dullards and possessors of handkerchiefs. They have a 'vivid interest in bushrangers and blackfellows', unaware that Australia in 1883—the year Collins purports to be recording—had freed herself from fears of such people. To establish Australia's respectability—or new orthodoxy, which Boldrewood had felt historical truth could not imperil and might perhaps enhance—Furphy is thus content to ignore the fact that Ned Kelly was bushranging in 1880. Like Mark Twain, he has much fun reproducing German English, unwilling to acknowledge, as Kingsley and Boldrewood were not, that two languages are better than one. Furphy's Germans are true sons of 'the microbe-laden atmosphere of Europe'. His Scotsmen are mean and 'impracticable', though Stewart of Kooltopa is the exception. He is the Australian equivalent of Scott's John, Duke of Argyle. There is a deal of racial theorizing in the book which Furphy may have caught from Zola, one of whose novels turns up as Collins's 'swapping-book'. Collins later repudiates the habit as practised by 'Marcus Clarke, or Trollope, or Froude, or Francis Adams', but concludes that 'The coming Australian is a problem', a remark which Compton Mackenzie in his *Gallipoli Memories*, writing of the Australian troops, almost echoes, though with a handsome and no more than just qualification: 'They really were rather difficult; and so, no doubt, was Achilles.'[1] With so much evidence of Furphy's unpleasant nationalism, it is puzzling that he continues to be seen as 'supremely right—seizing on' what is called 'this sense in the best of us that we are equals'. It is said to be his 'deepest theme'.[2] But some of us seem to remain more equal than others. The image of the 'coming Australian' is nevertheless firmly outlined:

'God is eternal,' says a fine French apophthegm, 'but man is very old.'

And very new. Mary O'Halloran was perfect Young-Australian. To describe her from after-knowledge—she was a very creature of the phenomena which had environed her own dawning intelligence. She was a child of the wilderness, a dryad among her kindred trees. The long-descended poetry of her nature made the bush vocal with pure gladness of life; endowed each tree with sympathy, respondent to her own fellowship. She had noticed the dusky aspect of the iron-wood; the volumed cumuli of rich olive-green, crowning the lordly curra-jong; the darker shade of the wilga's massy foliage-cataract; the clearer tint of the tapering pine; the clean-spotted column of the

[1] London 1929, p. 73. [2] Judith Wright, op cit., p. xx.

leopard tree, creamy white on slate, from base to topmost twig. She pitied the unlovely balah, when the wind sighed through its coarse, scanty, grey-green tresses; and she loved to contemplate the silvery plumage of the two drooping myalls. . . . For the last two or three springs of her vivacious existence, she had watched the deepening crimson of the quondong, amidst its thick contexture of Nile-green leaves; she had marked the unfolding bloom of the scrub, in its many-hued beauty; she had revelled in the audacious black-and-scarlet glory of the desert pea. She knew the dwelling-place of every loved companion. . . . To her it was a new world, and she saw that it was good. All those impressions which endear the memory of early scenes to the careworn heart were hers in their vivid present, intensified by the strong ideality of her nature, and undisturbed by other companionship, save that of her father.

. . . Rory was her guide, philosopher, and crony. He was her overwhelming ideal of power, wisdom, and goodness; he was her help in ages past, her hope for years to come (no irreverence intended here; quite the reverse, for if true family life existed, we should better apprehend the meaning of 'Our Father, who art in heaven'); he was her Ancient of Days; her shield, and her exceeding great reward.[1]

This passage of heightened prose is Furphy's nearest approach to a lyrical description of love. As in earlier Australian novels, the love is between a man and a little girl. That the girl is the man's daughter makes real what Marcus Clarke and Boldrewood had suggested was love's ideal. Man is to be to her as a god.

The passage is also significant in Australian fiction as being the first glad description of the Australian landscape, a landscape that is itself an extension of the 'up-country' man's dream of himself. Furphy describes it not because it is strange, exotic, or interesting, but because it has lost every alien quality. It is 'home', the home of a new race. For them it is Eden, the home of God and his child. The O'Hallorans live in 'Utopia paddock', where bliss would be complete were Mrs. O'Halloran not there. For the first time we hear that boast, which has since so often been an excuse, 'She's a young country', a land of promise and no fulfilment: 'think how immeasurably higher are the possibilities of a Future than the memories of any Past since history began. By comparison, the Past though glozed

[1] *Life*, p. 91.

beyond all semblance of truth, is a clinging heritage of canonised ignorance, brutality and baseness; a drag rather than a stimulus.'[1] Australia had a century of history behind her when Furphy was writing this; but, to create his own ideal, he glozes over the country's convict origins, the extermination of the aborigines, and the pouring influx of people mad with the gold fever. The future he saw had to be protected from Englishmen, Scotsmen, Irishmen, Germans, and Chinese, all lumbered with their pasts and, in their various ways, responsible for the necessity he felt to gloze over his own.

As if to make concrete the secret joys Australia holds, Furphy introduces what Boldrewood called the Terrible Hollow. One of his friends uses it for hiding horses, just as old Dan Marston used it in *Robbery under Arms*. But Furphy's Hollow cannot be equated with England, as Boldrewood's can; it is not the scene of distant green thoughts in a green shade, even less of past terrors. Australia 'is cursed by no memories of fanaticism and persecution'. He calls his Hollow 'that secluded Eden'; but 'At the time I write of, it was impossible to ride to this island of verdure, and no white man could track a horse through the labyrinth that led to it'.[2] Like those prisoners who escaped in *For the Term of his Natural Life*, he has learned to love his prison; and, through his racism, he insists that it fulfil all its functions. It must hold in the likes of Mary O'Halloran, and keep others out. Only the black man who formerly owned it can track well enough to find its heart and display to the white its secret joys. He has the words which Mary recognizes: the currajong, the wilga, the balah, the myalls, and the quondong. Furphy's hero, Warrigal Alf, who in name and action, 'comes as near the blackfellow as it's possible for a white man to get', is, like 'the supple-jointed, keen-sighted children . . . distinctly affirming that disquieting theory which assumes evolution of immigrating races toward the aboriginal type'. As the Jindyworobaks were to assume thirty years later, this is a reparation that the white man can make to those whose lands and lives he has taken. For Furphy, that land was the comparatively comfortable Riverina. Yet even there, in following the lubra tracking the white child lost in the bush, the white man's discovery that the land has killed the child is as significant as

[1] Ibid., pp. 81–2. [2] Ibid., p. 104.

Voss's death in the 'centre' or Heriot's journey to the islands. For all its trees and blossoms, Australia remains a chastening land, whose promise is ambiguous.

While professing scientific optimism, Furphy, like Boldrewood and other 'old hands', discounts its manifestations in Australia. Irrigation as much as cities is felt to be irrelevant to Australia. Like Lawson's mateship and Boldrewood's love, both ask something else of a man than that he should be like his country, 'so grave, subdued, self-centred'. A liking for social concourse, if not gregariousness, would be necessary. But Furphy, in proposing the new orthodoxy, or respectability, mixes an amalgam of mateship and love which allows the Australian—by definition an up-country man—to achieve his national consciousness undisturbed by what most would regard as the orthodox, or, to be tendentious, the natural, claims of either. Apart from his variations on love, there are specific and briefly sympathetic references to mateship of a kind that both Kingsley and Lawson would have understood. Dixon, a bullock-driver and 'sojer's son', takes Willoughby, the officer's son, for a mate. Andrew Glover, the old muddled swagman, is mates with the young immigrant Tom Armstrong. They are each concerned for the welfare of the other; but, by being critical of the values all of them follow, Furphy hedges his own sympathy. What he seems to be saying is that the land demands heroes for whom manly women must slave in a love as barren as the men's. Whatever their Byronic ancestry, these Australian heroes are imprisoned in their chastity. Shunning cities and the power of women, they enjoy only the 'hurly-burly' of brief masculine encounter, each within himself seeking 'full consciousness of his own nationality'. War is their logical, and unfruitful, end. But, while appreciating its unfruitfulness, Furphy, unlike Kingsley, Boldrewood, and even Lawson, denied its logic. For him, 'the symbol of deepest ignominy has become the proudest insignia of Court-moths and professional assassins'. He wants to preserve 'the deepest ignominy' of the cross, but ignores the part professional assassins necessarily played if 'deepest ignominy' was to be conferred. Like others who believe that 'State Socialism' is 'true Christianity', he missed the irony of the Crucifixion. Such heroism as it entailed is inseparable from ignominy. This is why it was necessary to invent eternal life, both damned and blessed. The refusal to accept either in the place of what even Furphy admits is second-best led to the Byronic hero of the nineteenth century becoming the Outsider of the twentieth—led, indeed, to Warrigal Alf becoming Richard Mahony.

9 William Hay, *The Escape of the Notorious Sir William Heans*

WILLIAM HAY'S *The Escape of the Notorious Sir William Heans (and the Mystery of Mr. Daunt)*[1] is a difficult novel to take seriously, especially on first reading; and to find a reason why it should be read again is perhaps its chief difficulty. Since Miss F. Earle Hooper's address on Hay, however, called 'Our Greatest Romantic Novelist', delivered to the English Association in Sydney in 1944, an increasing few have overcome the difficulty. And they have urged others to do the same. Yet the reasons offered have for the most part been inadequate. Because, for instance, Hay is thought a 'Romantic Novelist', even 'Our Greatest', is by itself insufficient. To take a romantic novel seriously is the wrong response to that form. Bernardin de St. Pierre's romantic novel, *Paul et Virginie*, to which Hay refers, is for example not without charm; but its pastoral elements, which sustain the innocent love of the young couple, cannot be taken seriously now, any more than in 1787 when it was first published. They are a game of 'let's pretend' only justified by what it was thought Rousseau had said; to take such a game seriously is to be misled into pompousness or worse. R. G. Howarth, in the Introduction to his edition of Hay's novel[2] seems aware of the possibility. For Howarth, Hay's novel shows instead a 'deep preoccupation with the moral order of life'. But despite references to Hawthorne and Henry James, the claim remains weak.

Nor is the novel 'primarily a study of human passion',[3] as E. Morris Miller calls it. Miller adds an exhausting exploration of the history and geography of Australia in the early 1840s, the period in which the novel is set. The exploration suggests why the novel should be taken seriously: it has a historical importance. In a letter to Miss Earle Hooper, from which Howarth quotes the following passage, Hay wrote:

[1] London 1919. [2] Melbourne 1955 (hereafter referred to as *Escape*).
[3] *Southerly*, 1946, no. 3. The essay is attached to R. G. Howarth's edition.

When I began writing, just before the beginning of this century, Australian novels had relapsed entirely into fifth-rate tales of the 'paddock and stockyard variety', in spurious imitation of Rolf Boldrewood's distinguished work. I felt it was necessary to try and raise Australian literature out of that desolate bog, and turned to her ballad-like and tragic history and its proper costumes. (Neither Marcus Clarke nor Kingsley nor Chas. Reade nor Boldrewood attempted civil or military costume.)

Hay's contempt for tales of the 'paddock and stockyard variety' is easy to understand. They proliferate still. This is unfortunate not because they are of the paddock and stockyard, but because, unlike the pastoral for instance, they do nothing with paddock or stockyard. Rather their creators say, as Darcy Niland or Jon Cleary do today or as 'Tasma' did yesterday: 'This is a paddock and that is a stockyard, while in the foreground is a gum tree.' Hay's objection is that they attempt a realism which implies, in choice of subject, an acknowledgement of, if not a sympathy with, a democratic political attitude, like that in Furphy or even Boldrewood. This is an attitude which is defined and continually emphasized by the ability of men, and occasionally women, of various social origins to exist among new experience. When Rufus Dawes, in *For the Term of his Natural Life*, holds off starvation both from himself and from the party with whom he is marooned, he does it not from inherited position or power, but because he knows his way around: 'Maurice Frere's authority of gentility soon succumbed to Rufus Dawes's authority of knowledge.'[1] Hay, on the other hand, was writing of

an age of stiff and laudable pedantry; when Adolphus and Achilles were Christian names of the vulgar; when man, in a fine endeavour to ornament his speech, to elevate his person, to 'exalt his Maker', often dropped to mere, cold precisionism—even hypocrisy; when common women read Scott, and spread his poems by the heart. We can afford to laugh—we, who, in our own time, with our wild equalizing of human temperaments, are threatened with a drab end of formlessness![2]

Thus Hay's concern with form expresses itself in his letter to Miss Hooper as a concern for 'proper costumes . . . civil or

[1] *For the Term of his Natural Life*, p. 197. [2] *Escape*, p. 80.

military'. Costume announces the differences men wish to perpetuate among themselves. Sir William Heans, with his eye-glass, 'his high black collarless stock, matchless claw-hammer, plaid breeks and hunting air',[1] is, in Howarth's words, 'a wealthy Irish baronet transported for the abduction of a married woman, one of his own rank, who had accused him to save her own reputation'.[2] Of this event, Howarth quotes Hay as saying: 'I had to find a crime that I could bear in a man for hero.'

Heans is befriended by the Hyde-Shaxtons. Matilda Hyde-Shaxton is his cousin, and her husband finally becomes the Commandant of the prison at Port Arthur. Heans falls in love with Matilda, and with her help attempts his first escape. He fails, and is assigned as a servant to Charles Oughtryn, himself a former convict. He becomes gentleman instructor to Oughtryn's nearly blind daughter, Abelia. Their home is the former house, or cottage, of Governor Collins, who died, or was murdered, there. During his stay, Heans receives from Mrs. Quaid, his former landlady, his treasured copies of Plutarch, books which she had bought from a soldier years before. He finds written inside them a clue to Governor Collins's possible murderer, the convict Walter Surridge, whose escape route through the caves above Oughtryns' stables he also discovers. Two others at Oughtryn's place are interested in Walter Surridge: Conapanny, an old aboriginal woman, and Spafield, a soldier posted to prevent Heans's escape. It transpires that Conapanny, a princess of her tribe, had loved Surridge, who had perished in his escape tunnel; and that Spafield, as the boy Spars, had seen Collins die, perhaps murdered by Surridge. Spafield was also Mrs. Quaid's bookseller and the books had belonged to Collins. Making use of Surridge's tunnel, Heans attempts another escape, but is prevented by Abelia's cries for help, as Spafield assaults her in some vigorous but uncertain manner. Heans returns to kill Spafield only in self-defence we are to understand, and is consequently sent to Port Arthur. He eventually escapes with the clandestine help of Commandant Hyde-Shaxton himself, and is guided through the scrub by Conapanny to a waiting boat. He is last heard of in the South of France, living a retired and peaceful life. The *diabolus ex machina* who thwarts Heans for so long and who is responsible for

[1] *Escape*, p. 5. [2] Introduction, p. xii.

stationing Spafield at Oughtryn's place, is Mr Daunt, the Chief of Police. He and Heans, Morris Miller tells us, 'secretly loathe one another as contenders for the sole pleasure of a woman's society'.[1]

Miller, who sees the novel as mainly a 'socio-domestic drama', appears to suggest in his conclusion, in the phrase of the romantic novelist, that *The Escape of the Notorious Sir William Heans* is an eternal triangle. It breaks only with Daunt's death from a heart-attack as he is on the point of defending whatever honour a Chief of Police may be thought to possess. His antagonist is Hyde-Shaxton, who is defending his wife's honour by impugning Daunt's. The fragments of the triangle that remain, Heans and Matilda, are thus free only to part.

Summarized in this way, the novel appears as fifth-rate as any of the 'paddock and stockyard variety' Hay despised and believed he had bettered. While such an appearance would be unfair, possibly to both, it is worth recalling that Hay's novel was published in 1919, after Freud, Kafka, Eliot, and the First World War. To read it with this in mind is to wonder sometimes whether Hay had even heard of the French Revolution. What he did in his attempt to revitalize Australian literature was not merely to go back to earlier models, in particular to Scott, but to invest the age he was describing with all the values he felt his own lacked. But Scott was a historical novelist precisely because the values he admired, like those he distrusted, were still close enough to matter, both to him and to the nation whose history he was relating. As Georg Lukács remarks, referring to Scott, 'without a felt relationship to the present, a portrayal of history is impossible'.[2] Scott's concern for 'proper costumes', for which he has been criticized as much as he criticized Richardson, is understandable. The English prohibition after the '45 Rebellion on the wearing of the tartan was an attempt to sever the present from the past. At the time Scott wrote such severance was still incomplete. The values which that costume distinguished were still alive. To Hay and to Australia in 1919, these values were not close; they were what the age lacked—an age when even the army had exchanged its colourful jackets for the same khaki the enemy wore. Such

[1] 'The Historical Background', p. xxxiv.

[2] *The Historical Novel*, London 1962, p. 53.

values were acquired not among men, who are the living proof that the past is 'the prehistory of the present',[1] but from books. It is no coincidence that the one object in the novel nearest to becoming a symbol is itself a book, Plutarch's *Lives*. For Hay, as for his hero, Mr. Daunt's essential evil is not that he contends for Matilda Hyde-Shaxton's company, or love, but that he is an upstart, ambitious for the privilege, and envying its inherited nature, of 'the good folk, to whose level he had won'.[2] It is no surprise that Heans should early liken him to a 'fine reptile', or that another, equally well-bred, should refer to him as Satan. Hay's upper classes often appear to the reader, and sometimes to themselves, more like injured gods than real people.

Realism is only incidental to Hay's novel. Unlike Marcus Clarke, he is not concerned with the wickednesses of the System. They are seldom mentioned except as an abstract called Evil, against which the Good (Matilda) complains. We are never told what Heans is escaping from, or any of the details of his failure, or even what it feels like to fail and be punished. But the novel is not without some of those appurtenances of realism which, as Lukács reminds us, 'Pushkin cruelly ridiculed in the work of Scott's incompetent imitators'.[3] As Morris Miller has shown, it is possible to find one's way around old Hobart and what remains of Port Arthur using only Hay's novel as a guide. We are told the names of the grubs and other wild life which Conapanny catches to sustain Heans and herself on their last journey. We are encouraged to hope that we might do the same in like circumstances, so long as we had the novel to consult. In the same fashion we are told whether Heans, in the caves or Oughtryn's haunted house, looked left or right, or to the left of his right, or the right of his left. Unhappily, for part of the time we do not know whether he is coming down feet first or on his head; nor do we know whether the directions are given from Heans's perhaps inverted point of view, or from that of an omniscient author observing Heans. Not only is the effect finally stultifying, it also emphasizes Hay's inability to distinguish between himself and his hero at those times when it would have been easiest as well as most useful to have done so. *The Escape of the Notorious Sir William Heans*

[1] *The Historical Novel*, London 1962, p. 53.
[2] *Escape*, p. 145. [3] Op. cit., p. 53.

is no more a realistic novel than it is a historical novel: rather, it is a 'Romance of Tasmania', as Hay subtitled it.

To call a work of fiction a Romance is to invoke Hawthorne's shade. It duly appears for Howarth, and he tells us Hay read Hawthorne. There are certainly superficial correspondences. In the large section set at Oughtryn's place, where Governor Collins died, or was murdered in his chair, a secret on his lips, *The House of the Seven Gables* comes to mind. Madame Ruth, the mysterious convict woman who is punished for a crime of love, who paints and makes herself useful among her fellows, may recall Hester Prynne. Even the Puritan atmosphere is invoked when Madame Ruth says to Matilda Hyde-Shaxton: 'I protest, you are as stern as the gentlemen. Do you too tell me I can sadden myself at my will? The gentlemen are John Knoxes, every one of them; to them a woman's will is her one reason.'[1] Certainly, too, Mr. Daunt's concern for his prisoners, at least for some of them, seems as assiduous as that of Judge Pyncheon for his unfortunate cousins in *The House of the Seven Gables*; and his end is the same. All this, however, was available in Scott, whom Hay openly admits to admiring, and whose precedents he followed. A grim old house, as Hay calls Oughtryn's place, is the New World equivalent of Scott's grim old castles, Lochleven, for instance, where Mary Stuart was imprisoned,[2] an event which Hay twice indirectly recalls. He remarks that Matilda was compassionate towards Daunt and his ambitiousness, 'as history tells great Queens have been of those prisoners who had been their companions, and who had turned aside to be unkind to them, even "to grudge the continuance of their lives" '.[3] Again, Spafield, the soldier, is likened to 'the Black-adder to some official Bothwell,'[4] but this time Heans is responsible. Heans has the advantage over all other Australian fictional heroes in that his aunt actually knew Scott: '. . . she would meet Scott wherever she went according to her own account, though, as she would say, "he has lately written such dreadful things about us women!" "The great poet", she would say, "was there with Lady Buccleugh: I knew him by his *déshabillé* and faithful eyes".'[5] The 'faithful eyes' are important, they are the marks of a gentleman. But which novels was Heans's

[1] Ibid., p. 295.
[2] See Sir Walter Scott, *The Abbot*.
[3] *Escape*, p. 292.
[4] Ibid., p. 227.
[5] Ibid., p. 6.

aunt thinking of? Although Scott is always penetratingly exact about women who are socially unimportant, to ladies he is never less than deadeningly polite, as every critic since Balzac has complained. Rose Bradwardine, the first of these well-bred nonentities, is merely the fictionalized version of the Lady of the Lake. Hay follows the habit unquestioningly in his Matilda Hyde-Shaxton, but seems to regret the type's rarity in life:

She seemed, in a word, to have an unnatural distaste for 'practising', even where the interests of those she loved were concerned. This is, I suspect, as much as should be expected of any good woman, just as we may well expect something more, in like difficulty, than the lying, stab-in-the-back methods, the treacherous use of youth's belief in her saintship, of the ordinary wicked one. Surely life holds few contrasting facts so confusing as its vulgar-minded woman—than which no man can be so little or so base—and its angel, rich or poor.[1]

Only the angels play much part in Hay's novel; and they are as ineffectual as one would expect where women are divided into the ordinarily wicked and unnaturally good.

As for the superficial likeness between the death of Colonel Pyncheon and that of Governor Collins, it is enough to refer to Hay's footnote:

The Author may be accused by some, of confounding fiction with reality. He therefore thinks it necessary to state that the circumstances of the death of Governor Collins as described in the text are, as far as he knows, entirely imaginary. But it is well known that the Governor was found dead in his chair about the date mentioned, and how he died is still a mystery. A similar note to this is to be found in Sir Walter Scott's 'Waverley', explanatory to a parallel historical narrative half-true, half-unknown.[2]

This note perhaps also tells us something about Hawthorne, but nothing at all about the moral significance of 'Maule's curse'. Earlier, of Madame Ruth, Hay tells us that her 'life-sentence had been given her for homicide, and the history of her crime closely resembled that of Lucy Ashton, or rather the legend on which the great weaver, Scott, wove his saddest and most poetical tapestry. She had shot her dissipated husband.'[3] When we allow that Madame Ruth is a less important character in Hay's novel than Hester Prynne in Hawthorne's, we may still

[1] *Escape*, p. 40. [2] Ibid., p. 225. [3] Ibid., p. 112.

remark on the absence of any moral regeneration in Madame Ruth or, what is more important, the feeling anywhere in the novel that there is any need for moral regeneration. One reason is that we are never convinced that there was any moral degeneration in the first place, either in Madame Ruth or in the System. We are told that she killed her husband, and the fact is softened by the knowledge that he was dissipated: the case involves special pleading even at its start. We learn nothing more about her, except that she paints and is useful in unspecified ways to her fellow prisoners. But there can be no real comparison between Hay and Hawthorne; New England, founded to the glory of God, turned into its opposite, and Australia, founded to the glory of nothing, became the shame of many; and the violence of the System on which Australia was founded nowhere impinges in its ugly detail on Madame Ruth, any more than it does on Sir William Heans. All that we are told is that Madame Ruth is rescued from her Australian captivity. Like Heans, she never suffers from the system of solitary confinement which Commandant Hyde-Shaxton designed with Heans's help. Her rescuer is not the Earl of Daisley, who had followed her in his own ship to Australia, but Mr. Carnt, who is of her own station in life. In the same way, Heans is freed, not by Mr. Carnt, who tried, nor by Abelia Oughtryn, who was sympathetic, nor certainly by his own exertions, for his code rendered him incapable of any, even of knocking a garrulous parson on the head. Heans is freed by the Hyde-Shaxtons, members of his own class. Matilda, to show her continuing love for or fidelity towards Heans, suggests to her husband that he should himself show Heans how to escape; Hyde-Shaxton, as an indication of his love for or fidelity towards Matilda, readily obliges. None of this is brought about by a recognition in the Hyde-Shaxtons that Heans has been morally regenerated as the result of his experiences. Therefore, there can be no useful comparison between Hay's novel and Hawthorne's *The Marble Faun*, a comparison which Howarth proposes.

Nor does Madame Ruth's reference to the 'gentlemen' all being John Knoxes justify any real comparisons with Hawthorne. Knox was a Scotsman, not one of the Pilgrim Fathers. Though Scott is aware of Knox's influences on Scotland, even on his own father, he nowhere convinces us that he understood it or felt it personally the way James Hogg, say, in *The Confessions of a Justified Sinner* understood and felt it. He did, however, understand patriotism, and in such novels as *The Monastery* and *Woodstock* this understanding has the function which religious fanaticism has in some of his other novels. Hay, on the other hand, imitating the 'great weaver' yet unable to understand fanaticism of any kind, religious or political, relies on the mere mention of Knox to disguise his own deficiency. Of the 'gentlemen', those who worked the System, we meet only one, Mr. Daunt, and of his prisoners only two, Madame Ruth and Heans. His main concern is with Heans; and envy and ambition are the motives he supplies. The novel contains no further evidence of Knox or the Puritan belief, which permeates *The Scarlet Letter*, that 'a woman's will is her one reason'.

Hay quite openly displays his debt to Scott. Talfourd's play, *Glencoe; or the Fate of the Macdonalds*, which is introduced into the later stages of the novel, was itself sufficiently indebted to Scott's poem on the subject to be a dramatic pastiche. Of Port Arthur, Hay mentions 'the still arm of a ramparted and foliaged sea much resembling the landscape of Loch Lomond'.[1] The phrase owes its origin to literature, not to experience, for there is no resemblance at all. Hay curiously seems to recognize this, possibly because he looked up his Scott again: he immediately withdraws his former emphasis on the 'foliaged sea' by saying, 'Perhaps the mountains were a trace too weird and goblin in shape, too close and darkly massed with trees.' Whatever a goblin-shaped mountain is, Ben Lomond was bald even in Johnson's time.

On Heans's last visit to the prison chapel, when Matilda nods to him to show that he need only walk away to that freedom which members of his own class have decided is more important than the System they have devised for those less fortunate, 'A hymn was sung, a stern old hymn by Sir Walter Scott'.[2] The hymn is evidently the one which begins,

> That day of wrath, that dreadful day,
> When heaven and earth shall pass away . . .

We are not told this, however; nor are we told what significance the hymn might have. The only significance it can have lies,

[1] *Escape*, p. 368. [2] Ibid., p. 383.

not in its sternness—for there are many sterner to be found in *Hymns Ancient and Modern*—but in its author. The reference is a purely literary one. Similarly, even Conapanny, an aborigine, though a princess, is at one with Heans's aged aunt, the friend of Lady Buccleugh, in counting *Rokeby* among her favourite reading.

This emphasis on Hay's superfical indebtedness to Scott is intended to show that the novel exists within a persistent tradition in Australian fiction; but it also helps to understand it and value it properly. The task has been complicated and made more difficult by what Hay and others have written about the novel, but even more by the nature of that indebtedness. Despite his many references to Scott and his wish to make both the history and geography of Australia resemble Scotland's, Hay understands his model and Australia less than most of his predecessors with whom we have dealt and who are separated off from him in Morris Miller's *Bibliography* of Australian literature as 'Colonial' writers. He fails, as they did not, to recognize what was new in the history and geography of his country; and he compounds his failure by his inability to recognize the true worth of Scott. Balzac first defined that worth in his criticism of Stendhal's *La Chartreuse de Parme*, which Georg Lukács summarizes thus: 'the broad delineation of manners and circumstances attendant upon events, the dramatic character of action and, in close connection with this, the new and important role of dialogue in the novel.'[1] In Hay's novel there are no events, no crises, no conflicts, even between the prisoner and his circumstances.

One reason for this is Hay's choice of hero. As Lukács reminds us, 'The "hero" of a Scott novel is always a more or less average English gentleman'; but Hay's hero is the 'notorious' Sir William Heans, an apparently Byronic hero, a philanderer, an adulterer: 'It is strange how the world will give a man a second chance—especially if he be a good-looking one. This perennial instance of man's patience is no more evident in our male clubs and criminal courts than in the cabinets of the women.'[2] The equation of the world with clubs, courts, and cabinets is racily alliterative, but narrow; yet it is in this world, narrower than Byron's or Scott's, that Sir William

[1] Op. cit., p. 31. [2] *Escape*, p. 3.

is introduced to us. He is well born, one who, according to the Earl of Daisley in his unlikely Australian disguise as the Jewish-looking Homely O'Crone, was 'a man, by repute, peculiarly sought after by women'.[1] He is 'pale, proud, yet still on his dignity'.[2] A little later, he is 'fine, pale, and wonderfully dignified',[2] has a 'grey, grand way', is 'pale, gentle, and handsome',[3] and soon 'unutterably dignified'. Of this, R. G. Howarth says,

> The adjective 'grey' becomes attached to Heans, as descriptive of his moods of resentment, offendedness, grief, anger, and others of that cast, varied by 'pale'. Matilda and others, too, have their characteristic emotional marks. It is a matter less of subtlety than of extremely close observation and interpretation, some of which is supplied by the novelist, some by the reader.[4]

Seldom has a reader been asked to supply so much. Howarth is asking the reader to turn the novel into a study in realism; but that it is not should be clear very early when Hay describes Matilda Hyde-Shaxton:

> Her sweet face seldom smiled. It was high, small, bright, and shyly serious. She seemed taller than she was; would have been active if she had not been delicate; and was straight as a needle. You would see her talking with someone in her drawing-room, near a chandelier, with that fine antagonistic eye of hers wild and full of a strained yearning.[5]

The observation which the reader supplies, to be later confirmed by the novelist, is that she too is pale. That Heans's paleness is in no way a 'characteristic emotional mark' is recognized by Miller when he writes: 'Every character's expression of face, whether of strength or weakness, pales somehow sometime somewhere.'[6] He resolutely attributes this general debility to the all-pervasiveness of the System; but Miller is writing from his knowledge of the System and his recollection of Marcus Clarke's *For the Term of his Natural Life*. He is obliged to do so in the first place because Hay seems to have been unable to accept details of prison life as fit for his

[1] *Escape*, p. 86. [2] Ibid., p. 5. [3] Ibid., pp. 13–14.
[4] Introduction, p. xvii. [5] *Escape*, p. 4.
[6] 'The Historical Background', p. xxiv.

kind of novel: abduction was the only crime he could accept in a hero,[1] but he was determined to see Australia's convict history as 'a romantic, deeply enthralling, and, in many cases, heroic history'.[2] In the second place, Miller is pressed by his conviction that so much paleness 'cannot be without design'. He nevertheless concludes that 'one cannot altogether cease to plead for some lessening of the adjective's repetitions'.

Of the pallid cousins, Heans and Matilda, it must be said that they begin as the Byronic hero and his consanguineous lady. They are present in McCombie's *Arabin* as they are in *For the Term of his Natural Life*; but because Hay, by using the words 'perhaps' or 'possibly' as often as he does, has been aggrandized into a 'psychological' novelist,[3] the likeness has been overlooked. The pallor, at least of the two main characters, is part of their 'proper costume'. In the absence of experience or imagination, Hay relied on his reading of Marcus Clarke, Kingsley, Charles Reade, and Boldrewood. All of these assure him that despite the Australian climate heroes are distinctively pale. Having learnt from Scott that all heroines are similarly pale, Hay seems to conclude that any character will pale when temporarily influenced by those emotions which are associated with, and even define, heroes and heroines. Misunderstanding the Byronic convention as thoroughly as he misunderstood Scott, he communicates the significance of an emotion by the word 'pale'. The result is that his novel reads like a faded medieval sampler, all the colours that once gave it emblematic meaning now reduced to a pale grey.

Heans, however, has more than his pallor to announce his literary antecedents. True to his lonely type, he had 'received slight after slight on landing'.[4] Dismounting his horse, Suffolk, which like Starlight he loves but, as a convict, is singularly and unaccountably fortunate to have, Heans is flattered by another convict:

> Behind his volatile flattery, he was significantly, if half-sneeringly hostile: a form of approach familiar to Heans from the prisoners.

[1] This was the only crime which James Ballantyne felt he could not accept in Scott's first outline of *St. Ronan's Well.*

[2] William Hay, *Herridge of Reality Swamp,* London 1907; quoted Howarth, Introduction to *Escape,* p. x.

[3] E. Morris Miller, 'The Historical Background', p. xxiv.

[4] *Escape,* p. 5.

It was as if the convict[1]—unable to help forcing the fact that he knew him, as did many in the town—would have given this man his championing as a fellow-prisoner, and one, moreover, who carried it off so cleverly, could he only have resisted the chance Heans' situation gave him of making one of the 'swell-mob' feel his position. The temptation seemed tragically irresistible.[2]

The motive for such unpleasantness, Hay seems to suggest, is class envy. Heans, however, is much more obtuse: despite the frequency of similar experiences, he never appears to learn either to expect them or to understand them. Spafield, the soldier, for instance is later sarcastic about a fainting fit from which Heans has barely recovered: 'At the moment Heans thought it singular the man should exercise his resentment when he saw he was discomposed.'[3] Fifty pages later, when Spafield has again been ungracious, we learn that Heans 'had known this type of cunning, gabbling fellow to show his fangs at sight of men of his like'. Not content with reducing a fellow to a fox, Hay adds: 'We all know the strange shock of being brought face to face with hate with no motive.'[4] It is significant that Hay not only identifies completely with his hero, but expects his readers to do so; yet the task remains impossible even for those among them who are continually exposed to similar unpleasantness. Hay appears to forget that he has already provided a motive, class envy. He also appears to forget that the Byronic hero is above all things aware of his separateness and is unsurprised by it.

So much forgetfulness needs explanation; if real, it could be easily accepted by the reader. As it is, it indicates a much more fundamental weakness in the novel: Hay is intent on turning his apparently Byronic hero into a gentleman. This transformation, which others have called 'moral regeneration', is ostensibly what the novel is about. It fails in a way that McCombie's *Arabin* for instance, does not. Although McCombie is no more a 'psychological' novelist than Hay, he does not involve himself in impossibility by confusing his types. He provides his novel with two main characters, one based, as he says, on Waverley, the other on the Byronic hero.

[1] Hay here seems to forget that Heans is also a convict.
[2] *Escape*, p. 77. [3] Ibid., p. 185.
[4] Ibid., p. 243.

Hay's recognition of the existence of the two types in literature is early illustrated in an interview between Sir John Franklin and Heans, on whose behalf Matilda has spoken:

'You will not move your proud foot thus far,' said the Governor, 'in pursuit of an honoured life!'

'Your Excellency said "honoured life",' said Heans, dropping his glass, with a wild, little bow. 'Is there such a thing? And will you find it, sir—great traveller as you are—for a convict in this town? I put little value on existence. My dignity and honour none of your laws can touch. If I lose them, I shall cry out to no one. When they are gone, the more vulgar officials can use no worse methods against me than have been used hitherto. Do not fear for me, kind sir. I am grown too old and grim' (with a bow) 'with the grey side of difficulty to play with the young ladies. The worth of a man's life—what is it? I pray you credit me with a certain happiness in my own way of it.'

To this Byronic credo, Franklin opposes that of the gentleman: 'I will give you my idea of [honour] in a man. It is that he should not wound his friends by his falling. If a man have bravery and not compunction, he is no gentleman. What to him becomes mere life, must be to his friends a perpetual tragedy.'[1] The creator of Waverley, that 'sneaking piece of imbecility', as Scott called him, would have agreed. Hay's mistake is to present Heans as the proud, friendless Byronic hero and immediately introduce him among friends. In other words, despite pallor, pride, dignity, and the rest, he is at heart a gentleman, but one who has let the side down; but the side will continue to receive him, despite his 'notoriety'. As Captain Grimes in Waugh's *Decline and Fall* says of the public schools, they may kick you out, but they will never let you down. His pallor, pride, loneliness, and 'notoriety' are not Heans's 'proper costume', merely bits and pieces Hay has salvaged from his reading. He is using a convention without understanding the circumstances that once gave it meaning; and without this understanding, he cannot invest it with any new meaning. One phrase particularly exemplifies Hay's confusion of types, and produces in the reader a response normally elicited by farce. Heans has sacrificed his own chance of escape in order to free Abelia from the improper hands of Spafield. Clutching a stable fork, he strove 'to hide the calm trembling

[1] Ibid., p. 81.

of his hands'.[1] The Byronic hero is always calm: 'His blood in temperate seeming now would flow',[2] whereas, as Sir John Franklin explains, a gentleman trembles for his friends.

Hay leaves us in no doubt as to what a gentleman is. Even the lowly Oughtryn has a definition: '... putting aside notableness—it's him that cheats less than he could—including of his mortal life.'[3] In sacrificing himself to Abelia's safety and earlier to Matilda's honour when Daunt impugns it, Heans 'cheats less than he could'. His own view of the gentlemanly code is expressed in a letter to a friend: '. . . a fellow may engage himself in being simply a generous, temperate, and noble person, passing his leisure in reading and talking for entertainment, and yet fall short of a difficult ideal.' Hay adds: 'It will serve our turn to suppose he engaged himself in some effort of this nature.'[4] The significance of Scott's 'faithful eyes' is now apparent: compunction, generosity, and faithfulness are one and the same gentlemanly quality.

This quality is, of course, laudable if its complexity is acknowledged; but to Hay, as to Heans the quality is simplified by the nature of the friends. All are from the one class, as they are not in Scott: even Waverley recognizes the 'superiority of knowledge' which Donald Bean Lean possesses. There is no suggestion that compunction could be, or even need be, extended beyond the one social group which is never endangered by economic hardship. On the one occasion when Heans does appear to sacrifice himself to the lower orders, in the form of Abelia, not only is Abelia a woman, but she has hopes of being a lady. Heans is employed by Oughtryn so that she may learn that code which has been diminished neither by his 'notoriety' nor by imprisonment nor by any of the circumstances which made Australia what it was in the eighteen-forties. Because this quality is never tested, it reduces the novel to a stasis. The condition is emphasized by the fact that Heans, as Howarth says, has been 'transported for the abduction of a married woman, one of his own rank, who had accused him to save her own reputation'. This is to say that the 'notorious' Sir William Heans had kept faith with her and had accepted his punishment to preserve her honour. Thus the change which the hero is

[1] *Escape*, p. 345. [2] *Lara*, Canto I, xviii. [3] *Escape*, p. 304.
[4] Ibid., p. 406.

supposed to undergo as a result of his suffering is as illusory as the suffering itself. Daunt's particular misfortune is that he only partially recognizes the indestructibility of the '*ton*' of a gentleman born. To Captain Sturt, who has commented on Heans: '. . . you mean you're sceptical about his gentility?', Daunt replies: 'Not of its endurance, but of its honesty. That man will fight me with it as long as he can scrape a satin stock together . . . It's wonderful how long they keep it up—almost as if it were part of the blood.'[1] This is indeed what it is. It cannot be acquired in any other way even by a man as assiduous and ambitious as Mr. Daunt.

Having introduced the Byronic stage-properties, however, Hay does not fail to supply his hero with another change to remind the reader that something is supposed to have happened to him. Thus Heans acquires a 'port-wine face' at a time when everyone else is paling into significance. His matchless claw-hammer, plaid breeks, and the rest are replaced towards the end by a 'second-class suit of smooth cords, a sort of collar, and that sort of clever cravat which tries to hide a linenless shirt. No cane. No glass. No gloves.'[2] Such is the measure of the man's degradation under the miseries of the System. Well may Commandant Shaxton feel 'much hipped at seeing how little he was really altered'.[2] Rufus Dawes had no skin on his back; and we are told why, and how he came to lose it. More than this, we see a spiritual and mental change, from the gentleman who values his title of 'Mr.' and kept his mother's secret, to the Byronic hero who entrusted his own to no one. Hay and Clarke are using the same Byronic convention, but Clarke infuses his re-creation of the System with a moral anger intended to prevent its recrudescence and thereby enlarges the convention till it matches its Byronic sources. Georg Lukács says of the treatment Pushkin and Stendhal accorded the Byronic hero: 'They interpreted the problem of the eccentricity of this type in a social-historical, objective-epic way: that is, they saw the present historically and revealed all the social determinants of the tragedy (or tragi-comedy) of this protest.'[3] This is also Clarke's way. Of Scott's 'recognition or rather sense of the eccentricity of this type', Lukács remarks that its result is that

[1] *Nature*, p. 140. [2] Ibid., p. 370.
[3] Op. cit., p. 34.

he 'endeavours to portray the struggles and antagonisms of history by means of characters who, in their psychology and destiny, always represent social trends and historical forces'. Because of his sense of what is 'proper' in literature and his demure attitude to history, and, one suspects, to life, Hay manages to do neither.

But it would be wrong to suppose that Hay's lack of dynamism is anything but deliberate. Incapable he may have been of doing otherwise, a view his other novels support; but the incapacity arises from a deliberate, and what his letter to Miss Hooper suggests, was a necessary denial of progress. The division of the novel into three parts, 'High Water', 'Neap Tide', and 'Low Water', seems to emphasize time's progression, but really does the opposite. It insists that the history of man is cyclical: that what happened yesterday may not happen today, but is bound to happen tomorrow. The course of Hay's narrative is also cyclical, unchronological, indirect, and often circumstantial, so much so that some readers have made oblique and on the whole misleading references to Henry James's naturalism. It is burdened with the language of flowers: valerian 'for hope', mignonette, ragged Robin; Daunt's boots 'bruise the rosemary', 'the thorn of a white lady slits his sleeve'; Matilda is 'beautiful as a lily', etc. When mannerisms like these are mere literary playfulness on the part of 'us lovers of Nature',[1] the attempts at naturalism, i.e. authorial absence, or at least impartiality or ignorance, appear incongruous. When they are seriously meant, as when crane's-bill is crushed so that Heans's 'track was starred with little drops of red',[2] or when we are reminded that red valerian, 'for hope', is also called 'bloody warrior', we recognize the dead literary reference to a world which, for the mad Ophelia at least, was reassuringly static with emblems. We respond to the literary reference, perhaps, by recreating that world which was emblematic because unchanging and unambiguous. Yet at the same time we are being asked to accept Heans as a complex inhabitant of a complicated world, one in which change can occur. We finally abandon the attempt when we recall that this strange Australian world, at least in its flora, is older than a Tudor cottage garden. Though climatically Tasmania does in parts resemble Westmorland, as Heans

[1] *Escape*, pp. 102–3. [2] Ibid., p. 253.

is happy to remark, it also has its own flora which, to the unliterary visitor, is more noticeable than that imported from abroad. It can be argued that Hay was being true to his facts: that the early settlers often did recreate those gardens they had been too poor to keep up in England; but it can also be argued that in the eighteen-forties, Australia's historical and geographical circumstances destroyed the dream that Australia was another England. The wattle was more significant than red valerian. To believe that Heans is changed by his Australian experiences, we would require more than the withered language of European flowers.

All this disparate evidence makes it fair to suggest that Hay, far from being concerned with the 'moral order of life' and 'moral development', is concerned rather to assert that the social order should not change. Unlike Scott, he has not 'made his own land romantic'; for, though the country is Australia, the world, as he has learnt of it from books, remains in its 'proper costume'. Matilda, extending her sympathy to Madame Ruth, can say of her prison bars that they 'shut so much out that we might not have seen or been vexed with'.[1] Thus the Factory, at least for a visitor, becomes a nunnery, but without its Elizabethan ambiguity. For Hay, an Australian born and bred, but with a Cambridge education, a private income and a country house, his library had become a monastic cell.

Though it may be only an unfortunate coincidence that no great fiction has come from such a source, in *The Escape of the Notorious Sir William Heans* there may also be evidence that Hay had to choose the lesser form of romance—a chaste love-affair set in the age of caste—because he could not write anything else. If we momentarily accept Howarth's theory of moral progress, there is one incident which assumes more importance than any other. Heans, hearing Abelia's cries for help as Spafield assaults her, comes down from his cave above the stable and rescues her. This is the occasion when more is demanded of him than an inherited class response, which can be said to explain his defence of Matilda against Daunt's suspicions. Abelia is the daughter of an ex-convict, a 'drab' in her father's description, and almost blind. In other words although Heans has been instructing her in how to be a lady

[1] Ibid., p. 298.

she can be considered the antithesis of Matilda. Heans's response, if it is to convince, must be to her endangered humanity. This is how Hay describes the incident:

> The fellow staggered upright, the facings of his coat vying with her groping visage. He pulled her near to him. Heans saw her face drop. She struggled. He kissed her poor, weak eyes. She gave a slight cry, and he put his hand upon her mouth.
>
> There came a groan from the wall.
>
> Sir William Heans began to return, and with a side-wrench struggled back behind the sag. Somewhere here he stopped an instant, and in a sad distinct voice said, 'Be calm, miss. I am close beside you. You will soon have aid.' He added, as calmly: 'God pity you, you beggarly villain.' Looking out again, he saw the girl duck and (taking advantage, perhaps, of a spasm of amazement in the red-coat) near pull apart, wrestling a few steps over to the wall, but in the wrong direction, to the east of the port-hole. Spafield wavered slowly after her, his steady leaden glance on the wall behind. 'Ah,' said he, swift and harshly, 'I hears an old cat mewing. So that's where my noble was? I thought you was a dook—very near. You're coming to interfere between me and the drab!' He caught the girl again, and she hid her face. He dragged her hands away and again covered her mouth. The feeble girl struggled back, cowering into a corner of the black door.
>
> Sir William swiftly pushed his way down under the sloping roof, and when presently he reached the cavern midway between the narrows, he altered his posture head-downward, and so slid and struggled his way to the narrows below, into which—retaining his balance of mind I know not how—he entered on his chest and stomach, feeling for the hand-fasts, and guiding his person roughly from left to right, and vice-versa, by his recollection of the ascent; steadily at first, for fear of a sprained hand, but, catching, with the fourth hand-fast, a glimmer of straw through the hole at the bottom, pushing and sliding with a jam and a heavy fall against the mouth or funnel; thence, flinging, rather than climbing into the cavern . . .[1]

This 'great scene' as Howarth calls it, 'enfolded in a richness of detail and setting unexcelled in our fiction', continues for another ten pages and culminates in Spafield's death. Abelia, whose danger is the cause of everything—including Heans's regeneration—is mentioned three times: once when Heans tells her to run away; once when Spafield threatens her if she does; and once when Heans, in the chapter's last sentence, says: 'Do

[1] *Escape*, pp. 343–4.

not weep, miss.' This suggests that Abelia is only incidental to the struggle; which in turn would suggest that the struggle has another cause. It is not a struggle between good and bad, so much as a struggle between knighthood and the 'fellow', who before he dies has been reduced to 'a grunt and a whinny'.[1] Heans's 'God pity you, you beggarly villain' and the villain's reply: 'I hears an old cat mewing. I though you was a dook—very near', almost become an occasion for music-hall cheers and hisses as Hay presents his version of the class war. We are not surprised that 'there came a groan from the wall'.

That drama is intended, despite the puppetry, is evident in the changes of style. The first paragraph is built up of short simple sentences, the third of dialogue, the fourth of long complex sentences. The artifice is not only obvious, but ineffectual. 'The fellow staggered upright' is unclear. Spafield seems to have been lying down and is staggering into an upright position; but this is not so. He has just been described as standing with his 'loving hand' on Abelia's mouth. Presumably the sentence means: 'He staggered.' We do not know why. Unless the reader is aware—and there seems no reason why he should be—of Spafield's 'proper costume', 'the facings of his coat vying with her visage' is also unclear. Is Abelia, hot, cold, or bruised, red, white, or blue? 'He pulled her near to him' sounds clear enough; but he has a hand over her face. How much nearer is it possible for them to be? And how is it accomplished? If he is standing behind her, which would seem the probable position, it is impossible for him to 'pull' her any closer. 'Wrench' would seem more precise a word. 'Heans saw her face drop' is similarly meaningless. It is a cliché, where it is not a disruptive joke. 'She struggled', despite its apparent simplicity, again poses the question: How? in what manner?

The last paragraph, in which the clauses are run together to indicate the relentless continuity of Heans's descent, is a hotchpotch of information. It leaves the reader exhausted, dizzy, aware only that 'he entered on his chest and stomach' while 'retaining his balance of mind I know not how'.

And so on. Despite Howarth's enjoinder that 'there is subtlety in almost every line of the book, which compels minute reading', to go on with such criticism would be useless. Far

[1] Ibid., p. 347.

from being a dramatic scene of moral regeneration, it is a description of a fatal brawl between a gentleman and a lout. The reader can no more believe in it than he can in the puppets locked in their wooden struggle. Eventually he feels that he, like them, is having not one but both legs pulled.

10 'Henry Handel Richardson'[1], *The Fortunes of Richard Mahony*

ALTHOUGH Henry Handel Richardson conceived *The Fortunes of Richard Mahony*[2] as a whole, it was written and originally published in three parts: *Australia Felix* in 1917, *The Way Home* in 1925, and *Ultima Thule* in 1929. In the first part Richard Mahony, a twenty-eight-year-old Anglo-Irishman persuaded by tales of Australia Felix to adandon the medical profession in the Old World for the 1850 Ballarat gold-fields, has also abandoned his brief life as a digger. Its rewards have matched neither its promises nor his expectations; he becomes a store-keeper on the diggings in the hope of a competency large enough to take him back home. For he believed that Australia was still 'too great and ambitious for affection, yet not great enough for respect'.[3]

Mahony's younger English friend, Purdy, once his well-fed but lowly-housed school-comrade in Dublin, persuades him to visit the Beamish Family Hotel, which, besides Mr. and Mrs. Beamish and their two daughters Tilly and Jinny, contains Polly, or Mary, Turnham, a sixteen-year-old English girl. She is one of a large family of children. The eldest of this family, John, is a successful businessman in Melbourne, who, during the novel's progress, achieves political eminence. Over the years two other brothers arrive, one feckless and a wastrel, the other dependable and eventually a bank manager. Because their mother is in England, Mary becomes their confidante and comforter. Purdy sees her as his friend's future wife. Mahony meets her, falls in love with her, and takes this pretty 'child' as his 'girl-wife'.

Back in the Ballarat shop, or shack, they find business declines, partly because Mahony thinks it unprincipled to sell alcohol, partly because the diggers remember that Mahony criticized their cause at the Eureka rising, in which Purdy, full of enthusiasm, has been accidentally wounded by one of his own side.

[1] The pseudonym of Ethel Florence Lindesay, who married J. G. Robertson, the German scholar.

[2] London 1930.

[3] Charles Darwin, *The Voyage of the Beagle*, 1839; London 1961, p. 434.

Mahony removes the bullet, his scorn intensified, his business declining. He also unwillingly returns to doctoring when his wife miscarries. He saves her but is too late to save the child. Sued by a Melbourne supplier for payment of goods never delivered, Mahony wins his case with the help of a sharp lawyer, Henry Ocock, and the pitifully inept character presented in court by the old, drunken, and broken supplier. Disheartened by the principles of the law, which are also those of trade, and by shrinking custom, he resumes practice. He becomes rich enough to amaze his wife by announcing that he is ready to return home with her, to England.

The second part of the novel, *The Way Home*, covers two journeys to and from England. The Mahonys return to Australia the first time because neither can come to terms with industrial England, or with the rural class-system, or with their mothers' small worlds. Back in Australia Mahony finds that bad shares he has held for years have miraculously gone up, and he has both wealth and leisure. There is money enough to fit the ambitions of a fallen Anglo-Irish gentleman, and time enough to ponder man's spiritual aspirations. Renouncing doctoring and, to his wife's dismay, embracing spiritualism, he plants himself a garden round a splendid house, decks his wife's beauty in rich clothes, and fathers a family. This is his Eden, though he calls it Ultima Thule. His capacity for quiet enjoyment is short-lived, however. He moves his family once more back to England, this time to London society and the sights of Europe, to both of which money and the friends of money give him the key. Climbing the tower of Strasbourg cathedral, he discovers what his wife has long suspected, that he has no head for heights, despite his constant need to try to scale them. Only in Venice does he feel at home, the city with neither streets nor heights to challenge him, the ancient water-borne city where merchant princes had flourished, Goethe lived, and Wagner died. Mahony, with his passion for music, sailing, and bathing, happy to follow the advice of Conrad's Stein, 'in the destructive element immerse', instead receives news that the stockbroker to whom, on Purdy's recommendation, he had entrusted his money and shares, has sold the scrip and fled to America. *The Way Home*, its title as ironic as *Australia Felix*, ends with Mahony returning to Australian poverty, his wife and family to follow.

The third part, *Ultima Thule*, completes the irony of fate. Mahony spends what money he has left on a mortgage and withholds the knowledge from his wife. Older and out of skill, he returns to doctoring, first in Melbourne, then in the bush, then back in Melbourne again, each attempt worse than the last. His gentlemanly ambitions, his instinctive need to try to scale heights, are taken for pretensions, and he offends by his brusqueness the people of a country he feels has wronged him. One of his daughters dies and he is powerless to save her, which further undermines his own and his patients' confidence. Trying to contact the spirit of the dead child, he scares the woman who looks after him while his wife is in Melbourne recuperating with her friend Tilly Beamish, who is now, after a rich widowhood, Purdy's disillusioned wife. The woman says the house is haunted, that she has seen the devil. Mahony's practice declines to nothing. After illness and an attempt at suicide, Mahony returns to Melbourne to become port doctor, his job being, ironically, to pronounce on those unfit to enter Australia. It also involves his putting to sea in a small boat in all weathers, which he would once have enjoyed, but now neither the task nor the symbolism fits him. He slips on the deck, injures himself, and is attacked once more by the vertigo he has recognized and sometimes acknowledged. His oddity develops into abnormality. In order to get money, his wife decides to take in boarders, thus offending the pretensions that are by now becoming Mahony's only reality. He decides to revenge himself on her by burning what remains of their shares along with the house from which he cannot escape. She returns from taking the children to bathe, leaving them behind to enjoy the warm sensations of a country they have known from birth. She finds Mahony laughing hysterically and shouting her name in the smoke-filled house. Her arrival precipitates his final scream of insanity and the paralysing stroke that accompanies it.

Mary eventually has him certified insane and, to keep her family, learns to be a postmistress. Through the good nature and good offices of Henry Ocock, the sharp lawyer turned politician, Mary is given a job in the bush. To this post-office, as much shack as shop, she brings the enfeebled Mahony after much difficulty with the medical and legal authorities. To them he is a raving lunatic. To himself he is 'Richard Townshend Mahony, F.R.C.S., M.D., Edinburgh, R. T. Mahony, M.D. and Accoucheur; Specialist for the Diseases of Women; Consulting Physician to the Ballarat Hospital',[1] whose accomplishments are exhausted only when his thin voice can sing them no more. To his wife, he is her child-husband. On his death he is buried 'within sound of what he had perhaps loved best on earth —the open sea';[2] while 'The rich and kindly earth of his adopted country absorbed his perishable body, as the country itself had never contrived to make its own, his wayward, vagrant spirit'.[3]

Such a brief summary inevitably diminishes what is grandly conceived; but it may draw attention to the structural firmness which in more than eight hundred pages tends to be unnoticed beneath the rich fabric it supports. In a summary, the novel appears to rely for its unity solely on the character of Richard Mahony, whose name dominates its title; but his fortunes have about them a fearful symmetry. Materially he goes from big house to shack to big house to shack again. Spiritually, he goes from the idealism and unquestioning love of early manhood, which force the change from the big house and make the shack bearable; through the mature assurance that wealth confers in order that maturity, assurance, and wealth may be questioned; to the aged certainty of spiritual salvation which allows a broken mind and a broken body to inhabit a shack contentedly and with a sense of wonder unimpaired. Having thrown away the chloroform with which he had planned to kill himself, Mahony experiences a

> beatific certainty that his pain, his sufferings . . . had their niche in God's Scheme (pain the bond that linked humanity: not in joy, in sorrow alone were we yoke-fellows)—that all creation, down to the frailest protoplasmic thread, was one with God; and he himself, and everything he had been and would ever be, as surely contained in God, as a drop of water in a wave, a note of music in a mighty cadence. More: he now yearned as avidly for this submergedness, this union of all things living, as he had hitherto shrunk from it.[4]

That this vision should be conveyed in terms of Mahony's twin passions, for water and for music, illustrates Richardson's care

[1] 'Henry Handel Richardson', *The Fortunes of Richard Mahony*, London. 1961, p. 821 (hereafter referred to as *Fortunes*).

[2] *Fortunes*, p. 830. [3] Ibid., p. 831. [4] Ibid., p. 740.

for structure. After this experience, Mahony appears to his son 'just like the picture of Tomfool in the "King of Lear" '.[1] In his aged madness, he becomes, it seems to his wife, a peaceful child, re-experiencing that childhood which the novel omits, but without those pains of childhood which Mahony recalls throughout his adult life and tries, ever less successfully as his own fortune works itself out, to protect his son against.

Throughout the novel there are structural parallels of this kind, ironies of fate or variations on the theme of fortune. Australia Felix is not happy. The glittering gold is there, but not for Mahony until he takes to healing those who have been injured in their search for it. Without their sickness, he could never even hope to be well. *The Way Home* ends not in Europe but in Australia. Ultima Thule is not the big house of wealth and time, but poverty in a shack and eternity in a narrow box that is yet too big to go through any door in the shack. Though healing others, Mahony could not heal himself. Though he attended many funerals, his own doctor could not attend his. The parson and the bank manager go instead, representing those two interests with which Mahony had had little luck and no sympathy.

Richardson, however, is saying more than that these are just life's little ironies, or that 'such is life'. By employing such examples of parallel situation, of coincidental response, of fatal irony, so carefully and for so long, she is conferring on her novel a unity of action that embodies a seriousness of purpose and wholeness of intention. She does not commit 'the error of all poets who have . . . imagined that as Herakles was one man, the story of Herakles must also be a unity'. Her theme is fortune, primarily that of Mahony, but including too that of a host of his wife's friends and relatives and his own acquaintances. They are proud examples or bitter victims—often both within the same lifetime—of Australia's 'boom and bust' history in which a competency is pursued as intensely as saints pursue salvation. Richardson's concentration on Australian history's most volatile period gives added point to Mahony's remark to his wife about friends: '*Panta rei* is the eternal truth: *semper idem* the lie we long to see confirmed. . . . No, the real friend is one you pick up at certain points in your life, whose way runs along with yours—

[1] Ibid., p. 742.

for a time. A time only. . . . Few or none march together the whole way.'[1] The friends, like the fortune, are whittled away, till at the end his wife has only two, Henry Ocock and Tilly Beamish. Mahony has none, except his wife.

Richardson does not scorn the 'competency'. She has Mahony fulfil himself most completely as a social being during that time when he is at his wealthiest. It is also the time when he is most able 'to think a few thoughts through to the end'; but it is also part of Mahony's tragedy—in other terms, the 'fatal flaw' in his character—that he is incapable of appreciating the connection between sufficient wealth and sufficient well-being, wishing rather with Lear to shake all cares and business from his age so long as he retains 'the name, and all the addition to a king'. His attitude is that which de Tocqueville attributes to members of an aristocracy: 'The comforts of life are not to them the end of life, but simply a way of living; they regard them as existence itself—enjoyed, but scarcely thought of.'[2] Mahony, however, is an aristocrat fallen among democrats, to whom, as de Tocqueville points out, the amassing of wealth and goods is the only distinction democracy permits, and who 'are, therefore, always straining to pursue or to retain gratifications so delightful, so imperfect, so fugitive'.[3] By setting the beginning of her novel in a sun-drenched shop on the Ballarat gold-fields of 1852 and the end twenty-eight years later in a shop threatened by Kelly's money-hunting gang, Richardson is doing rather more than record a glittering period in Australia's history or compose an extended epitaph to her father. Gold, earth, and sunlight are the symbols of fortune. Equally symbolic is Mahony's instinctive preference for the world of spiritualism and music, the silver of moonlight, starlight, and water.

Whether Richardson had read the works of her contemporary Thomas Mann, who, as the last of the Decadents or the first of the Moderns, exploits such symbolism for similar ends, is not important. So many of her critics have already spent so much time and ingenuity in isolating her possible sources and models that her achievement as a novelist is well on the way to being overshadowed by her extraneous achievement as a historian of early Australia, or as her father's chronicler, or

[1] *Fortunes*, p. 485. [2] *Democracy in America*, p. 398.
[3] Ibid., p. 399.

as the naughty former student of the Melbourne Presbyterian Ladies' College. Perhaps because she lived most of her life abroad, such attempts to establish her indebtedness to her father's letters, her own diaries, even the *Ballarat Star*, have been persistent among Australian critics; and, perhaps because she is the only Australian woman to have written a novel worth much attention, such attempts have relied on the persistence of women. Were it not for the splendid example of Henry Handel Richardson herself, it might be impossible to resist the temptation to agree with Yeats that 'women do not keep their sanity in the presence of the abstract'. Grateful though we must be to Nettie Palmer,[1] Edna Purdie, Olga Roncoroni,[2] and Leonie Gibson[3] for providing so many facts to prove that Richardson like any other novelist used facts, it is time to assert that, until Patrick White, this is the finest novel written by an Australian, man or woman. Despite its much-stressed infelicities of style and its old-fashioned air of completeness, it remains great: not merely because, like a thousand others, it increases an 'awareness of the possibilities of life',[4] but because, in doing so, it exploits myth and symbol, history and geography, *Zeitgeist* and *Weltgeist*, to enhance that awareness in a way that makes the English part of the Great Tradition look as local an affair as the Great Western Railway. It is an epic, comparable with others like *The Magic Mountain*, *Dog Years*, and *Riders in the Chariot*. It also has as much to do with the twentieth century as they.

Mahony, as a boy, 'when he reached home, closed the door of one of the largest houses in the most exclusive square in Dublin', yet 'on the glossy damask of the big house, often not enough food was set to satisfy the growing appetites of himself and his sisters'.[5] His widowed mother and family approve only of the army as a profession. Mahony offends them by choosing medicine, a profession which, his wife later says in a metaphor more his than hers, 'fitted him like coursing does a hound'. Nevertheless, 'ingrained in him, and not to be eradicated, was the conviction that he was a gentleman first, doctor second'.

[1] *Henry Handel Richardson, A Study*, Sydney 1950.

[2] *Henry Handel Richardson: Some Personal Impressions*, Sydney 1957.

[3] *Henry Handel Richardson and Some of Her Sources*, Melbourne 1954.

[4] F. R. Leavis *The Great Tradition*, London, 4th Impression 1960, p. 2.

[5] *Fortunes*, pp. 32–3.

True to character, and nineteenth-century Australian literary tradition, Mahony happily bores his wife with readings from *Waverley*. His advice to his small uncomprehending son is: 'I want you never to forget that you are a gentleman—a gentleman first and foremost—no matter what you do or where you go, or who your companions may be. *Noblesse oblige*. With that for your motto you cannot go far wrong.'[1] Along with these gentlemanly qualities, and sometimes in opposition to them, Mahony has what Furphy's Stewart of Kooltopa calls in Warrigal Alf 'a damnable disposition'. It links him with the other Byronic heroes and their distant Miltonic ancestor. Like Starlight, he likes 'poetry and the higher fiction'. He lacks the dark hair and commanding eye, though he has a fair skin and arresting presence. He is slight rather than tall, possesses surprising resilience, and is crippled only by madness. By making him a doctor, constantly concerned with the ills of others, Richardson seems to underline his healthiness; but she loosens the conventions only in order to emphasize the tragic irony of his fate, the symbolism of which allies him closer to a more recent type. As a doctor, he is aware that what began, in Novalis's words, as *So wird alles in der Entfernung Poesie . . . ferne Berge, ferne Menschen, ferne Begebenheiten usw.* (*alles wird romantisch*),[2] has become incipient madness. It is part of his tragedy to have recognized its symptoms. Unable to prescribe a cure, he is without even the comfort of Doctor Rieux's existentialism—or pessimistic humanism—in Camus's *The Plague*. He knows that he has had one significant, or 'real experience', as Kierkegaard calls it.

Like the Byronic hero, he is by nature a 'recluse', 'lonely', and when young capable 'for good or evil, of swift decision'; and 'compromise he would not . . . or could not'. As Gracey Marriner tells him while they are discussing music and spiritualism: 'it is with you as the German poet sings: "There, where thou art not, there alone is bliss." ' He is no Don Juan, but he is popular with women: 'He met them with the deference he believed due to their sex.'[3] In contemplating suicide, he analyses himself and in doing so hints at the Satanic origins of the Byronic hero:

[1] *Fortunes*, p. 719.
[2] *Schriften*, Jena 1923, vol. 2, *Fragmente vermischten Inhalts*, No. 390, pp. 301–2.
[3] *Fortunes*, p. 274.

None would miss him, or mourn his passing—thanks to his own *noli me tangere* attitude towards the rest of mankind. For there had been no real love in him: never a feeler thrown out to his fellow-men. Such sympathy as he felt, he had been too backward to show: had given of it only in thought, and from afar. Pride, again!—oh! rightly was a pride like his reckoned among the seven capital sins. For what *was* it, but an iron determination to live untouched and untrammelled . . . to preserve one's liberty, of body and of mind, at the expense of all human sentiment. To be sufficient unto oneself, asking neither help nor regard, and spending none. A fierce, Lucifer-like inhibition. Yes, this . . . but more besides. Pride also meant the shuddering withdrawal of oneself, because of a rawness . . . a skinlessness . . . on which the touch of any rough hand could cause agony; even the chance contacts of every-day prove a source of exquisite discomfort.[1]

Nevertheless, 'little by little, with pangs unspeakable, did the death-throes of his crucified pride cease, and he emerge from the struggle, spent and beaten, but seeing himself at last in his true colours. Too good . . . too proud to live? Then, let him also be too proud to die: in this ignominious fashion . . . .'[2] He throws the phial away, not because 'conscience does make cowards of us all', but because 'of dauntless courage and considerate pride'.[3] He then experiences his vision of being at one with God. His conviction is strong enough to allow him to face the certainty of jeers from those who will count him an even worse failure because he, a doctor, has not only tried to kill himself, but failed. His conviction can withstand even more: 'As if to test him to the utmost, even the hideous spectre of his blackest nights took visible form, and persisted, till, for the first time, he dared to look it in the face.—And death seemed a trifle in comparison'.[4] In the juxtaposition of 'Lucifer-like inhibition' and 'crucified pride' and in the way such pride is rewarded, Richardson disrupts the smoothness of a convention with the ambiguity of myth. It was not the pride of Lucifer but the humility of Christ that was crucified. Yet the cry St. Matthew records, 'My God, why hast thou forsaken me?', expresses the condition of Satan. It is also the cry of pride; but in making it at all, Christ is expressing a human concern not only for the absence but for the restoration of God's grace, while St. John

[1] Ibid., p. 738.
[2] Ibid., p. 739.
[3] *Paradise Lost*, Book I, line 603.
[4] *Fortunes*, p. 741.

records the cry that is said to have confirmed Christ's divinity; '*Consummatum est.*' The irony of the Christian myth is that Christ was crucified because he was a man among men; but he was also crucified in order that 'the scripture should be fulfilled', that his divine task of reconciling fallen man with God should be completed. Mahony shares the humanity, is shown to partake of the divine and the damnable. By using the sin of pride to fight the sin of self-murder, he discovers a humility that is both reward and support in the further trial of impending madness. He has '*known*' that he will not be forsaken by God, but only by that faculty which might persuade him that he is. Thus is the foul fiend defied: 'while the light lasted, he *understood*'. This is the lasting part of his fortunes, not the glitter of gold but 'a radiance thick as milk, unearthly as moonlight'.[1]

This understanding, however, does not prevent him living out the demands of his 'damnable disposition'. His final act between sanity and insanity, the burning of his shares, is the fulfilment of 'considerate pride / Waiting revenge'. Shrouded in smoke, his hands in the ashes, he laughs and shouts his wife's name. What so many of his credulous neighbours had suspected seems here confirmed: he is the devil. Mary's first remark on seeing him thus is packed with an irony that seems intended to underline this: 'Richard! My God! What have you done?' This is the man of whom Richardson had written: 'He touched the hem of peace at last.' That in his sanity he has been Mary's god is reinforced by her remark when she sees him fall in 'a confused and crumpled heap on the floor': 'Richard! My *darling*! What is it, oh, what is it?' Richardson will not allow us to escape the association. She immediately follows this with the chapter's concluding sentence: 'But to these words, with which she had so often sought enlightenment, sought understanding, there was now no reply.'[2] Two pages later, Richardson restates this, thus defining Mahony's character most clearly: 'For twenty-five years and more she had had him at her side, to give the truth if she asked for it.' Those who withhold it from her now are, ironically, doctors she has called in to examine her husband.

To have made old types new is only a part of Richardson's achievement; she has also out of an old situation created a new

[1] *Fortunes*, p. 740. [2] Ibid., p. 781.

awareness of it, and thereby said something new about the situation. Richardson's Byronic hero becomes the Outsider. Mahony is a man who himself experiences the difference de Tocqueville cites when he says: 'Aristocracy had made a chain of all the members of the community, from the peasant to the king: democracy breaks that chain, and severs every link of it.' Mahony lives to recognize that 'not only does democracy make every man forget his ancestors, but it hides his descendants, and separates his contemporaries from him; it throws him back for ever upon himself alone, and threatens in the end to confine him entirely within the solitude of his own heart'.[1] This is Kierkegaard's 'levelling process', whose result is that 'No longer can the individual, as in former times, turn to the great for help when he grows confused. That is past; he is either lost in the dizziness of unending abstraction or saved for ever in the reality of religion.'[2] The change from Byronic hero to Outsider is emphasized by Richardson's allowing us to see Mahony an old man—at least when compared with the heroes of the other novels we have considered. The Byronic hero is always young, potent, clear-eyed, pale, smooth-skinned. The Outsider can be any age, but as an old man, like Voss, or Heriot in Stow's *To the Islands*, his condition is emphasized. His potency is gone, his hair grey, his eyes dim and inward-turned, his skin shrivelled; but we assume he was once otherwise, and found no joy that was not illusory, a confirmation of his separateness, a revelation of his 'forlornness and despair'. Richardson lets us see the change.

Arguing with Mahony about the political meetings which were to lead to the Eureka rising, his friend Purdy complains:

> 'If only you weren't so damned detached, Dick Mahony!'
>
> 'You're restless, and want excitement, my boy—that's the root of the trouble.'
>
> 'Well, I'm jiggered! If ever I knew a restless mortal, it's yourself.'[3]

Mahony later recognizes the rightness of the judgement and tries to find in outside events some explanation that will account for his restlessness. In doing so, he illustrates his detachment. The particular example he chooses is the circumstances in which he abandoned medicine:

[1] Op. cit., p. 368.

[2] Kierkegaard, *The Present Age*, p. 93.

[3] *Fortunes*, p. 20.

The only excuse he could find for his apostasy was that he had been caught in an epidemic of unrest, which had swept through the country, upsetting the balance of men's reason. He had since wondered if the Great Exhibition of '51 had not had something to do with it, by unduly whetting people's imaginations; so that but a single cry of 'Gold!' was needed, to loose the spirit of vagrancy that lurks in every Briton's blood. His case had perhaps been peculiar in this: no one had come forward to warn or dissuade. His next relatives—mother and sisters—were, he thought, glad to know him well away. In their eyes he had lowered himself by taking up medicine; to them it was still of a piece with barber's pole and cupping-basin. Before his time no member of the family had entered any profession but the army. Oh, that infernal Irish pride! . . . and Irish poverty. It had choke-damped his youth, blighted the prospects of his sisters.[1]

The spirit of the times, avarice, race, family—all are possible explanations of the restlessness that brought him to Australia; but, at the time of making them, it is the fact that he is still there that worries him. In Australia to secure a competency that he is slow to find, he sees himself not so much as a restless man but rather as an exile, to whom freedom means a return 'Home'. During his wife's first pregnancy, when he is afraid she will die, he thinks: 'If this is to be the price exacted of him—the price of his escape from exile—then . . . then . . .'[2] The dilemma is as harsh as the exile. Tangye, the local chemist, whose school Latin is the broken man's only comfort, connects the exile with the restlessness in quoting '*Coelum, non animum, mutant, qui trans mare currunt*'. He continues:

I grant you it's an antiquated point o' view; but doesn't that go to prove what I've been sayin'; that you and me are old-fashioned, too—out o' place here, out o' date? The modern sort, the sort that gets on in this country, is a prime hand at cuttin' his coat to suit his cloth; for all that the stop-at-homes, like the writer o' that line and other ancients, prate about the Ethiopian's hide or the leopard and his spots. . . . Harder'n nails, they are, and sharp as needles. You ask me why I do my walkin' out in the night-time? It's so's to avoid the sight o' their mean little eyes, and their greedy, graspin' faces.[3]

Mahony, in a spirit of detachment, refutes Tangye, but assimilates the argument into his own thinking, even to the point of believing that he has learnt the Latin tag at school—

[1] *Fortunes*, p. 142. [2] Ibid., p. 138. [3] Ibid., pp. 257–8.

as he probably did, but not well enough to remember it before recognizing it in Tangye as one of the few remaining traces of a gentlemanly origin. As his madness advances he is also haunted by the eyes of his fellow men, for which early in the novel Richardson has provided the historical justification: 'the thought he had to spare for his fellow-men was of small account: his fate was not bound to theirs by the altruism of a later generation. It was a time of intense individualism. . . .'[1] So many reasons are there, all bedded in the facts of history, for Mahony's discontent, that it is not surprising that the novel has been seen as a historical novel or a 'naturalistic' novel. It is worth recalling, however, Georg Lukács's remark that 'there are deep differences between epic and [historical] novel. The all-national . . . themes of epic, the relation between individual and nation in the age of heroes require that the most important figure should occupy the central position, while in the historical novel he is necessarily only a minor character.'[2] *The Fortunes of Richard Mahony* is an epic novel, but an epic of the twentieth century. 'The relation between individual and nation in the age of heroes' has been profoundly changed in the age of anti-heroes. To point to this change is the purpose of the irony in the title of the middle section of the novel, *The Way Home*: 'No sooner ashore . . . than [Mahony] had felt himself outsider and alien. England had no welcome for her homing sons, or any need of them: their places were long since filled.'[3] But Mahony had never had a place in England. It had all been the dream of an Anglo-Irishman, to whom exile is the reality into which he is born. On visiting his mother and sisters in Ireland, however, he finds that he is as much an outsider and alien among exiles as he was among natives:

For they were even more deeply rapt than of old in the mysteries and ecstasies of religion. On its conduct they lavished their remaining vitality; while the mother faith, which flourished so abundantly around them, supplied them with an outlet for the bitter hatred which life's hardships had engendered in them. Popery was an invention of the Arch-Fiend; its priests were the 'men of sin'—To Mahony, who had learnt to regard all sects and denominations as branches of the one great tree, such an attitude was intolerable.[4]

[1] Ibid., p. 163. [2] *The Historical Novel*, p. 45. [3] *Fortunes*, p. 416.
[4] Ibid., pp. 383–4.

The metaphor is apt in an age of Darwinian revelation; it contributed to the evolution of the Outsider. If all men are equal, so are their organized faiths. As Purdy the Englishman had said, Mahony is 'so damned detached', damned by being detached, detached because he is damned.

A further example of just how detached Mahony has become is provided when he revisits Edinburgh on this first journey 'Home'. He had been a student there, but revisting the city 'made him feel like a shade permitted to revisit the haunts of youth'. Born an Anglo-Irishman, educated in Scotland, shipped to Australia, who yet refers to England as 'home', Mahony is the complete Outsider. He has neither home nor nation. After his journey to England and his return to Australia, he admits it: 'no place could ever be "home" to him as long as he lived. He was once more an outcast and a wanderer.'[1] The words 'once more' underline what is by now clear, even to him: that he was born an Outsider. His last journey to England is made as a visitor, while his return to Australia ends in insanity. The modern situation in which he finds himself permits only one fleeting vision of peace, of being an 'insider'—and only then when on the verge of suicide, of changing the situation altogether, a state to which detached reflection has driven him. As Kierkegaard remarks, 'Nowadays not even a suicide kills himself in desperation. Before taking the step he deliberates so long and so carefully that he literally chokes with thought. It is even questionable whether he ought to be called a suicide, since it is really thought which takes his life. He does not die *with* deliberation but *from* deliberation.'[2]

In his detached analysis of his response to London, Mahony comes nearest to providing a clue to the puzzle of his birth:

> 'This sense of insignificance regularly haunts me. I'm paying, I expect, for having lived so long in a place like Ballarat, where it was easy to imagine oneself a personage of importance. Here, all such vanity is soon crushed out of one. The truth of the matter is, London's too big for me; I don't feel equal to it—I believe one can lose the habit of great cities, just like any other.'[3]

Back in Australia, the first thing he does is settle in Melbourne, which, at least to W. S. Jevens, the British economist, had even

[1] *Fortunes*, p. 417. [2] Op. cit., p. 33. [3] *Fortunes*, p. 362.

in 1858 'a metropolitan character', its shops 'equal to the best in London'.[1] It was the city which in 1880, the year of Mahony's death, held its own International Exhibition: 'On the opening day . . . twenty thousand people were in the streets, watching the great procession led by nine brass bands.'[2] And yet, as Mahony says of himself, he has a great unwillingness to 'go back on his traces'. He can say with Antoine Roquentin, the hero of Sartre's *Nausea*: 'I have crossed the seas, I have left cities behind me . . . always making for other cities . . . and I could never turn back, any more than a record can spin in reverse.'[3] Mahony's nameless discontent is Roquentin's: 'I want to leave, to go somewhere where I should be really *in my place*, where I would fit in . . . but my place is nowhere: I am unwanted.'[4] 'The great city determines everything,' Le Corbusier wrote. It is the culmination, the most obvious and proudest manifestation of the 'levelling process'. Dublin, Edinburgh, London, Melbourne, 'where the old restlessness was strong on him again', where 'he was tired of everything he knew': the city determines his discontent and defines his insignificance. Mahony takes no Dickensian delight in cities and streets. He is of a different century. The motto from Céline's *The Church*, which introduces *Nausea*, could equally well apply to Mahony's 'fortune': 'He is a fellow without any collective significance, barely an individual.'

The one solace Mahony has is music. He has 'a pleasant tenor' and 'skill as a flute player'; but it is not in such 'amusement', as the Anglo-Irishman Dr. Goldsmith called it, that Mahony delights, but in music as a 'wordless language'. Sartre's Roquentin sums up the appeal thus: 'melodies alone can proudly carry their own death within them like an internal necessity; only they don't exist. Every existent is born without reason, prolongs itself out of weakness and dies by chance . . . existence is a repletion which man can never abandon.'[5] Thomas Mann in *Buddenbrooks* earlier expressed the same absurd appeal:

> The fanatical worship of this worthless trifle, this scrap of melody, this brief, childish harmonic invention only a bar and a half in length,

[1] Quoted Asa Briggs, *Victorian Cities*, p. 287.
[2] Quoted ibid., p. 306, from *Melbourne Argus*.
[3] Jean-Paul Sartre, *Nausea*, Harmondsworth 1965, p. 34.
[4] Op. cit., p. 175.
[5] Op. cit., p. 191.

had about it something stupid and gross, and at the same time something ascetic and religious—something that contained the essence of faith and renunciation. There was a quality of the perverse in the insatiability with which it was produced and revelled in: there was a sort of cynical despair; there was a longing for joy, a yielding to desire, in the way the last drop of sweetness was, as it were, extracted from the melody, till exhaustion, disgust, and satiety supervened. Then, at last; at last, in the weariness after excess, a long, soft *arpeggio* in the minor trickled through, mounted a tone, resolved itself in the major, and died in a mournful lingering away.[1]

Neither Mann nor Sartre, however, offers the most useful comparison with Richardson's *The Fortunes of Richard Mahony.* They deal with the condition of the artist, specifically that of the artist as writer. In general terms, they are more helpful in a consideration of Richardson's *Maurice Guest*[2] or *The Young Cosima*,[3] the first of which, however, owes little to Australia, the second nothing. Mahony is not an artist, although 'The law governing artistic production applies, on a smaller scale, to every one in daily life. Every man who has a real experience experiences at the same time all its possibilities in an ideal sense, including the opposite possibility.'[4] This is the irony already referred to in Mahony's 'real experience', when 'he *understood*'. Mahony is the *Steppenwolf*, 'the beast astray who finds neither home nor joy nor nourishment in a world that is strange and incomprehensible to him'.[5] For Mahony, as for Hermann Hesse's Steppenwolf, there can be no comfort in artistic creation, that struggle with words which assumes the possibility of triumph; and, because Mahony's passion for music is 'natural' and uninformed, the recreation of music and its vicarious triumph can offer him only undifferentiated solace.

Hermann Hesse's novel, *Steppenwolf*, combining allegory and myth, has been variously interpreted—Hesse said 'misunderstood'—for the very reason that makes it most useful as a comparison with *The Fortunes of Richard Mahony.* Its main character, Harry Haller, is, because of the book's allegorical nature, the clearest expression of the Outsider, but his condition is not complicated by the artist's realization that 'language could but

[1] Thomas Mann, *Buddenbrooks*, 1902, Harmondsworth 1957, p. 584.
[2] London 1908. [3] London 1939. [4] Kierkegaard, op. cit., p. 79.
[5] Hermann Hesse, *Steppenwolf*, 1927; Harmondsworth 1965, p. 39.

extol, not reproduce, the beauties of the sense'.[1] As Hesse wrote of *Steppenwolf* in 1961: 'It is not a book of man despairing, but of a man believing'.[2] Like *The Fortunes of Richard Mahony*, it is the story of an intellectual who surrenders to 'the hegemony of music'. Haller, in his detached analysis of his condition, says: 'We intellectuals, instead of fighting this tendency like men and rendering obedience to the spirit, the Logos, the Word, and gaining a hearing for it, are all dreaming of a speech without words that utters the inexpressible and gives form to the formless'.[3] The reason for such surrender is equally clear: 'None of us intellectuals is at home in reality. We are strange to it and hostile.' Or as Kierkegaard expresses it: 'Life's existential tasks have lost the interest of reality.'[4] Whether one accepts Hesse's claim that his novel is 'of a man believing' must depend on whether one accepts the assumption that there is something to believe in. For Camus, at least in *The Outsider*, there was not, except perhaps 'the inability to regret anything'.[5] Camus's Outsider was a late manifestation of the type, however, or possibly an old-fashioned nihilist. Here it is enough to remark that Camus did not repeat the type in fiction. Richardson shares Hesse's assumption: Mahony is god-haunted. His last mumbled words to his wife are an assertion 'of a man believing': 'Not grieve . . . for me . . . I'm going . . . into Eternity.' A moment later he says, 'Dear wife.' Braving the charge of sentimentality, Richardson continues:

> Eternity was something vast, cold, impersonal. But this little phrase, from the long past days of love and comradeship, these homely, familiar words, fell like balsam on her heart. All his love for her, his gratitude to her, was in them: they were her reward, and a full and ample one, for a lifetime of unwearied sacrifice.[6]

Hermine, who instructs Harry Haller in the meaning as well as the practice of love, says of eternity:

> The pious call it, the kingdom of God. . . . In eternity there is no posterity . . . it is the kingdom on the other side of time and appearances. There is our home. It is that which our heart strives for. And

[1] Thomas Mann, *Death in Venice*, 1912; Harmondsworth 1955, p. 58.
[2] Author's Note; p. 6. [3] *Steppenwolf*, p. 159.
[4] *Op. cit.*, p. 90.
[5] Albert Camus, *The Outsider*, 1942; Harmondsworth 1961, p. 101.
[6] *Fortunes*, p. 827.

for that reason, Steppenwolf, we long for death . . . we have to stumble through so much dirt and humbug before we reach home. And we have no one to guide us. Our only guide is our home-sickness.[1]

This is Wagner's *Sehnsuchtsmotiv* in *Tristan und Isolde*, 'such a morbid and profoundly equivocal work'.[2] It is not surprising that Richardson, a concert pianist whose 'aversion to being stared at settled into a definite idiosyncrasy', should have chosen Wagner as the hero of her last novel, *The Young Cosima.*

In *The Fortunes of Richard Mahony*, however, Richardson is interested not in Wagner's *tiefe Zweideutigkeit*, but in the music of Schumann, who like Richardson had studied at Leipzig. Like Mahony, he ended his life insane. Richardson uses his music as catalyst for the theme of what Beckett calls 'the poisonous ingenuity of Time', and griefless, impersonal eternity.

The family is visited by Baron von Krause, a German botanist who has heard of Mahony's earlier interest in lepidoptera. In conventional terms, the Baron is the German scientific figure so frequent in Australian fiction, a remnant of the Faust legend, but a Faust to whom knowledge has brought peace. Besides being a botanist, Baron von Krause is a musician. While with the Mahonys, he discovers that their son, Cuffy, has a great musical talent. This does not surprise his mother, who at a party, when asked to play, 'did not wait to be pressed; it was her business to set the ball rolling; and she stood up and went to the piano as unconcernedly as she would have gone to sweep a room or make a bed'.[3] As Mahony says hotly, the Baron is not talking about Cuffy's 'cleverness', as Mary thinks he is, but about 'music, and the musical faculty . . . ear, instinct, inborn receptivity'. He adds, what the whole novel is intended to illustrate, that 'it sometimes seems as if we spoke a different language'. The Baron plays for the child what seems to be Schumann's piano Concerto, Opus 54. It makes Cuffy cry, because, as the Baron explains, it tells of 'the sufferings of a so unhappy man—the fears that are coming by night to devour the peace . . so great were they, so unhappy he, that at the last his brain has burst.'[4] The Baron calls him 'Our dear madman'. Cuffy's reply is: 'Shooh man.—What's mad?' Richardson is here doing more

[1] *Steppenwolf*, pp. 179–80.
[2] Thomas Mann, *Tonio Kröger*, 1903; Harmondsworth 1955, p. 155.
[3] *Fortunes*, p. 249.
[4] Ibid., p. 658.

than record Junior's cuteness. She is exploiting the *double-entendre* to relate the themes of music, eternity, and madness. She has externalized and simplified the complexity of Mahony's problem, the problem of his own character. The Baron continues: 'But will you be that one, my son, you must first have given up all else for it . . . all the joys and pleasures that make the life glad. These will be for the others not for you, my dear . . . you must only go wizout . . . renounce . . . look on.'[1] Or as Sartre's Roquentin puts it: 'You have to choose: to live or to recount.'[2] Schumann chose to recount, and went mad. Mahony chooses to live; and the result is the same. Which is to say that the human condition is absurd. It is also tragic, in that choice involves 'the fact that one value runs counter to another'. One 'cannot have two things at once',[3] though one is aware of the others in the ideal sense. Such awareness compounds the irony, and emphasizes the tragedy. *The Fortunes of Richard Mahony* may not be 'a work of tragic force', but it encompasses tragedy by recognizing the absurd. It is a supremely ironical work, essentially modern even in its historical details.

As the Baron recognizes, the child has a choice. He offers to pay for his musical education, which would, as Mary realizes, begin by his having to go away from home and renounce his family. She forbids it: to eschew or 'shooh' man is to her obviously mad. The sole trace left on Cuffy's life is a game he plays with his sisters, which goes 'Shooh, man!', 'Shooh, woman!'.[4] Gracey Marriner's much earlier diagnosis of Mahony's condition comes again to mind: 'It is with you as the German poet sings: "There, where thou art not, there alone is bliss." '[5] The line, evidently from Schubert's *Der Wanderer*,[6] reinforces the part music plays in the novel.

[1] Ibid., p. 658.
[2] Jean-Paul Sartre, *Nausea*, p. 61.
[3] Cesare Pavese, *This Business of Living*, London 1961, p. 193.
[4] *Fortunes*, p. 660.
[5] Ibid., p. 513.
[6] The line, 'There, where thou art not, there alone is bliss', had a long history. Evariste Vicomete de Parny's

La peine est aux lieux qu'en habite
Et le bonheur ou l'on n'est pas.
(*Poésies*, Paris 1777, Lettre 4)

became in German

Die Qual ist überall, wo wir auch hausen,
Und wo wir nicht sind, ist das Glück.

In 1808, Schmidt von Lübeck adopted it in his *Taschenbuch zum geselligen Vergnügen*

This use of what Mann called, following Wagner, *Leitmotiv*, makes *The Fortunes of Richard Mahony* cohere. Four years separated the publication of the second book, *The Way Home*, in which Gracey Marriner makes her remark, from the publication of the third book, *Ultima Thule*, in which the childish game appears. Richardson's use of the *Leitmotiv*, the phrase which symbolizes ideas and establishes unity of action, distinguishes her work from any that had preceded it in Australia, and from much that followed. It does not, however, isolate her from the Australian tradition. The novel's time scheme is roughly thirty years, from the Great Exhibition in London in 1851 to the International Exhibition of 1880 in Melbourne. Gold is the symbol of that period in Australian history. Apart from a reference to the 'scum of Norfolk Island', there is no mention of Australia's convict origins. Mahony was not the kind of man to relish them. Yet Richardson uses these origins in elaborating her symbol of gold and in defining the nature of the Outsider. Such is her artistry, however, that she can be accused by one Australian critic of her novel of lacking 'invention' and by another of lacking 'imagination'.

Of the diggers, she writes: 'And the intention of all alike had been: to snatch a golden fortune from the earth and then, hey, presto! for the old world again. But they were reckoning without their host: only too many of those who entered the country went out no more. They became prisoners to the soil.'[1] And again:

> . . . the 'unholy hunger' . . . was like a form of revenge taken on them, for their loveless schemes of robbing and fleeing; a revenge contrived by the ancient, barbaric country they had so lightly invaded. Now, she held them captive—without chains; ensorcelled—without witchcraft; and, lying stretched like some primeval monster in the sun, her breasts freely bared, she watched, with a malignant eye, the efforts made by these puny mortals to tear their lips away.[2]

Mahony has abandoned the digger's life and might be thought

so that it became: '*Da, wo du nicht bist, ist das Glück*!' Zelter composed a poem on the subject which Schubert then changed slightly and set to music under the title of '*Der Wanderer*' in which the line appears more or less as it does in the English translation:

Dort, wo du nicht bist, dort ist das Glück!

In Turgenev's *Fathers and Sons*, the line is referred to as a 'proverb', which it probably was in 1862; it is used as an ironic summary of the Romantic ideal.

[1] *Fortunes*, p. 13. [2] Ibid.

free from such servitude; but this is the very thing that has not happened:

Oh! he had adapted himself supremely well to the standards of this Australia, so-called Felix. And he must not complain if, in so doing, he had been stripped, not only of his rosy dreams, but also of that spiritual force on which he could once have drawn at will. Like a fool he had believed it possible to serve mammon with impunity, and for as long at it suited him. He knew better now. At this moment he was undergoing the sensations of one who, having taken shelter in what he thinks a light and flimsy structure, finds that it is built of the solidest stone. Worse still: that he has been walled up inside.[1]

Leaving Ballarat the first time for England and freedom, Mahony sees the town dominated by a bare hill. He comments to his wife: 'There goes the last of old Warrenheip. Thank the Lord, I shall never set eyes on it again. Upon my word, I believe I came to think that hill the most tiresome feature of the place. Whatever street one turned into, up it bobbed at the foot. Like a peep-show . . . or a bad dream . . . or a prison wall.'[2] Thus far—to the end of the first part—it is possible to see the continuing tradition of Australia as the chastening, imprisoning land, whose deity is female. It is a land most delightful to leave, to get away from. As Mahony thinks on leaving it: '. . . he had every reason to feel thankful. For many and many a man, though escaping with his life, had left youth and health and hope on these difficult shores. He had got off scot-free.'[3] He is leaving for 'Home', away from 'the troubled seas that break on the reef-bound coasts of this old, new world'. Like Camus's imprisoned Outsider, Mahony suffers from the 'habit of thinking like a free man'.[4]

Even in the first part, however, Mahony, 'as utterly alien as any Jew of old who wept by the rivers of Babylon', tends to personify in himself his imprisonment, and thereby admit his own as well as the country's difference. Following the Australian convention, Richardson has him see not only Australia as woman, but woman as his gaoler. When he first thinks of escape, he is 'foiled by Mary's pleadings and his own inertia' and 'let himself be bound anew'.[5] He returns to this explanation when, proposing escape again, he hears Mary suggest he consult her brother: 'No you don't, madam, no you don't! . . . You

[1] Ibid., p. 317. [2] Ibid., p. 336. [3] Ibid., p. 341.
[4] *The Outsider*, p. 79. [5] *Fortunes*, p. 319.

had me once . . . crippled me . . . handcuffed me—you and your brother John between you! It shan't happen again.'[1] This time, 'he saw that he dared delay no longer in setting free the imprisoned elements in him, was he ever to grow to that complete whole which each mortal aspires to be'.[2]

Once in England, however, Mahony, like Mr. Dorrit, the Father of the Marshalsea, finds that English society has its 'cast-iron barriers with which the various cliques hedged themselves round, to keep those a step lower in the scale from coming too near'.[3] As de Tocqueville says of the American in Europe: 'He is like a man surrounded by traps: society is not a recreation for him, but a serious toil.'[4] Unlike de Tocqueville's American, however, Mahony owed nothing to forebears or predecessors who 'went forth to seek some rude and unfrequented part of the world, where they could live according to their own opinions, and worship God in freedom'. The beginnings of his adopted country's history were different. In de Tocqueville's sentence: 'The criminal courts of England originally supplied the population of Australia.'[5] He was without the assurance that comes from having as a first national object 'the triumph of an idea'. In so far as he is an Australian, society remains a serious, and endless, toil. He is kept outside until wealth admits him as a visitor, briefly, on his second trip to England. Having bought his way in, he is immediately restless to buy his way out again, to be on the move from one city to another. As he asks himself when he has returned to Australia and poverty:

> Wherein lay the fault, the defect, that had made of him throughout his life a hunted man? . . . Himself he was the hunter and the hunted: the merciless in pursuit and the panting prey . . . The plain truth was: the life-instinct had been too strong for him. Rather than face death and the death-fear, in an attempt to flee the unfleeable he had thrown every other consideration to the winds, and ridden tantivy into the unknown.
>
> But now all chance of flight was over. He sat here as fast a prisoner as though chained to a stake—an old and weary man, with his fiftieth birthday behind him.[6]

Having begun in Australia as one of de Tocqueville's 'speculators and adventurers greedy of gain', Mahony finds his early

[1] *Fortunes*, p. 324. [2] Ibid., p. 318. [3] Ibid., p. 391.
[4] *Democracy in America*, p. 441. [5] Ibid., p. 34.
[6] *Fortunes*, pp. 692–3.

life there defining itself in terms more suited to the experiences of Effie Deans or Quintus Servinton. But the image of the prison is not just the heart of Midlothian or Botany Bay: it is in the nineteenth century the heart of what Dickens[1] called 'the social condition'.[1] Richardson extends the image till it becomes the heart of the human condition: 'And all men kill the thing they love', as Wilde has it. Mahony's 'fault, the defect', is the approaching scream of madness, the final loneliness of freedom, escape, and imprisonment. Once he is certified, his books and clothing are returned to his wife: 'He had been stripped, not only of his rosy dreams'. As his wife says: 'Prisoners—no, she meant patients—were not allowed any superfluous belongings.' Freed from the asylum, he is returned to her 'roped' like a beast by 'his keepers'. He 'was a lamb in her hands, a little child, whom she could twist round her finger'. 'He was now the least troubled of men. Content and happiness had come to him at last, in full measure. No more doubts, or questionings, or wrestlings with the dark powers in himself. . . .'[2] To see him thus 'was Mary's reward'. After his final fall in the mud—recalling the occasion of his vision and as well Hermine's remark to the Steppenwolf, 'We have to stumble through so much dirt and humbug before we reach home'—Mary sees him a 'very prisoner to [his] chair', and finally to his bed and to death. For Mahony they are stages to freedom. He abandons the image of the prison for others to use, as they had used it in the book's opening paragraph, realism disguising its symbolism:

In a shaft on the Gravel Pits, a man had been buried alive. At work in a deep wet hole, he had recklessly omitted to slab the walls of

[1] Or R. H. Hone, in the article he and Dickens wrote called 'The Great Exhibition and the Little One', *Household Words*, 5 July 1851, the first paragraph of which reads: 'It was seen by a few philosophers long since, that the abstract faculties of man could not be increased in number, neither could they be enlarged and refined beyond a given extent; and it was therefore concluded that the advances of mankind in their practical social condition were limited to the ordinary characteristics of a high condition of civilization.' Dickens had reservations about the general acceptance of this event as being the symbol of progress. He knew the cupidity, avarice and criminality on which it was partly based and which it was meant to disguise. (See his other article with W. H. Wills, 'The Metropolitan Protectives', *Household Words*, 26 April 1851, which is meant to assure 'all having the fear of the forthcoming Industrial Invasion' of 'the adequate efficiency of the London Police', while pointing up the social degradation of the times.) In blaming the Exhibition for his decision to go to Australia, Mahony is aware that gold was as powerful an attraction as restlessness was a stimulus.

[2] *Fortunes*, p. 821.

a drive; uprights and tailors yielded under the lateral pressure, and the rotten earth collapsed, bringing down the roof in its train. The digger fell forward on his face, his ribs jammed across his pick, his arms pinned to his sides, nose and mouth pressed into the sticky mud as into a mask; and over his defenceless body, with a roar that burst his ear-drums, broke stupendous masses of earth.[1]

The young digger here is Long Jim's mate, Young Bill with 'his lily-white hands and finical speech' whose end in what Mahony much later calls 'the land of sudden accident and death'[2] provokes Long Jim into saying: 'It's 'ell for white men—'ell, that's what it is.' Their only escape is in death. As for the black men, the aborigines, they are of no interest to Richardson. They molest neither the white man's activities, as in earlier Australian literature, nor his conscience as in later literature. For the aborigines, there was neither use nor symbolism in gold. To dig for it, or to weigh human fortune against it, is to them mad, incomprehensible. Richardson is not prepared to act on Voss's dictum: 'It is necessary to communicate without knowledge of the language.'

Nor is she much interested in mateship. Mahony, who also possesses 'lily-white hands and finical speech', eventually assumes responsibility for Long Jim, who becomes his paid servant first in the shop, then in the doctor's house. Mahony also pays his fare to England and back again, believing like Rowcroft's gentlemanly heroes that master and servant should, in de Tocqueville's phrase, 'stand firmly by one another'. Long Jim, however, believes that 'in democracies servants are not only equal among themselves, but . . . that they are in some sort the equals of their masters . . . At any moment [a servant] may become a master.'[3] Investing in shares as Mahony does, though more wisely than he, this is indeed what Long Jim does become.

Mahony has his friend, Purdy, whom he has known in Ireland, 'he the senior, Purdy the junior'; but this is not the mateship of Long Jim and Young Bill, who 'had boiled a common billy and slept side by side in rain-soaked blankets', who had stood 'by his mate through . . . disasters'. Mahony's relationship with Purdy is that of a man who 'had no talent for friendship', whose 'nature has a twist in it which directly hindered friendship'. While the Byronic hero may, in A. D. Hope's

[1] *Fortunes*, p. 7. [2] Ibid., p. 907. [3] De Tocqueville, op. cit., p. 446.

words, 'long for the companionship of men, their sexless friendliness',[1] the nature of the type prevents any satisfaction in it. Similarly, the nature of the Outsider prevents him sharing even the Byronic hero's transitory solace, whose

> thoughts are women, he breathes, is clothed with them,
> he sinks on something female in the dust.[2]

For as Camus writes, what is really irksome to the Outsider is his 'habit of thinking like a free man'. There is no alternative, even in prison.

The themes of mateship, friendship, and love, like the crowd of characters in the early part of the novel, are introduced to emphasize 'the deep significance of [Mahony's] solitude'. Like the drunken squatter, Glendinning, Tangye the broken chemist, Young Bill, the buried digger, they are projections of possibilities Mahony's own character contains. He cannot realize these possibilities because to do so would involve the accommodation of 'death and the death-fear'. Glendinning's drunkenness and Tangye's bitter cynicism are the peace each has made with life, the 'repletion' which each has tried to abandon. Even suicide, Young Werther's antidote to *Weltschmerz*, 'needs humility, not pride';[3] but as de Tocqueville had written one hundred and fifty years earlier of man so tempted in a democratic world; 'The will resists—reason frequently gives way.'[4]

Despite her affinity with the greatest of modern European writers, Richardson is also working within an Australian tradition; but, because in technique and concern she is so much more sophisticated than any earlier creators of that tradition, her belonging to it is not so apparent. Yet it is Richardson who most clearly marks the fulfilment of one possibility and the recognition and acceptance of another. Australian literature began with Scott and Byron.[5] The Australian scene was novel

[1] A. D. Hope, *Poems*, London 1960, 'The Damnation of Byron'.

[2] Ibid. [3] Cesare Pavese, op. cit., p. 220. [4] op. cit., p. 409.

[5] Lockhart movingly tells how similar they could appear even to Scott: 'Among other songs, Mrs. Arkwright . . . delighted Sir Walter with her own set of—

> "Farewell! Farewell!—the voice you hear
> Has left its last soft tone with you,
> Its next must join the seaward cheer,
> And shout among the shouting crew," etc.

He was sitting by me, at some distance from the lady, and whispered as she closed, "capital words—whose are they?—Byron's, I suppose, but I don't remember

to European readers and readers lately European. Its novelty was increasingly exploited as Scott had exploited Scotland's; and as Byron made his peace with Scott, so the Byronic hero made his peace with Australia, till in Furphy's *Such is Life*, the scene has become old, local, and endearing, its starkness for the most part softened, the triumph of man almost complete. Because its five fingers, Perth, Adelaide, Melbourne, Sydney, and Brisbane, twitch with life, and its arteries—the rivers, roads, and tracks—run freely, the continent's dead heart is forgotten. The heart's existence and condition, symbolically so much like modern western man's, has become the concern only of Australia's most recent writers, who, by education, temperament, and the world's smallness, owe as much to Baudelaire as to Banjo Paterson. Stephen Heriot, the hero of Randolph Stow's early novel, makes the journey through the dead heart to the islands of the dead which, according to aboriginal legend, lie beyond the heart. His reference to 'this cursed Baudelaire whining in his head like a mosquitoe preaching despair' can provisionally stand as an epigraph to the literature of what Richardson calls 'this old, new world':

J'ai plus de souvenirs que si j'avais mille ans.[1]

them." He was astonished when I told him that they were his own in the Pirate—he seemed pleased at the moment—but said next minute—"You have distressed me—if memory goes, all is up with me, for that was always my strong point." ' (Lockhart, vol. vii, p. 129).

[1] Randolph Stow, *To the Islands*, 1958: Harmondsworth 1962, p. 13.

Bibliography

THE following bibliography contains all those works which I have found immediately helpful in trying to define a fragment of a large and elusive subject. Where two dates appear, the first indicates original publication or standard text, the second the text which I have used.

TEXTS to which specific attention has been paid:

'Boldrewood, Rolf' (T. A. Browne):

Robbery under arms: a story of life and adventure in the bush and in the goldfields of Australia, 3 vols., London 1888; 1 vol., London 1961.
The miner's right: a tale of the Australian goldfields, 3 vols., London 1890.
A colonial reformer, 3 vols., London 1890; 1 vol., London 1890.
A Sydney-side Saxon, London 1891.
Nevermore, 3 vols., London 1892.
The crooked stick, or Pollie's probation, London 1895.
The sphinx of Eaglehawk: a tale of old Bendigo, London 1895.
My run home, London 1897.
Plain living: a bush idyll, London 1898.
A romance of Canvas Town, and other stories, London 1898.
Babes in the bush, London 1900.
In bad company, and other stories, London 1901.
The ghost camp, or the avengers, London 1902.

Clarke, Marcus:

The peripatetic philosopher by 'Q', Melbourne 1869.
The man with the oblong box, Melbourne 1878.
For the term of his natural life, London, Melbourne 1885; London 1952.
The mystery of Major Molineaux and human repetends, Melbourne 1881.
Sensational tales, Adelaide 1886.

Furphy, Joseph ('Tom Collins'):

Such is life: being certain extracts from the diary of Tom Collins, Sydney 1903; 1962.
Rigby's romance: a 'Made in Australia' novel, Melbourne 1921; Sydney 1946.
The Buln-buln and the Brolga, Sydney 1948.

Hay, William:

The escape of the notorious Sir William Heans and the mystery of Mr. Daunt: A romance of Tasmania, London 1907; Melbourne 1955.
Herridge of Reality Swamp, London 1907.

Kingsley, Henry:

The recollections of Geoffry Hamlyn, 3 vols., Cambridge, London 1859, 1 vol., London 1924.
The Hillyars and the Burtons, 3 vols., London 1865.

Ravenshoe, 3 vols., Cambridge, London 1862.
The boy in grey, London 1871.
Hetty and other stories, London 1871.

McCombie, Thomas:

Arabin, or the adventures of a colonist in New South Wales. With an essay on the aborigines of Australia, London, Edinburgh, Aberdeen 1845.

'Richardson, Henry Handel' (Mrs. Ethel F. L. Robertson):

Maurice Guest, London 1908.
The getting of wisdom, London 1910.
The fortunes of Richard Mahony, London 1930; 1961.
The end of a childhood and other stories, London 1934.
The young Cosima, London 1939.

Rowcroft, Charles:

Tales of the colonies, or the adventures of an emigrant. Ed. by a late colonial magistrate, 3 vols., London 1843.
The bushranger of Van Diemen's Land, 3 vols., London 1846.
The confessions of an Etonian, 3 vols, London 1852.

Savery, Henry:

Quintus Servinton: a tale founded upon incidents of real occurrence (Anon.), 3 vols., Hobart Town 1830–1; ed. C. Hadgraft, 1 vol., Brisbane, Melbourne 1962.

Tucker, James:

Ralph Rashleigh, or the life of an exile, ed. Colin Roderick, Sydney, London 1952, 1962.

BOOKS AND ARTICLES of a general kind:

Adolphus, J. L., *Letters to Richard Heber*, London 1821.
Allen, Walter, *The English novel*, London 1954, Harmondsworth 1958.
Baynton, Barbara, *Bush studies*, London 1902, Sydney 1965.
Bentham, Jeremy, *Rationale of punishment*, trans. from French by Richard Smith, London 1830.
Borrow, George, *The Zincali, or an account of the gypsies in Spain*, London 1841.
Brennan, Christopher, *Poems*, Sydney (title-page dated 1913, published 1914).
Briggs, Asa, *Victorian people*, London 1954.
—— *Age of improvement*, London 1959.
—— *Victorian cities*, London 1963.
Brown, Max, *Australian son: The story of Ned Kelly*, Melbourne 1948.
Buckley, Vincent, *Henry Handel Richardson*, Melbourne 1961.
Byron, Lord, *The poetical works of Lord Byron*, ed. E. H. Coleridge, London 1905.
Cambridge, Ada, *Thirty years in Australia*, London 1903.

Camus, Albert, *The outsider*, Paris 1947, trans. Stuart Gilbert, London 1946, Harmondsworth 1961.

Carlyle, Thomas, 'Characteristics', *Edinburgh Review*, liv, December 1831.

Chesterton, G. K., *The Victorian age in literature*, London 1913.

Clacy, Charles (Mrs.), *A lady's visit to the gold diggings of Australia in 1852–1853*, London 1853; ed. Patricia Thomson, Melbourne 1963.

Clark, Manning, *A short history of Australia*, Sydney 1963.

Cole, G. D. H., *A short history of the British working class movement, 1789–1947*, London 1948.

Cole, G. D. H., and Raymond Postgate, *The common people 1746–1946*, London 1938, 1949.

Cooper, Fenimore, *The Deerslayer*, Philadelphia 1841.

Craig, W., *My adventures on the Australian goldfields*, London 1903.

Crawford, Thomas, *Scott*, Edinburgh, London 1965.

Croce, B., *European literature in the nineteenth century*, Bari 1923; trans. Douglas Ainslie, London 1924.

Cusack, Dymphna, *The sun is not enough*, London 1967.

Dark, Eleanor, *The timeless land*, London 1941.

—— *Storm of time*, London 1949.

Darwin, Charles, *The voyage of the Beagle*, London 1839, 1961.

Defoe, Daniel, *Robinson Crusoe*, London 1719, (Everyman) 1960.

Dennis, C. J., *The songs of a sentimental bloke*, Sydney 1916.

Digby, Kenelm Henry, *The broadstone of honour: or, the true sense and practice of chivalry*, 4 vols., London 1826–9.

Dutton, Geoffrey (ed.), *The literature of Australia*, Ringwood 1964.

Elliott, Brian, *Singing to the cattle, and other essays*, Melbourne 1947.

—— *Marcus Clarke*, Oxford 1958.

Ellis, S. M., *Henry Kingsley, 1830–1876: towards a vindication*, London 1931.

Empson, William, *Some Versions of Pastoral*, London 1935, Harmondsworth 1966.

Fitzpatrick, Brian, *British imperialism and Australia*, 1783–1833, London 1939.

Gibson, Leonie J., *Henry Handel Richardson and some of her sources*, Melbourne 1954.

Gordon, Adam Lindsay, *Poems*, Melbourne 1887, London 1912.

Gosse, Edmund, *Father and son*, London 1907, 1912.

Grant, Douglas, 'Sir Walter Scott and Nathaniel Hawthorne', *The University of Leeds Review*, June 1962.

Grattan, C. Hartley, ed., *Australia*, California 1947.

—— *Australian literature*, Seattle 1929.

Graves, Robert, *Goodbye to all that*, London 1929; 1957.

Green, H. M., *A history of Australian literature*, 2 vols., Sydney, Melbourne, London 1961.

Gross, John, John Holloway, Graham Hough, Lawrence Lerner, Christopher Ricks, Ian Watt, *The novelist as innovator*, London 1965.

Hadgraft, Cecil, *Australian literature*, London 1962.

Hancock, W. K., *Australia*, London 1930.

Hardy, Frank J., *Power without glory*, Melbourne 1950; 2 vols., Leipzig 1956.

Harris, Alexander, *The emigrant family: or, the story of an Australian settler*, 3 vols., London 1849.

—— *Settlers and convicts: or recollections of sixteen years' labour in the Australian backwoods*, London 1847; ed. C. M. H. Clark, Melbourne 1953.

Hazlitt, William, *The spirit of the age*, 1825; London (Worlds' Classics) 1966.

Hesse, Hermann, *Steppenwolf*, Berlin 1927; trans. Basil Creighton, Harmondsworth 1965.

Hobsbawm, Eric J., *The age of revolution, 1789–1848*, London 1962.

Hope, A. D., *Poems*, London 1960.

—— *Australian literature, 1950–62*, Melbourne 1963.

—— *The cave and the spring*, Adelaide 1965.

Horace, *Horace's collected works*, trans. Lord Dunsany and Michael Oakley, London 1961.

Horne, Donald, *The lucky country*, Ringwood 1964.

Houghton, W. E., *The Victorian frame of mind, 1830–1870*, New Haven 1957.

Howitt, Richard, *Impressions of Australia felix, etc.*, London 1845.

Howitt, William, *Land, labour and gold: or, two years in Victoria, etc.* 2 vols., London 1855.

—— *History of discovery in Australia, Tasmania and New Zealand, etc.*, 2 vols., London 1865.

Hughes, Thomas, *Tom Brown's schooldays*, London, Cambridge 1857.

Hunt, Leigh, *The autobiography of Leigh Hunt*, 2 vols., London 1850.

Jack, Ian, *English literature, 1815–1832* (*Oxford history of English literature*, vol. x, ed. F. P. Wilson and Bonamy Dobrée), Oxford 1963.

James, Louis, *Fiction for the working man*, London 1963.

Jeffares, A. N., 'Australian Literature', *Études Anglaises*, 6, 1953.

Johnston, Grahame (ed.), *Australian literary criticism*, Melbourne 1962.

de Juvenel, Bertrand, 'Jean-Jacques Rousseau', *Encounter*, December 1962.

Landor, E. W., *The bushman or life in a new country*, London 1847.

Lang, John, *The forger's wife, or Emily Orford*, London 1855.

Lang, J. D., *Transportation and colonisation*, London 1837.

Lawson, Henry, *Prose works of Henry Lawson*, Sydney, London 1948.

Leakey, Caroline ('Oliné Keese'), *The broad arrow; being passages from the history of Maida Gwynnham, a lifer*, 2 vols., London 1859.

Leavis, F. R., *The great tradition*, London 1948; 1960.

Levine, George (ed.), *The emergence of Victorian consciousness*, New York, 1967.

Lockhart, J. G., *The life of Sir Walter Scott*, 7 vols., London 1837–8.

Lukács, Georg, *The historical novel*, trans. Hannah and Stanley Mitchell, London 1962.

—— *The meaning of contemporary realism*, trans. John and Necke Mander, London 1962.

Mann, Leonard, *Flesh in armour*, Melbourne 1932, 1944.

Mann, Thomas, *Death in Venice* (with *Tristan* and *Tonio Kröger*) trans. H. T. Lowe-Porter, London 1928; Harmondsworth 1955.

Mann, Thomas, *Buddenbrooks*, Berlin 1903; trans. H. T. Lowe-Porter 1924; Harmondsworth 1957.

Macaulay, T. B., *Works*, 10 vols., London 1903.

McCombie, Thomas, *The history of the colony of Victoria from its settlement to the death of Sir Charles Hotham*, London 1858.

Mackenzie, Compton, *Gallipoli memories*, London 1929.

McLeod, A. L. (ed.), *The commonwealth pen: an introduction to the literature of the British Commonwealth*, New York 1961.

Matthews, John, *Tradition in exile*, London 1962.

Mill, John Stuart, 'Civilisation: Signs of the Times', *Westminster Review*, xxv, April 1836.

—— *Autobiography*, 1873.

Miller, E. Morris, *Australian literature from its beginnings: a bibliography to 1938; extended to 1950*, ed. Frederick T. Macartney, Sydney 1956.

—— *Pressmen and governors*, Sydney 1952.

Mountford, Charles P., *Brown men and red sand*, London 1950.

Mudie, James, *The felonry of New South Wales, etc.*, London 1837.

Mudie, Robert, *The modern Athens: a dissection and demonstration of men and things in the Scotch capital*, London 1825.

Newman, J. H., *The idea of a university*, London 1873.

Novalis, *Schriften*, Berlin 1802; 3 vols., Jena 1923.

Palmer, Nettie, *Henry Handel Richardson: a study*, Sydney 1950.

Palmer, Vance, *The legend of the nineties*, Melbourne 1954.

Parkes, Sir Henry, *Fifty years in the making of Australian history*, London 1892.

Pavese, Cesare, *The business of living*, Turin 1952; trans. Alma E. Murch, London 1961.

Phillips, A. A., *The Australian tradition: studies in a colonial culture*, Melbourne 1958.

Pike, Douglas, *Australia: the quiet continent*, London 1962.

Praed, Rosa, *My Australian girlhood*, London 1902.

Praz, Mario, *The romantic agony*, Milan, Rome 1930, trans. Angus Davidson, London 1933, 1960.

Purdie, Edna, and Olga Roncoroni, *Henry Handel Richardson: some personal impressions*, Sydney 1957.

Roderick, Colin, *An introduction to Australian fiction*, Sydney 1950.

Rousseau, Jean-Jacques, *Émile, or education*, Paris 1762; trans. Barbara Foxley, London 1911, 1966.

Sartre, Jean-Paul, *Nausea*, Paris 1948; trans. Robert Baldick, Harmondsworth 1965.

Scott, Walter, *Waverley*, Edinburgh 1814.

—— *The Heart of Midlothian*, Edinburgh 1818.

—— *Rob Roy*, Edinburgh 1817.

—— *Poems*, London 1880.

Semmler, Clement (ed.), *Twentieth century Australian literary criticism*, Melbourne 1967.

Shaw, A. G. L., *Convicts and the Colonies*, London 1966

Shelley, Percy Bysshe, *Poems*, vols. 1–4, London 1965.

Southey, Robert, *Essays moral and political*, 2 vols., London 1832.
Spate, O. H. K., *Australia*, London 1968.
Stone, Louis, *Jonah*, London 1911, Sydney 1965.
Stow, Randolph, *To the islands*, London 1958, Ringwood 1962.
—— (ed.) *Australian poetry* 1964, Sydney, Melbourne, London 1964.
de Tocqueville, Alexis, *Democracy in America*, Brussels 1835; (abridged) trans. Henry Reeve, London 1961.
Trevelyan, G. M., *British history in the nineteenth century and after* (1872–1919), London 1938.
—— *History of England*, London 1926, 1952.
Trollope, Anthony, *Australia and New Zealand*, Melbourne 1876.
—— *An autobiography*, London 1883; 1962.
—— *John Caldigate*, 3 vols., London 1879.
—— *Harry Heathcote of Gangoil: a tale of Australian bush life*, London 1874; Melbourne 1963.
Turner, E. S., *Gallant gentlemen*, London 1956.
Turner, F. J., *The frontier in American history*, New York 1928.
Twain, Mark, *Life on the Mississippi*, London 1883.
Vidler, Alexander, *The church in an age of revolution*, London 1962.
Walpole, Spencer, *A history of England from the conclusion of the Great War in 1815*, 6 vols. London 1890.
Ward, Russel, *The Australian legend*, Melbourne 1958.
'Warung, Price' (William Astley), *Tales of the convict system*, Sydney 1892, *Convict days*, Sydney 1960.
—— *Tales of the early days*, Melbourne 1894.
—— *Tales of the old regime*, Melbourne 1897.
—— *Tales of the Isle of Death*, Melbourne 1898.
Webb, R. K., *The British working class reader, 1790–1848: literacy and social tension*, London 1955.
White, Patrick, *Happy valley*, London 1939.
—— *Voss*, Harmondsworth 1962.
—— *Riders in the chariot*, Harmondsworth 1964.
Willey, Basil, *Nineteenth century studies*, London 1949.
—— *Ideas and beliefs of the Victorians*, London 1949.
—— *More nineteenth century studies*, London 1956.
Williams, Raymond, *Culture and society*, London 1958.
Wilson, David, *Thoughts on British colonial slavery*, London 1828.
Wright, Judith, *Preoccupations in Australian poetry*, Melbourne 1965.
Young, G. F., *Under the coolibah tree*, London 1953.
Young, G. M., *Victorian England: portrait of an age*, London 1936.
—— (ed.) *Early Victorian England, 1830–1865*, 2 vols., London 1934.

JOURNALS

In an article called '*Meanjin* and the Australian Literary Scene', which appeared in *The Journal of Commonwealth Literature* (Dec. 1967, no. 4), A. M. Gibbs wrote: 'But the essays on Richardson, Furphy, Lawson and White have been steadily accumulating in the pages of *Meanjin* (and elsewhere) over the last fifteen years . . . how many more reconsiderations and revisitations, one wonders, are these writers going to be able to bear for the time being, and will the lesser giantlings of Australian literature provide sufficient alternative grist for the mill?' The following is a list of helpful articles in Australian publications. It sustains Gibbs's suggestion that a few writers have received much critical attention, perhaps too much, and 'the lesser giantlings' little or none.

Australian Literary Studies:

Horner, J. C., '*Geoffry Hamlyn* and its Australian setting', 1963, no. 1.

Kiernan, Brian, 'Society and nature in *Such is life*', 1963, no. 2.

Robson, L. L., 'The historical basis of *For the term of his natural life*', 1963, no. 2.

Australian Quarterly:

Howarth, R. G., 'H. H. Richardson's *Richard Mahony* and *The end of a childhood*', March 1955.

Meanjin:

Barnes, John, 'The structure of Joseph Furphy's *Such is life*', 1956, no. 4.

'Furphy number', 1943, no. 3.

'Henry Handel Richardson number,' 1963, no. 1.

Mares, F. H., '*The fortunes of Richard Mahony*: a reconsideration', 1962, no. 1.

Palmer, Vance, 'Marcus Clarke and his critics', 1946.

Southerly:

Howarth, R. G., 'Marcus Clarke's *For the term of his natural life*', 1954, no. 4.

Mitchell, A. G., '*Such is life*: the title and structure of the book', 1945, no. 3 ('Joseph Furphy number').

Oliver, H. J., 'Joseph Furphy and "Tom Collins" ', 1944, no. 3.

'William Hay number', 1946, no. 3.

Index